The
Advisory
Book

BUILDING A COMMUNITY
OF LEARNERS GRADES 5-9

Linda Crawford

ISBN: 978-0-938541-12-7
Library of Congress Control Number: 2008929365

Photography by Jennifer Bush, with contributions from Jo Devlin and Ellen Shulman
Cover and book design: Heidi Neilson

ORIGINS
DEVELOPMENTAL DESIGNS®

The Origins Program
3805 Grand Avenue South
Minneapolis, Minnesota 55409
800-543-8715
www.originsonline.org

12 11 10   5 4 3

The

Advisory
Book

BUILDING A COMMUNITY
OF LEARNERS GRADES 5-9

Linda Crawford

BEST PRACTICES SERIES

ACKNOWLEDGMENTS

To make this book as useful as possible to teachers, I knew that in addition to being authentic, it had to be practical, detailed, and thorough. Writing such a book became a team effort, and I am eager to thank my fellow players.

Middle school teachers were an abundant source of ideas for greetings, share topics, and activities that had been tested in real classrooms with real adolescents. To Kandace Logan, Shelly Drake, Matthew Christen, Lourdes Ramirez, Diana O'Donnell, I offer special thanks for their contributions of CPR ideas. And for the true stories of classroom life which bring color and energy to these pages, my thanks go to Matthew Christen, Sharon Greaves, Christopher Hagedorn, Erin Klug, Ana Knapp, Kristen Konop, and Scott Tyink.

There was also a group of middle level and high school students who responded to our request to hear about their experiences. The following students shared with us their school advisory stories. Thanks to:

Cole Chiasson, Alyssa Dalton, Marisa Duplisea, Nate Otenti, JFK MS, Hudson MA
Karin Hecht, Logan Middle School, LaCrosse WI
Priyanka Sen, Maria L. Baldwin School, Cambridge MA
Eden Rome, New City School, Minneapolis MN
Dayna Alcott, Jenna Kleiner, and Amber Mixon, Olson M.S., Tabernacle NJ
Shalana Lussier, Red Lake High School, Red Lake MN
Harley Hart and Sierra Strong, Red Lake Middle School, Red Lake MN
Tia James, Richard Green Central Park Community School, Minneapolis MN

Scott Tyink's helpful suggestions for every chapter in the book reflect his commitment to this project as well as his deep understanding of and appreciation for middle level students and their teachers.

Christopher Hagedorn was a tireless describer of games, greetings, and other activities. His patience with all the details gave me heart.

Jo Devlin went far beyond providing meticulous copy editing. She kept us true to best writing practices throughout, and helped us through patches of weariness with her wholehearted enthusiasm for the mission.

Our designer, Heidi Neilson, was a pleasure to work with. Her combination of skill, patience, and lively creativity brought us to as attractive a final version as I could imagine.

Most of all I take pleasure in expressing my deep gratitude for the fates that brought me the tireless, meticulous, insightful (and funny) editor, Elizabeth Crawford. Her insistence on quality in the content, language, and design of this book was steadfast, and no amount of work was too much to achieve it. It is hard to imagine how *The Advisory Book* could have been created without her.

Finally, I want to acknowledge the intended audience for this book, teachers of young adolescents whose insistence on authenticity, evidence, practicality, and fun kept the book steady to its purpose—creating the kind of learning community in which middle level learners can thrive.

For adolescents and their teachers

TABLE OF CONTENTS

Chapter Five: 170 Advisory Themes   137

Use advisory to forge relationships to peers and school,
build autonomy, competence, and to infuse learning with
fun

CHAPTER ONE

An Argument for Advisory

I have to say it [CPR in advisory] is pretty fun because you get to know your classmates better and you get to play games that are fun and also funny, and you can tell your plans and other things you like to do. It makes a difference. It wakes you up because you get to feel the joy in the room.

—middle school advisory student, Red Lake MN

THE POWER OF HEALTHY COMMUNITY

Young adolescents exhibit many of the signs of adulthood. Some have reached their adult height; many have part-time jobs and social lives separate from their families. They clearly are no longer little kids, but it is a mistake to think that they need less support and tending from their teachers and parents than their younger counterparts. The key is balance. We have to allow them as much independence as they can responsibly handle, and at the same time support and guide them along the way. With our help, they can experience what it's like to operate successfully within a caring, inclusive, safe school community to which they feel connected, a community within which they can grow and have fun at the same time.

In a small K-8 school, the Circle of Power and Respect (CPR) meeting formed the heart of the advisory program. In the circle, students shared what was going on in their lives, good and bad. They greeted each other every morning, and even if you weren't there, you knew the group was saying hi to you. In the circle they had their best laughs, and they played games—sometimes silly, sometimes challenging games, in which no one ever really lost and everyone was included. The circle was the heart of their community.

One day Angela, an 8th grader at the school, acted up on the bus ride home, and as a result she forfeited her right to ride the school bus for a week. On the third day of that week, a public bus strike began, and Angela had no transportation. Her father agreed to give her a ride downtown, and then she called the principal to request a pickup downtown. "I really want to be there! Could somebody please, please come get me? I'm not far away!" Someone did.

On another day, a 7th grader listened to an announcement that no school buses would be coming into her area until the debris from the big storm the night before was hauled away. She grabbed her hat and coat, and announced to her mother that she was walking the six miles to school. "I'm not going to miss school just because of that stupid storm!" She set out on the walk, which got her to school just in time for the beginning of CPR.

"Good morning, Bethany. What's up?" one of the boys in the circle said.

"Good morning, Roberto. I'm glad to be here—I walked the whole way from my house!"

— 7th/8th grade advisory, Minneapolis MN

Those are stories of a pull towards school strong enough to overcome big obstacles. That's the kind of connection a caring learning community can create. And a good part of the energy behind it was a lively, friendly, interesting advisory that met the needs of its adolescent participants.

This Book and Adolescent Needs: Designing a Path to Student Success

The Advisory Book is rooted in the belief that every idea for teaching middle level students is only as good as its capacity to meet the needs of young adolescents in a constructive way. It offers practical ways to meet the social and emotional needs of middle level students every school day. Through an advisory period of 15 to 30 minutes a day, teachers can offer students a consistent, dependable opportunity to get to know themselves and each other, to build social strengths, to warm up their thinking selves in a wide variety of mentally challenging games and relevant activities, and to have fun doing so. Two structures for advisory—Circle of Power and Respect and Activity Plus—are described in detail and with great variety. Once familiar, they become powerful formats for helping to ensure that each school day is productive, safe, and enjoyable for everyone.

> Dr. James P. Comer of the Yale Child Study Center Project proposes that "many practices in education that have been developed over the past two decades have been less successful than they might have been because they have focused primarily on curriculum, instruction, assessment, and modes of service delivery," neglecting to base their instructional work on the principles of child and adolescent development. (Comer 2005, 758)

We have chosen to use these two basic structures as the bones of the advisory program, because once a teacher has mastered them, they can serve as containers for any content a teacher wishes to use. A repeatable format becomes simple to implement, and when there is a rich variety of possibilities within that format, you have the best of both worlds: a comfortable routine, and a large variety of activities for breadth, depth, and enjoyment. Then out of the various advisories communities, a school community is born, a place where students feel connected and appreciated—a place where they want to be.

A meta-analysis of 207 studies of social-emotional learning (SEL) programs which involved a broadly representative group of almost 300,000 students from urban, suburban, and rural elementary and secondary schools found that students who participate in school-based social-emotional learning programs (compared to students who do not experience SEL) profit in multiple ways (CASEL, 2007). They improve significantly in:

1. Social and emotional skills

2. Attitudes about themselves, others, and school

3. Social and classroom behavior

4. Achievement-test scores and school grades

It isn't enough to offer only academic course work, no matter its quality. For adolescents to succeed, we have to carefully orchestrate their social as well as their intellectual climate. If they get help in working and playing with their peers, and if they learn the social skills necessary to navigate their relationships with a wide variety of people, they stand a good chance of doing well in school. Most of the adolescents referred to in this book are young ones, ages 11-14, but much of what is offered is also applicable to older adolescents, who share many of the same needs as their younger counterparts.

ADDRESSING ADOLESCENT NEEDS CONSTRUCTIVELY AND CONSISTENTLY

Adolescent needs are differently named by different researchers, but basically they come down to four that are always present, like hungry mouths to feed, all day long in middle school: Autonomy, Competence, Relationship, and Fun.

Autonomy

Young adolescents long for independence, and they'll grab for it irresponsibly unless we provide carefully orchestrated ways for them to grow into it. A baby is totally dependent upon others; a young child can do some things for herself, but needs constant supervision. By the time children are entering adolescence, they are capable of doing many things on their own, but might be marginally capable of doing so responsibly. They don't want to be directed all the time, and they take advantage of opportunities to push off into directing their own lives and making their own decisions. The adults around them must protect them from the negative and sometimes tragic outcomes of inappropriate judgments, while helping them to stand on their own.

> High rates of boredom, alienation, and disconnection from meaningful challenge are not signs of psychopathology, at least not in most cases, but rather signs of a deficiency in positive development. The same might be said for many cases of problem behavior ... [which is a response] to the absence of engagement in a positive life trajectory. Many youth do their schoolwork, comply with their parents, hang out with their friends, and get through the day, but are not invested in paths into the future that excite them or feel like they originate from within. A central question of youth development is how to get adolescents' fires lit, how to have them develop the complex of dispositions and skills needed to take charge of their lives. [Young people need activities with] enough structure so that youths are challenged, but also enough flexibility so that, as youths gain experience, they assume responsibility for the direction of the activity. (Larson 2000, 170)

The best response to the urge for autonomy is to grant it incrementally, with sufficient structure and supervision to make the probability of responsible independence most likely. When you build it bit by bit, there is room for backsliding and mistakes, and the promise of days ahead when the young person can run the show. A carefully orchestrated advisory is a perfect context for this kind of growth.

Elena was a shy, extremely reserved girl who apparently lacked social confidence. As a 6th grader she hung back from participation, spoke very softly, and didn't volunteer. In our daily advisory meeting she shared only in situations where everyone was expected to participate.

By mid-year in advisory, I began having students take over leading the meeting. On the morning when it was Elena's turn to take over the circle, she sat quietly while everyone circled up and then put her hand in the air to signal for silence. I had taught students to respond to the signal for silence, and Elena had seen me do it countless times, but no other student had taken the initiative to begin the meeting that way. The signal was effective, and the meeting got underway. Elena led the greeting and introduced a topic for sharing. As someone began to share, another student whispered to a friend. "Take a break," said Elena immediately. Everyone watched as the whisperer paused for a second and then stood up and walked to the break chair. Elena resumed leading the meeting.

Apparently, Elena had been building confidence, empowered by the safety she felt with peers (and me) in our advisory. That morning she was able to come into her own and take charge. It was her turning point in the year and, it seemed, for the remainder of her middle school experience.

—8th grade advisory, LaCrosse WI

A ninth grade teacher described how math interest, confidence, and performance increased in her students when she invited them to do their own pacing as they worked their way through the math curriculum. "I was convinced that these students, who were on the brink of adulthood and who desperately wanted to make decisions for themselves, would be more motivated if I gave them responsibility for their own learning." The results exceeded expectations: students enjoyed math with their new autonomy. Students assigned themselves more homework than the teacher ever did. Discipline problems were rare. Students passed exams (when formerly they had not). "What pleased me most was that the students' focus shifted from getting a grade to learning math."

—9th grade advisory (from "The Self-Paced Student," *Educational Leadership* 2005, 69)

Competence

Young adolescents want to feel that they are good at doing things, that they can think, create, solve problems, and understand. They want to feel that they've got what it takes to succeed in life. Feelings of incompetence can quickly be translated into giving up, depression, or acting out. Since middle level students are still developing the mental equipment to be competent people, and their capacity to weigh and consider will not be fully developed until they are adults, they need our help to move along a continuum designed to scaffold their way to competence.

> A major cause of underachievement is the inability of students to control one's own behavior. ...Research indicates that learning self-regulatory skills can lead to greater academic achievement and an increased sense of efficacy.... [W]e view academic self-regulation as the ability of students to control the factors or conditions affecting their learning. (Dembo and Eaton 2000, 69)

Young people don't seem to care about some things very much. Investment in "getting good" seems to occur around skills and activities and subjects for which they have a personal investment. That often means that teacher-driven tasks in school don't figure in their push towards competence, but sports, some aspects of technology, and after-school projects in arenas of high interest to them are the ones in which they strive to succeed.

I wanted my 7th and 8th graders to acquire some competencies in playing basketball. Some of them already played on teams, and had some bravado about their skills. Others had no confidence at all about handling a basketball. There was a big push towards playing real games, especially from the more experienced players, but from the start I put a low priority on competition and a high priority on developing personal skills. I set up leveled tasks around basketball skills such as dribbling, passing, and running, and everyone was challenged to build personal competence incrementally. The experienced players found that they had been talking a bigger game than they could play, and had to work hard, for example, to get good enough to dribble a ball in figure 8's through their legs. Everyone achieved success in the process of working towards higher levels of personal competence.

The basketball unit culminated in a game against staff. My desire was that everyone would play, whatever their perceived skills. It took a lot of discussing to get everyone to accept my decision that everyone would play the first half, and then those who wanted to could call for a substitute during the second half.

The big game held some surprises. The staff was impressed with the level of skill the students had attained—all of them, not just the ones who played on teams outside of school. The hotshots were surprised to see how well it worked to play as a team, pass to someone who had a better chance at a shot, and have everyone take a turn. Most of all, the ones who lack confidence, were happy with their playing (even scoring one or two baskets!) and with how much fun it all was. Nobody called for a substitute in the second half! Spirits soared right along with confidence and competence.

—7th/8th grade advisory, Minneapolis MN

<u>Researchers connect self-efficacy with competence and accomplishment</u>

According to Stanford psychologist Albert Bandura (2004), people with confidence in their competencies approach difficult tasks as challenges to be mastered rather than as threats to be avoided. They are more likely to work with focus because of their intrinsic interest in the activities, and they are not afraid to commit to challenging goals. How do you help young people develop such a strong sense of belief in their own capacities?

> The most effective way of creating a strong sense of efficacy is through mastery experiences. Successes build a robust belief in one's personal efficacy. (Bandura 1994, 72)
>
> It is in peer relationships that [young people] broaden self-knowledge of their capabilities. Peers serve several important efficacy functions. Those who are most experienced and competent provide models of efficacious styles of thinking and behavior. A vast amount of social learning occurs among peers. In addition, age-mates provide highly informative comparisons for judging and verifying one's self-efficacy. Children are, therefore, especially sensitive to their relative standing among their peers in activities that determine prestige and popularity. (Bandura 1998, 78)

The challenge for teachers of middle level students is to ease their young charges towards the experience of competency by scaffolding their way to success, both socially and academically. Incremental success in social as well as academic skills, orchestrated by adults, in the context of supportive peer relationships, brings young adolescents to successively higher levels of competence and self-efficacy. As students become more able, they can assume more responsibility, which means they achieve the independence for which they long. The reward of social and academic competency then becomes responsible independence. A carefully designed advisory program can bring such rewards, because it orchestrates incremental social success and fosters supportive peer relationships, another crucial element in the development of belief in one's own competence.

Relationship

Along with the search for competence comes the craving for relationship. Peers rule for young adolescents, but it is a mistake to underestimate the importance of relationships with adults to middle level students.

<u>The importance of links to adults</u>

The care and guidance of family and teachers are crucial to their survival (and they know it). They watch and listen to the adults around them. If those models use sarcasm and put-downs, they will imitate their tone and words. If the adults are consistently friendly and courteous with each other, the students are much more likely to be so. And if at least one adult shows interest in his success and keeps in touch regularly, a student feels connected to that person, and usually to the school as well. When adolescents bond with their schools and feel connected to the learning experience, there is always an element of teacher support involved, and that connection is crucial to success. Advisory is a perfect place to make the connections.

Friendly greetings in CPR and A+ advisories build relationship

The importance of links to peers

However important relationships with adults are for students, the people with whom young adolescents long to be connected all day, every day, are other adolescents. But even in peer relationships, adolescents need adult guidance. Left to themselves, they will grab onto some people and reject others, sometimes permanently, and often for poor reasons. One of their most frequently used tools for socializing is exclusion. Cliques abound. The largely unconscious rationale is:

I will occur to others as a valuable person when I appear in public with kids who are considered valuable. I don't want to be seen as a loser, so I must avoid appearing with kids who are already perceived that way. On the other hand, I have to show up with someone. The worst thing would be to be without any allies. You're no one unless you hang out with someone.

> [In academic performance and in the area of health behaviors], young people who feel connected to school, that they belong, and that teachers are supportive and treat them fairly, do better.
>
> Some contend the business of school is teaching for knowledge acquisition and that attention to the non-academic aspects of school is a low priority. However, the health and education literature suggests these factors contribute significantly to school success. (Libbey 2004, 282)

Our job as adults is to provide a way for our adolescent students to be with others without the poison of rejection, to create a community in which everyone is included, and the resulting diversity is okay—more than okay, it's great! In a study on the impact of friendship on middle schoolers, students without friends showed lower levels of prosocial behavior and academic achievement, and increased emotional distress two years later (Wentzel, McNamara, and Caldwell 2004). In an atmosphere that clears away some of the pain, students can get ready to learn. Advisory can create such an atmosphere.

The best thing that happened in a CPR meeting happened on Valentine's Day. I was not present on February 13, so I could not do the activity planned for that day. The activity was to write one nice thing about everyone in the class. I came to school February 14, and in the meeting my teacher handed out valentines. I got one and I almost cried—it was nice! Some of the things my classmates wrote were, "She's always smiling." "She's pretty." "She's smart." "She is hard-working." I don't know who wrote these things, but I do know there are nice people out there. You just have to get to know them.

—high school advisory student, Red Lake MN

Fun

If you leave the need for fun out of the equation, you leave out the element that gets us out of bed every morning. If you erased from our lives all the things we do that are play-related, energy, motivation, and even hope might disappear as well. School, in which young adolescents spend six hours a day, five days a week, for nine months of the year, cannot be a place devoid of fun. If we don't provide it in quick, healthy, educational ways, students will make their own fun, and it will often involve excess—going too far, being too loud, too physical, too emotional. Teacher-provided fun, although sometimes initially labeled as stupid or childish, will before long win over the play-loving hearts inside our students.

Scientists are very interested in the role of play in neurological development, and some researchers see play as a central part of brain development, one important way to build complex, creative, flexible brains that will help them negotiate adulthood (Marantz Henig 2008). Whatever such research helps us decide, the positive effects of play and other kinds of fun seem to consistently provide us with students who are more interested in life and more engaged. We'll take that quickened state and convert it into learning. And when the learning itself is fun, we have all we need to succeed.

Fun is the genetic reward for learning. (Glasser 1998, 41)

Adolescents pursue fun in both childlike and newer adult ways. Through this pursuit, the teenager learns about more complex relationships.... Having fun in relationships creates intimacy and forges a "pleasure bond" between the people that helps maintain the relationship. (Fall, Holden, and Marquis 2004, 252)

The greater the anxiety we feel, the more impaired is the brain's cognitive efficiency. .... Plotting the relationship between mental adeptness (and performance generally) and the spectrum of moods creates what looks like an upside-down U with its legs spread out a bit. Joy, cognitive efficiency, and outstanding performance occur at the peak of the inverted U. Along the downside of one leg lies boredom, along the other anxiety. The more apathy or angst we feel, the worse we do, whether on a term paper or an office memo. (Goleman 2006, 270)

[A]dolescents who feel as if their peers at school are supportive and caring tend to be interested in school and to pursue goals to be prosocial more often than those who do not. (Wentzel, Barry, Caldwell 2004, 202)

[P]eer-group climate ratings emerged as a significant predictor of rates of change in reading achievement, while family climate ratings had no significant effect. Students reporting more positive ratings of peer climate had more positive rates of change in reading achievement. (Fleming, Coork, and Stone 2002, 60)

Researchers Ryan and Deci state "intrinsic motivation [is] more likely to flourish in contexts characterized by a sense of security and relatedness." Their self-determination theory links intrinsic motivation and student success in school. (Ryan and Deci 2000, 71)

One year, I kept track during the fall of what reason students gave on their "Fix-it" plan sheets after breaking our rules, and having to be sent to the buddy room next door. In the first half of the year I used the buddy room 42 times. Students' explanations for why they broke the rules were as follows: 23 said they needed some fun; 12 said it was because of a need to talk to someone; 6 times it was because of a need to relax; 1 was because the person needed information. I see more clearly now that fun, talking, and relaxing are very important to middle school students, and sometimes these needs can get in the way of learning. They can also damage individual relationships and a learning community's fabric. The more I built into my lessons opportunities for fun, social interaction, and learning in a relaxed environment, the better learning climate I had.

—7th/8th grade advisory, Minneapolis MN

SEEKING A MODEL FOR SOCIAL-EMOTIONAL LEARNING AT MIDDLE LEVEL: LOOKING BACK, LOOKING FORWARD

The challenge within the context of schools is finding a manageable way to meet these fundamental adolescent needs, day in and day out. Ever since the Carnegie Foundation *Turning Points* study (Carnegie Council on Adolescent Development 1989) asserted the necessity for a socially safe community, middle schools have been trying to find a quick (because there's never enough time for everything), effective (not just pointless play or relaxation time), consistent (because different approaches among teachers can lead to confusion and conflict) method to consciously and efficiently build a healthy learning environment.

Homeroom

Historically, many middle level schools established a designated period for social-emotional growth and making connections. The homeroom model was originally designed to help bridge the transition from home to school, to give students a chance to talk and make social connections, and for teachers to connect to students within small groups. Sometimes a group of teachers designed a homeroom curriculum. In many cases, homeroom was simply a catch-all time for announcements, hanging out with friends, reading the newspaper, or getting a little extra sleep. Some teachers used the time to connect with individual students; some did not.

Advisory

Another structure that has been used at the middle level is an advisory system. The goal is for all students to establish a connection with at least one adult in the school, a person who gets to know them and can serve as a guide. Advisory groups sometimes meet in the mornings, but in many schools they consist of a designated time during the middle of the day once or twice a week where students can check in with their advisors.

Some school programs set out to create advisory periods that can also serve as a community-building time. In addition to the connections made with their advisory teacher, students have a chance to connect with each other, and learn the social skills necessary for success in any relationship. Some advisories with these goals have an explicit curriculum; many do not. Sometimes the curriculum provided is not used very much.

This Book and Advisory

This book offers the combined wisdom of researchers and dozens of middle level teachers about how to meet the developmental needs of young adolescents so they can thrive in school. It gathers together many of the best ideas for building community, teaching social skills, and engaging students in learning, and organizes them within two basic structures that teachers can use all year during a designated daily advisory or homeroom time of about twenty minutes: Circle of Power and Respect (CPR), a community-building *meeting*, and Activity Plus (A+), an extended community-building *activity* framed by an opening and a closing routine.

This format approach to daily advisory has maximum flexibility, consistency, and structure. Instead of relying on a particular curriculum which can grow repetitive or become irrelevant, the formats, repeated daily with variations, become so familiar that eventually, when they have the social skills necessary, students can begin to lead the advisory meeting (CPR) and at least part of the A+ advisories. When this happens, you are addressing the adolescent need for autonomy and teaching social skills and leadership, all at the same time.

The Advisory Book provides directions for establishing the two formats. It also gives you ideas for greetings, sharing, and games and activities from which to choose each day to flesh out the basic structures. You can pick and choose to create either a CPR meeting or to spend advisory time mostly on a longer activity in an A+ advisory. See Appendix D: Activities for dozens of activities that are leveled according to their risk and complexity so you can choose what fits for your students at any point in the year.

In addition, Chapter 5: 170+ Thematic Advisories provides specific CPR and A+ examples organized around themes of interest and relevance to adolescents, like Getting to Know Each Other, Social Skills, Careers, and Service. Teachers can plan a whole year's worth of advisories using different themes, or they can take a mixed approach, making up CPR's out of the leveled chart (page 209) (an approach that students will also use when they start leading CPR), and then switching to a thematic unit for a week or two to add variety and focus and to investigate specific adolescent needs and interests in a coherent, organized manner. The possibilities are myriad!

Students gather in CPR and A+ advisories to build community and social skills and to get ready for the academic day

ADVISORY, A TIME FOR COMMUNITY AND GROWTH

Students are moving into the room in pairs and clusters, and settling themselves into the chairs arranged in a circle. They are a mixed group culturally, although more homogeneous in their poverty. There is chatting and laughing, and there are a few downcast looks in students who are keeping to themselves.

The teacher raises his hand, and everyone falls silent. It is time to begin CPR, the Circle of Power and Respect. A student takes charge of a greeting, which is a quick high five passed around the circle, along with a variety of "How're you doing?" "What's up, Carlos?" "How's it going, Adel?" Some look at the floor much of the time, but everyone makes eye contact at the moment of greeting. The greeting takes only a minute or two.

Then the student leader calls on a student who has volunteered to share, and a brief conversation ensues:

My mom is talking about moving again. I'm hoping it's just talk, but it may not be. I'm open for questions and comments.

Have you told your family that you don't want to move, Michael?

What did your mom say?

Is there any chance you could keep coming here even after you move?

No problems are solved for Michael that morning, or for the students who share about their lives after he does, but there is some comfort for him, a feeling that the community is there for these young people as they deal with issues or share fun times with their peers. Whatever problems occur for the people in this circle, they have a friendly, caring community.

Creating a Positive Culture

Schools are like towns, a group of people, often diverse, that spends a lot of time together working, talking, eating, and playing. Both need to create a climate that supports the productivity and well-being of the people who live there. If they don't have a healthy, safe climate, nothing of real quality can be sustained.

Schools have something of an advantage over towns in that the process of creating climate can be a conscious, deliberate one. Schools have the power to create structures that help people know one another, get along, work effectively, and grow. The structures described in this book are based upon the *Developmental Designs* approach developed by Origins, a non-profit educational organization founded in 1979. Origins' mission is to promote an equitable and humane multicultural society through quality education for all. *Developmental Designs* is an approach founded upon a set of beliefs which themselves are grounded in decades of research into adolescent development and best middle level practices.

Six Principles of the ⁜ORIGINS DEVELOPMENTAL DESIGNS® Approach

- Social learning is as important to success as academic learning.

- We learn best by constructing our own understanding through exploration, discovery, and application.

- The greatest cognitive growth occurs through social interactions within a supportive community.

- There is a set of personal and social skills that students need to learn and practice in order to be successful socially and academically:
  C—Cooperation A—Assertion R—Responsibility
  E—Empathy S—Self-control

- Knowing the physical, emotional, social, and intellectual needs of the students we teach is as important as knowing the content we teach.

- Trust among adults is a fundamental necessity for academic and social success in a learning community.

Purposes of Advisory

While providing adolescents with what they need to thrive, a good advisory program in middle level schools can create the context for quality learning. It can:

- Establish trust—student-to-student and student-to-adult, a trust that can extend into classes and become schoolwide.

- Teach social skills—skills necessary for students to enjoy relationships with peers and adults, in school and out, and negotiate the intricacies of daily life so that they can handle their lives with responsible independence.

- Make school meaningful and pleasurable—relevant to life outside of school, connected to what is interesting and important to young adolescents—and fun.

- Prepare students to learn—disencumber the passage from home to school, from purely social interactions to social and academic ones combined, from fear and self-doubt to efficacy and confidence.

Positive Outcomes of Effective Advisories

Are advisory periods worth the time spent on them? Yes, if they are structured for success.

> [S]ome of the most frequently mentioned purposes of advisories include:
>
> 1. Promoting opportunities for social development
>
> 2. Assisting students with academic programs
>
> 3. Facilitating positive involvement among teachers, administrators, and students
>
> 4. Providing an adult advocate for each student in the school
>
> 5. Promoting positive school climate
>
> (S. Clark and D. Clark 1994, 135-136)

Researchers have found ample connections between advisories and academic success. MacIver (1990) found that when teacher advisories focused on social and academic support activities, then a strong relationship existed that promoted the reduction of dropouts. Connors (1986) found evidence that advisory programs that helped students grow emotionally and socially contributed to a positive school climate, helped students learn about school and getting along with their classmates, and enhanced teacher-student relationships. George and Oldaker (1985) suggest that when advisory programs are combined with other components of the middle school concept, student self-concept improves, dropout rates decrease, and school climate becomes more positive (compiled by Anfara 2006).

Can a small piece of time at the beginning of the school day achieve all that? It can if the time is carefully structured. It can if the time has built into its routine the opportunity for students to greet each other, with no one left out. It can if there is provided a format for conversations in which all voices are not merely heard, but listened to with empathy. It can if the daily routine is fun. And perhaps most important, it can if the time is structured in such a way that all these benefits accrue under the direction, eventually, of the students themselves.

No advisory time?

If there is no designated advisory time at your school, you can create one. Finding time for advisory will probably mean some wrestling with the schedule, but schools that want this community-building find a way to make it happen. In one suburban middle school, a meeting to consider integrating a more effective community-building approach with students' experience resulted in some creative minute-finding—a few minutes borrowed from here, a few from there, and in less than an hour, time for a brief daily advisory was created. Don't let an already-existing schedule prevent you from building better student connections to school!

STRUCTURES FOR ADVISORY: CPR AND A+

Advisories in schools vary in length from about 15 to 30 minutes, and they usually occur first thing in the morning. Whatever the amount of time available, an effective advisory requires a structure explicitly designed to help students start the day by meeting their basic needs. Young adolescents want to relate to one another; they want to have some control (autonomy) over what they do; they need to keep growing in skills, both social and academic, to feel good about themselves; and they crave fun. The best way to ensure a good transition into the school day is to use a consistent structure to help them see that they can get what they want *constructively*. Here are two frameworks from the *Developmental Designs* approach that allow for a variety of productive, nourishing activities.

Circle of Power and Respect Format

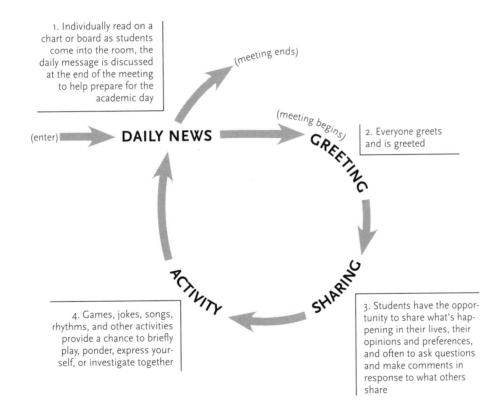

1. Individually read on a chart or board as students come into the room, the daily message is discussed at the end of the meeting to help prepare for the academic day

(meeting ends)

(enter)

DAILY NEWS

(meeting begins)

GREETING

2. Everyone greets and is greeted

SHARING

3. Students have the opportunity to share what's happening in their lives, their opinions and preferences, and often to ask questions and make comments in response to what others share

ACTIVITY

4. Games, jokes, songs, rhythms, and other activities provide a chance to briefly play, ponder, express yourself, or investigate together

Activity Plus (A+) Advisory Format

A main activity takes up most of the advisory time; it is framed by a greeting at the beginning and a reflection at the end.

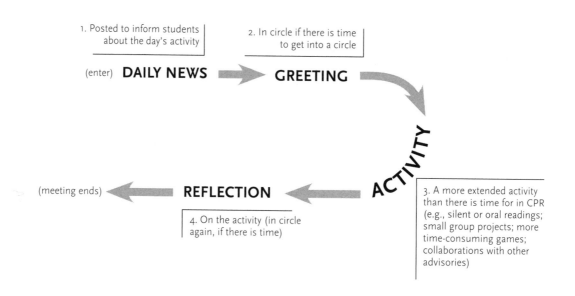

For maximum success, schedule at least three CPR meetings every week. For the first couple of weeks of school, use CPR structure *every day* to establish the rhythm of the meeting before introducing the second format, A+. The meetings provide the necessary connections between home and school, between personal lives and time in the academic setting. They maximize relationship-building and eventually provide a venue for students to show their competence and autonomy by leading the meetings themselves. CPR meetings are the adhesive of the community, and it seems to take steady use of at least three of them each week to keep the connective rhythm going.

Adhering to a basic pattern of CPR and A+ advisories provides a sense of order and safety as students know what to expect each day, and each day their needs are met within a varied but familiar format. Both include time for everyone to be together, often in a circle. In CPR, the whole advisory is dedicated to the circle meeting. On activity days, most of the time is spent on the extended activity, but that activity is framed by time together in the circle, if possible, for the greeting and a group reflection on the activity afterwards. In both, the community comes together and acknowledges each person's presence. Both provide closure and a carefully designed transition into the academic day. Chapters 2 and 3 provide ample detail for establishing and sustaining the CPR and A+ advisory formats.

SOCIAL CLIMATE IN ADVISORY

Teaching the Protocols and Routines: Assume nothing; model and practice everything

Time is short in the school day. The pressure to cram a lot into the time available pushes us to get right down to the assignment—whatever it is we want our students to do. However, as counter-intuitive as it feels, it is always dangerous to just barge ahead. When students approach the academic day with courtesy and self-control a great deal more time is saved than the minutes of CPR or A+!

The alternative is to go slow to go fast. What it looks like in a *Developmental Designs* advisory is that we take no social skills for granted; we introduce each move we want our students to make by modeling what it looks, feels, and sounds like to do it in a respectful, efficient way. If we don't show them, they'll make it up, and it may not be pretty!

> Modeling influences do more than provide a social standard against which to judge one's own capabilities.... Through their behavior and expressed ways of thinking, competent models transmit knowledge and teach observers effective skills and strategies for managing environmental demands. (Bandura 1994, 72)

Whatever the demands of your environment, whatever the space, the number of students, the assignment, you can count on things going better if you model for students exactly what you want them to do.

Modeling Routines

The typical day is full of routines, and we cannot assume either that students can figure them out for themselves or will follow the correct protocols without a good deal of support. Support comes in the form of modeling by teachers and students, practicing, and reflection. If you want students to do things right, you can't simply tell them. You have to model: coming into the room; starting the class routines; protocols for handling books and other materials; a signal for silence; taking a break as a redirection; handing in homework; getting the homework assignment; protocols for classroom participation, bathroom and other requests; and leaving the room to go to another class. Early in the year the advisory group can create the rules by which they will live. Even before those rules are made, however, the routines of the advisory have to be introduced. It's one of the tricky things about school start-up.

Modeling all the protocols and routines means we have to break them down into their small elements. We first demonstrate exactly how we want students to enter the classroom, for example, by entering the room ourselves, using exactly the moves we want them to use. Then we reinforce what they have witnessed by discussing it:

What did you notice that I did as I came in the room?

How long did it take me to get to my seat?

What did you observe that I did as I sat down?

This process of looking hard and then accurately describing what you have seen is good for students. Careful observation and accurate description is an essential skill for writers, scientists, historians, mathematicians, and so many others. It is a building block of good social skills. If we assume students already know how to do the routines of the classroom well, we invite mistakes. Better to make sure by showing, discussing, and completing the process by having a few students demonstrate the acceptable way to do the routine after you model it, and then direct everyone to practice it. At the end, you still take time to reinforce. Ask students to describe how the modeling went—in detail. That's where the difference lies between messy, noisy routines and quick, quiet ones.

How did we do in bringing our chairs to circle?

Did we follow the modeling exactly, or were there slip-ups?

How did it look and sound?

Establishing the Rules Democratically

In order to build a stable foundation for order and courtesy in an advisory, you need to establish early on some guidelines for behavior. A set of rules provides the context and the rationale for carefully observing the routines. Like most of us, adolescents dislike the confinement of rules. But unlike adults, they find themselves in the particularly irritating position of feeling capable of fully managing themselves but lacking the authority and autonomy to do so. They also lack the judgment, self-control, and experience, as the adults around them well know. However, when students participate in designing the advisory rules in the first place, they have a stronger identification with them and less resistance to the challenge of compliance and enforcement.

First, invite students to think about the possibilities for a group start to the day in a way that would help them get into a good mood, focused enough to begin learning.

Each day we're going to get together, say hello to one another, talk a little about what's happening in our lives, have some fun, and get ourselves ready for first hour. Let's talk about what guidelines groups generally need to make sure that everyone feels included and listened to. Think back to other classroom experiences. What made them go well and what were the problems?

As students describe past experiences, if they mention a negative experience, ask what guideline(s) might have made that experience better. When a positive experience is mentioned, identify the operating principle that allowed for that good experience.

A 7th grader shows
her agreement
with thumbs up

<u>Sample discussion of guidelines</u>

Student: *Nobody listens to what anyone else is saying. Everybody wants to talk at once.*

Teacher: *What rule might we set up to fix that?*

S: *One person speaks at a time.*

S: *It doesn't matter, because people don't listen anyway.*

T: *What rule would speak to that problem?*

S: *Listen to others.*

T: *Listen how?*

S: *Listen with your mouth shut.*

T: *In other words, listen respectfully?*

S: *Yeah, listen with some respect.*

The teacher lists these guidelines as they are articulated:

> One person speaks at a time.
>
> Listen with respect to others.

Consensus Agreement on the Rules

Keep listing the ideas until there are no more, or have students in pairs or small groups brainstorm ideas together and then list them all. Next, sort the ideas into categories. Finally, pare the list down to no more than five guidelines—that's as many as anybody will remember. This short list of rules needs to be broad enough to cover most situations, for example:

> Respect others
>
> Participate and work hard
>
> Take care of the school environment

It is not meant to be an itemized list of specific concerns about specific behaviors, but a broad umbrella that can be a reference for all the situations that might arise during the school year.

Once you have the final list of rules, use the consensus process of thumbs up, sideways, or down to indicate acceptance. Thumbs up is full acceptance. Thumbs sideways is guarded acceptance. Thumbs down is refusal to accept and signifies that the person's concern needs to be heard. Anyone who refuses must offer a replacement rule for any to which they object. If a student refuses to participate in the rule-making process, he surrenders his chance to have something to say about the rules, but must still comply with them. When there is consensus on the rules, write them in a large format, and ask all students to sign the rules poster to show their commitment to following the guidelines the group has chosen.

See the A+ sample advisory for creating the rules on page 144.

Keeping the Peace: Time for more modeling

Once you have your advisory rules, you can guide students through the process of thinking about how these rules will play out in the day-to-day activities of the class. You may create *Y-charts* with descriptions of how each routine will look, sound, and feel if you are following the rules, and you need to model what the routine looks like—exactly—and require that students practice it to make it likely that they will proceed correctly. Such a process will do much more than punishment to reduce disruptions.

Timely, early modeling and practicing of routines and procedures even before you create rules together will pay off right away, because it establishes good habits that will support the guidelines agreement.

Now that you have a set of rules, it's time for more modeling about the routines of the CPR meeting or A+ advisories, this time in the context of the new rules:

What will it look and sound like when we move desks and bring chairs into a meeting circle in a way that follows our rule to respect others? What will make this process as quick, safe, and quiet as possible so that we're taking care of the school environment and each other?

Students brainstorm some ideas about standards for moving chairs which you can record in a Y-chart that labels "look," "sound," and "feel" in its three sections. Post the chart. Then the teacher can model moving a chair, following the Y-chart ideas.

Sample Y-Chart: Bringing chairs to circle

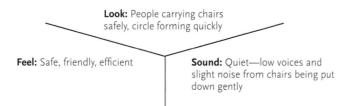

Look: People carrying chairs safely, circle forming quickly

Feel: Safe, friendly, efficient

Sound: Quiet—low voices and slight noise from chairs being put down gently

Solicit observations, then provide time for students to practice.
What did you notice about the way I moved my chair?
Who else is willing to demonstrate a quick, quiet way to get a chair to the circle?
Now let's all move our chairs into the circle, just as the demonstrators did. I'll call groups of four or five students and they will bring their chairs to the circle area.

By modeling routines and activities, you begin to create a familiar format for establishing safety and courtesy for any activity:

1. You help students think about it ahead of time.
   Rules: *Which of our rules will it be important to follow in this activity?*
   Social skills: *What social skills will be especially important? How will it look, sound, and feel if we do this activity well?*
   Student needs: *How can we have fun (or get good at, or build relationships) in this activity?*

2. You model and/or students model, and then everyone does the activity.

3. You help students reflect on the activity afterwards.
   Rules: *What rules did we follow during this game?*
   Social skills: *What social skills did we need to play this game well? How did it look, sound, and feel while we were doing this activity?*
   Student needs: *Was the activity fun? What might make it more fun to play? How can we get better at this? Did we forget any of our social skills?*

Using this before-and-after process, you increase the likelihood that the activity will go well, and that students will build the capacity to plan their actions and reflect on them afterwards as a habit of prudence and self-control.

Pathways to Self-control: Responding to rule-breaking

The proactive work of making the guidelines and then practicing them will head off most big problems. Every day, however, students will do or say things that violate the agreed-upon rules. None of these violations, no matter how small, can go unnoticed. Each rule-breaker must be redirected in order to maintain the integrity of the rules in the room. Tell your students this during the rule-making process. Describe the consequences of violating the rules, and promise students that you will protect the group by enforcing the rules that keep things safe, fair, and enjoyable for everyone.

Possible redirections

Verbal reminder: *Jim, how did we practice carrying the chair? Show me that you know the way we agreed upon so no one gets hurt and we get the job done quickly and quietly.*

Non-verbal reminder: Sometimes a non-verbal reminder will do. Pointing to someone who is carrying her chair incorrectly may trigger a change in careless behavior.

Time out of meeting: Sometimes, especially if this person has broken the rule before, you might ask her to sit out for a while and observe how others perform the task. It may be advisable, if the student has been reminded frequently about this protocol, to have her sit out for the whole meeting. If one refuses to follow the rules of advisory, one loses the privilege of participating in the advisory (which includes interesting, fun activities that students generally want to do).

Time out of advisory room: If a student can't tolerate sitting out, and becomes even more disruptive, it might be time to have her leave the room and try to regain composure in another room (a buddy classroom next door, for example, or a behavior room, if no buddy classroom has been established). The important principle is consistent respect for the rules and respect for the advisory, with no exceptions. It is the adult's responsibility to protect that principle at every moment of the advisory by addressing all breaks in the rules, in order to maintain their integrity and to support a climate of safety and inclusion. When teachers say what they mean and mean what they say, good times and learning can thrive.

Our purpose throughout this book is to integrate the teaching of academic and social learning. A well-designed, daily advisory provides the opportunity to move us from merely hoping students are ready to learn to fostering their readiness and reaping the benefits all day long.

Students meet in the Circle of Power and Respect

CHAPTER TWO

The Circle of Power and Respect

You know the old saying, "Life is a box of chocolates"? Middle school can be like that. Kids come in a variety of shapes, sizes, colors, cultures, and tastes. A middle school can be filled with cliques and clans, but there is a time each day when we all melt together and form a united community. CPR is a time when friends and loners, students and teachers can all blend together and leave negative perspectives behind.

—middle school advisory student, Hudson MA

THE CASE FOR STRUCTURE

Adolescents yearn to be free of the yoke of adult supremacy over what's going to happen, when, and how. Even though students may balk and complain at first, ultimately what will save them from the pain of cliques, exclusion, fear, and mistrust, and will make their days at school both productive and enjoyable, is a structure designed to produce a climate of inclusion, safety, challenge, and fun.

CPR is the glue of our school's project of community building; it's where we feel safe and confident with ourselves and others. We share what we think and feel without being judged.

—middle school advisory student, Hudson MA

To create new realities in the face of old, hardened ones, we have to experience the difference. A new reality is unlikely to happen by accident, so the components of the Circle of Power and Respect advisory are structured to provide it. Using the structure every day, or at least three times every week, infused with variety and challenge, provides a steady and novel way to build social and mental muscle. Instead of hoping for serendipity, design intentionally!

A sixth grade teacher struggling to build community in her homeroom with a student population that was diverse, poor, and gang-oriented had trouble getting some students to sit beside others during CPR. The best days were days when, for the activity portion of the meeting, they played chair-changing games. For example, they played a game called Where Are You From? in which one person in the center of the circle asked people that question at random, and everyone answered with the name of any state except the state in which they all resided. When a designated person said, "I'm from Minnesota," everyone had to take a new seat, including the person in the center. In the laughing scramble for a seat, gang affiliation slid away, and the students experienced themselves as a community. Every day, as they moved together through the structure of the four components of CPR, they enjoyed many opportunities to rise above their neighborhood exclusion code and reach towards each other.

—6th grade advisory, St. Paul MN

The Structure of CPR Is Designed to Meet Student Needs

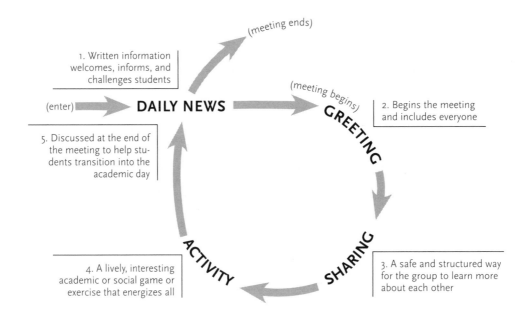

The four basic components of the Circle of Power and Respect speak to the basic needs of young adolescents. There is room for many variations within the four components, but the predictable format provides safety and reassurance. The structure keeps the meeting intact and effective, even when playful or idiosyncratic variations are introduced into it. You can count on the basic format of CPR to maintain peace, build connections, and provide the practice in speaking, listening, and thinking that is crucial to social and academic success.

Predictable CPR Structure Makes Student Leadership Possible

Because the structure is clearly defined and consistently practiced, students learn it and gradually become capable of leading all four parts of the meeting. To lead well, they must exercise many social skills—especially responsibility, assertion, and self-control. Leadership of the meeting provides a superb opportunity for young adolescents to experience themselves as successful leaders. See page 93 for details about building the capacity for student-led CPR.

A student responds to daily news message before CPR begins.

DAILY NEWS BEFORE THE MEETING

Purposes:

- To set a friendly tone at the beginning of the day
- To provide information about the day
- To stimulate student interest and thinking
- To improve skills in reading, writing, and following directions

The Basics

Students interact with the daily news message twice in advisory. They encounter it first as they enter the room, and their job is to read the message and write a response to a question or follow a direction before the advisory meeting gets underway. At the end of the meeting, the group reads the message together and discusses the news and the student contributions.

Reading the news and responding to a question or direction in it provides a productive task for every person in the group, a routine for beginning the day that downplays differences in the group and provides a purposeful alternative to just messing around as they come in. We call this morning task a "soft landing" from the bus and its commotion, from home, and from peer exchanges that might have left some people feeling unimportant or worse. Everyone has the same task. There's a job to do, and that job will become a part of the community meeting that is about to begin. It's as safe as it is predictable.

A welcoming message is a handy tool to get students started in the day or for a class hour. In addition to the date, the daily news message contains a friendly greeting to set a good tone and help students feel welcome. It has the appeal of a letter from a friend. It gives everyone an idea of how the day will go, thereby reducing the anxiety of the unknown. And it saves the teacher from having to respond repeatedly to the same questions. *What's the schedule today? Is this an A or a B day? Who's leading CPR? Are we doing Social Action Theater today?*

<u>Set-up for the Daily News</u>

Write the daily news message before advisory students enter the classroom, so it is there to greet them. Use the news to challenge students to see what they know about a topic, to think hard about an issue, and to organize themselves for the day.

Daily News Message Structure

<u>Essential</u>

- Friendly and welcoming tone
- Date
- Salutation
- Useful information about the meeting
- Stimulates thinking about a sharing topic or academic challenge
- Closing
- Signature
- System to monitor participation, if you invite student response
- Legible, accurate, and clearly written

<u>Optional</u>

- Mention something from yesterday or last week
- An interactive element (written, verbal, or reflective)
- Directions to think about or do something; an interactive question or exercise that is interesting and to which everyone responds
- A challenging word or two to build vocabulary (to be discussed during the processing of the news)
- An acknowledgment or reminder about behavior or academic performance
- Use Post-its to save time and avoid crowding when student interact with the news

Avoid using the message to post the entire day's schedule (not very interesting unless there's a change). Instead, post the daily schedule in the same place every day so students who need reminders about what is happening hour by hour can refer to it. The daily news message is different from a schedule. It's meant to be a friendly welcome to the classroom and the day.

Plan for Success

Paper, board, or electronic

Write your message so that it's convenient for you and your students. Chart paper is expensive, but it allows for the use of colorful markers and drawing, it's easy for students to write on, and they can be saved if you wish. Boards also allow for color (chalk or dry-erase), but have the drawback of smudging when they are touched. You can get around this by posting a paper next to the message for interactive responses. These you could save for review with students later in the year—a look back to see what we did and said at the beginning of the year. Another option is projecting the image of the news on a whiteboard.

Modeling and practicing the routine of daily news

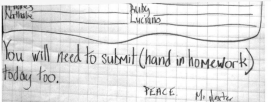

> STUDENTS CAN CREATE OUTCOME W/ GUIDANCE THROUGH MESSAGE IN HUDDLE - NEWS & ANNOUNCEMENTS

A daily news chart ready for student responses

Reading the news as students enter advisory or homeroom and responding to it is an important routine. For success, you need to introduce it, model, and practice the first time you do it, and thereafter whenever it seems necessary. Any routine takes a while to establish and needs to be reviewed and reinforced. If you skip the practice, you risk wasting time on the disagreeable task of correcting students because they ignored the protocol or didn't get it right. Like any routine or like the advisory guidelines themselves, the power lies in the practice. A good question to ask is: *How will this routine look, sound, and feel if we follow our advisory rules while doing it?*

Sample Daily News Message: First day of advisory

Date: Monday, September 7, 20___

Salutation: Ciao, Students!

Preview: Welcome to our advisory. This is a time to think a little, laugh a little, get to know each other, and prepare for a productive school day.

Call for Response: To begin, please sign in below under the season in which you were born, and write your birthday next to your name.

Summer	Fall	Winter	Spring
(July- September)	(October- December)	(January-March)	(April-June)

We'll be together for 15 minutes every day, and each day we'll start with a circle meeting. Directions: Please find your nametag on your chair, and wear it so all can see it.

Closing: Here's to a good year together!

Signature: Mrs. Lamongelo

Students can brainstorm some ideas about the daily news routine which you can record in a Y-chart that labels "look," "sound," and "feel" in its three sections. Post the chart on the wall. Then students can model the routines, following the Y-chart ideas.

Sample Y-Chart for Daily News Routine

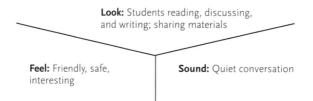

Now let's practice entering the classroom and reading and responding to the news following our Y-chart ideas. I'll call groups of four or five students at a time.

Finish with a brief reflection on what you have just practiced: *What did you notice about the way people read and responded to the news?*

This question is part of a process used throughout CPR and A+ advisories: *the reflective loop.* It involves setting up students to do something, doing it, and then reflecting on how you could improve it. The habit of such reflection will help them throughout their lives.

Let several students share their answers to the question. This will further reinforce the brainstorming of the Y-chart, the modeling, and the practicing. Now students are prepared for your expectations. Now you have greatly increased the likelihood that most, if not all, will responsibly follow the protocol of the daily news (and any other protocol approached with the same thorough care).

First day routine

As students enter her homeroom on the first day, Ms. Rueben meets them at the door and directs them to the daily news chart near where she stands by the door.

Good morning, Michael. Please read this message, and respond to the question I ask in it, as I have already done. Put your name in parentheses next to your answer. Then find the chair with your nametag on it in the circle. We'll begin our meeting in a couple of minutes.

Ms. Rueben greets the next couple of students the same way, and keeps an eye on the news chart to make sure that students are following the directions. When everyone has arrived and read and responded to the news, Ms. Rueben rings a bell and joins her students in the circle and begins the CPR meeting.

Teacher: *Thanks for following directions. As you look at the responses to the message, what do you notice?*

Student: *Not everybody signed their names.*

Teacher: *I noticed that, too. If you missed that part, you need to do it now. Devon, will you demonstrate for everyone what it looks like to respond to the daily news question or direction, and then identify your response?* (Devon adds his name to his response.) *What did you notice about how he did that?*

Student: He wrote small—there wasn't much room.

Teacher: I saw that. Tomorrow when you respond, please write small enough so there will be room for everyone. Reading the daily news message and responding to the message with your name attached is a requirement for everyone every day as you come into your advisory room.

Another possibility for that first modeling is that students take their assigned seats in the circle (indicated by nametags on chairs) and read the message from there, taking turns to write their responses. The first person to write a response should be the teacher, who models the process for everyone else.

Another approach is to have students come in and sit in the usual rows or groups until the teacher models for them how to read and respond to the message. Using this method, you also need to model how to move desks and bring chairs to the circle, followed by students bringing up their chairs before reading and responding to the chart. It's easier at first to have the chairs already arranged in a circle.

An orderly method of preceding a new routine with a *demonstration* of the correct way to do the routine will help head off trouble. Verbal instructions alone are insufficient. In any case, the teacher's job each day is to watch students read and interact in order to provide quality control and a chance to correct deviations, accidental or purposeful, from the routine.

A word about nametags

Nametags are annoying to most people, and middle level students especially resist wearing them. Even so, they must wear them in advisory during the first weeks of school. After enough time and CPR greetings and name games have transpired that everyone knows everyone else's name, it's fine to stop wearing nametags. But keep them handy. When a new student arrives, everyone needs to wear nametags for at least a couple of weeks, to give the new person a chance to learn names. When there is a guest speaker or a substitute, out come the nametags again. To maintain a safe and friendly climate, everyone needs access to everyone else's name—easily. And don't let students get away with wearing their tags in obscure locations such as on a back pocket or on a leg or under a shirt. The purpose of such locations is usually resistance or even rebellion. The response needs to be always a preservation of the standards.

Nametags are worn on the front near the right or left shoulder so they are visible to everyone. A clearly visible nametag is required for participation in CPR. A student who violates the nametag guidelines sits out of the circle until he or she displays a nametag properly.

Keep it simple

The daily news message doesn't have to be fancy, and it doesn't have to be long. It does need to have a welcoming tone, give information pertinent to the day so that everyone is informed, and ideally it prompts a response so that students start participating in school right at the start of the day.

One way to simplify it is to begin to gather from colleagues, books, magazines, newspapers, etc., questions or challenges that would interest young adolescents and would challenge them to use what they know in order to answer. Answers can be on a chart or overhead or on Post-its. Think about potential questions in four categories:

Personal: ask students to share a little about themselves—their likes and dislikes, things they do, people they know; not private information, but the sort of things they are willing to publicly share so that everyone in the group gets to know everyone else. *What is your favorite food, color, song, place to be, season, etc.?*

Tell us about a favorite person in your family.

Describe a pet you have, used to have, or wish you had.

If you could visit anywhere in the world, where would you go?

What is a habit you broke or wish you could break?

Social: ask for ideas about how to behave or responses about how students handle a social issue, or questions about social skills in general.

What's something to remember about your behavior in tomorrow's assembly?

In your opinion, how did we do in following the guidelines during yesterday's presentation in assembly?

How do students need to behave for the 8th grade dance to be a success?

What are some ways you handle conflicts with your friends or family?

What makes it hard for you to follow rules?

Academic review: ask students to remember content they have learned; you can designate a day for working on spelling or vocabulary or math each week. And whatever other academics you are focusing on, a daily word or two purposely included to stretch vocabularies will pay off in academic performance. You can circle and discuss these words when you process the message.

Put a checkmark next to the following words that are spelled correctly.

Matching: *Write the correct word next to its definition*

Choose a word below and write its synonym and antonym.

Make up a math word problem, write it on a card along with your name, and drop it in the basket. (Try a couple problems when you read the news message, and keep the rest for future meetings.)

Name a way that people can save energy, water, or other resources.

How many U.S. presidents can you think of? Write the number with your name next to it.

Be ready to add proper punctuation to a sentence in the chart.

Current events: prompt students to think about political and ethical issues.

Read the clipping, decide whether you agree or disagree that only the man driving the truck should have been arrested, and be ready to give your reasons.

If the election for President were held tomorrow, for whom would you vote? Be ready to give one reason for your choice.

Check below your choice for the main reason that the school levy didn't pass:

People don't have the money to pay more taxes;

People don't care about schools once their kids are finished with school;

Not very many people voted.

Payoffs of Consistency

The importance of reading and responding to the daily news chart is made clear only if the message is there every day for which you have planned an advisory meeting. Consistency breeds habit, and the habit of reading and responding to the message has lots of payoffs.

Students get practice in:

- reading for comprehension
- reading aloud
- building vocabulary

- thinking and then responding
- following directions
- solving problems
- reviewing content-area information and skills

They get geared up for the school day within a context that is relational and fun. They know just what to do when they walk into the room, and what there is to do helps them to grow personally and academically.

Reading and responding to daily news message is most successful when everyone is expected to participate. The message of such consistent expectations is that this community is dedicated to serious learning as well as social development, and we begin right now, as you step into the classroom. There's no time to lose!

When students mess up

If responding to the news is an assignment, then everyone is responsible for doing it. Many times you are asking students to think about something, or remember a piece of information, or evaluate or explain. In short, you are asking them to shift into school mode, so it's important, and, therefore, a requirement. Of course, you need to engage students in the topic question so they *want* to respond. Model the way you want students to read and respond to the message. Especially at first, stand near the message to supervise the quality of the work done with it. Ultimately, when you have students leading CPR meetings, they can also help set the questions or directions, which will add interest for other students.

If you give the direction to students to read and respond to the chart, you have to stick to it. Once you have set the expectation, you must keep track each day of whether you are getting what you require from the students. Some teachers assign class numbers and list each number next to a line on the message for each student's response; then it's clear whose response is missing.

Since responding is a requirement, you'll have to do something when some students skip the chart. For example, as a logical consequence for not responding you can require that everyone who has not responded do so before going on to their next class, a delay that is usually unpopular. It's easier to just do it when they first come in the room.

Reminding students who tend to skip the message, and personally overseeing their reading and responding, is the best way to get them into the habit of doing the task independently. What doesn't work is ignoring non-participation. If you show that response is optional (which is what you are doing by having no consequence for skipping it), you signal that it is acceptable to ignore it.

An unstructured beginning to advisory can be a setup for exclusion and confusion. A rigorous start is worth enforcing. When the news is an enforced routine, it helps equalize advisory. Everyone has something to do, and no one is left out.

Challenge Them

At first, students may not see the importance of reading the news and following the directions. Ask them to rise to the challenge anyway, to build for themselves the habit of following directions, to get their minds going at the start of the day, and to be fully participating members of the advisory. The daily news sets the tone for the day. It says, "Step up and be a student!" Accepting that invitation begins the day's learning.

Steady Progress

Once students have the routine established and everyone knows what to do and does it (with or without reminders), it's time to increase the challenge. Begin with simple questions for the interactive part of the message.

Name an insect.

What is a sign of spring?

What is your favorite sport?

Move on to questions that call for a little more risk-taking or are somewhat academically challenging.

Who is someone you admire, and why?

What is a skill you'd like to improve?

Select a newspaper clipping from the basket and be prepared to paraphrase what it says.

Write a challenging vocabulary word for us to learn and be ready to share its definition and use it in a sentence.

A sixth grader writes a learning goal on the daily news message

Turning it over to them

At first, only the teacher makes up the daily news message for the day, but as students show they can handle it, they can begin to create the questions for class response and eventually write the news. Everything, of course, is reviewed by the teacher, and the teacher can require the inclusion of certain information. See the guidelines for student-led CPR's starting on page 93 and CPR Student Plan Sheet on page 270.

Students enjoy creating the news, selecting an interesting question or direction, and writing the chart with colored markers or on the overhead or other methods. It's a chance to be creative and to have a little fun. As students take over the daily news, problems of non-participation are reduced, and the opportunity for self-directed intellectual growth increases. Remember, giving responsibility to students must be carefully graduated. Bit by bit, they become responsibly independent with regard to each component of CPR.

Scaffolding

When they seem ready, have students write interesting questions and challenges on index cards. Then you can select interactive portions for your news message from their questions.

Next, ask a student or two to come in early and transfer the message you have written on a piece of paper onto the board or chart paper or overhead master. Invite students to decorate the News with colorful drawings or designs.

Finally, when your community is strong and some students are willing to do the work, have partners create the whole message, in draft form the day before so you can have input and approve it. Watch the messages become even more relevant and interesting to students when they are written by peers! And watch the challenges increase—probably beyond what you would have given them—as they try to make innovative and exciting messages for their peers.

Q & A

Q. *I don't have time to write a message every day. Is there any way to make this part easier? I have so much to prepare already! What if I run out of interesting things to say or ask?*

There are several possibilities that could help. First, if you jot the message down the night before or during the previous day or at breakfast, the job becomes one of simply copying it onto a chart or the board—much quicker. Keep it as simple as you need to—just make sure it's interesting to your students. See the sample chart above on page 35 for a reminder of the basic parts of the message, a format that repeats day after day.

Another solution to the time problem is for teacher teams to either construct messages together that everyone uses, or take turns constructing messages for the whole team to use. One person could do the messages for everyone for a week, or you could establish a regular day of the week for each person. Sharing the responsibility means that students will get a variety of content questions, too—some days math, others science or social studies or language arts. Nothing too advanced—just the basics for review.

There are books that can help you with the interactive part. Some, like the *Chicken Soup* series, have little inspirational stories that you can use to get a response. Others have lists of questions that interest young adolescents. There are mind-bending problems, minute mysteries to solve, and all sorts of vocabulary challenges and riddles. You can even pose questions straight from old standardized tests! The following websites have puzzles, Mad Libs, and other ideas you can use for daily news messages:

> http://brainden.com/logic-puzzles.htm
>
> http://www.folj.com/puzzles
>
> http://www.madglibs.com
>
> http://www.wuzzlesandpuzzles.com

And then there is *this book!* It contains a daily news message (or the key sentences of a message) for 200 advisories. The main group is in Chapter 5: 170 Thematic Advisories.

It could be that the best source of help is the students themselves. Ask them to write on index cards questions they would find interesting to discuss. Request from your librarian books that have good resources for questions or quick stories, and have students comb through those and select a few that they think would be interesting. The resulting file of cards becomes your resource—the best kind, because they come directly from the people who will be answering or responding.

Q. *It all seems so haphazard! Do I just pick a question out of the hat each day?*

Your daily news messages can progress as sequentially or as randomly as you wish. If a sequence is helpful, you can focus on a topic for several days or organize a whole advisory series under a theme (see Chapter 4: Planning Advisories). Another approach is to designate a general category for each day of the week.

Monday: personal news

Students arrive with memories of the weekend. The interactive question can be:
What is one thing you enjoyed this weekend?
What is something you did with someone else this weekend?
How are you feeling after the weekend?

Tuesday: current events

Ask a question about a current event or direct students to read clippings and be ready to share one piece of information about them.

Wednesday: vocabulary-building

Define _____(students offer their best guesses to define an unfamiliar word).
Try to stump us with a word to define (students offer words, perhaps from the dictionary).
Name a synonym or antonym (each student contributes a pair)

Every day you can include a word or two in the news that would make a good addition to students' vocabularies. In the sample advisories in Chapter 5, each daily news message highlights a word that is useful academically. These words can be discussed, defined, and used in sentences. You can keep a running list, and encourage students to find ways to use them during advisory. When you hear one, be sure to notice and acknowledge it.

<u>Thursday: quotations or anecdotes</u>

Respond to a question asked about the quotation or story.

<u>Friday: homework tally</u>

Categories: Homework handed in; still outstanding and overdue; still outstanding and due next week. Students indicate the items they have in each category. Remind them on Thursday that there will be a homework tally on Friday—maybe they'll finish everything Thursday night!

<u>Other daily topics</u>

- Geography Day ("Where in the world is _____?")
- Math Day ("100 is the answer. What is the question? No repeats.")
- Famous People Day ("Name a U.S. president—no repeats.")
- Science Day ("Name a cycle that occurs in nature—no repeats.")
- Social Issues Day ("You know that a friend often feels left out. Do you tell her about things you've done with others?")
- Ethical Issues Day ("You know that a friend is secretly doing some unsafe things. Do you tell a teacher or some other concerned adult?")

Q. *Sometimes students write inappropriate things or write over what others have written on the chart, or take too long writing so others don't get a chance. How do you manage having everyone write on the same piece of paper or board?*

It does take management. If you are looking for anything more than a couple of words in response, use Post-it notes. Talk with students about behavior at the daily news.

We have about three minutes total for everyone to respond to the daily news board. What are some things that would speed the process?

If students still take too long, or if they violate guidelines in the other ways that you mentioned, they can lose the privilege of writing directly on the news. Instead, give them a piece of paper for a few days, and then give them another chance to write directly on the news board.

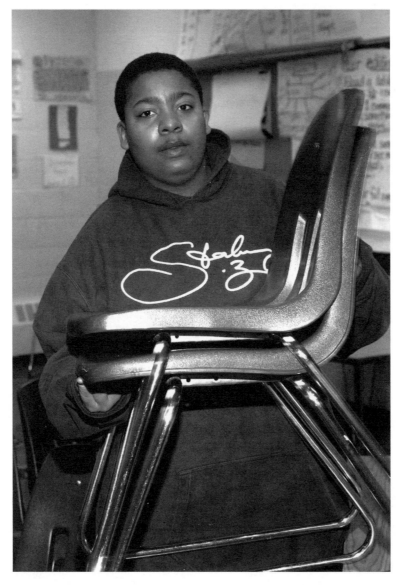

Moving chairs to form the
CPR circle

A Last Word of Encouragement

When Ms. D's advisory students come into the room on a Monday morning there is no daily news message. "Where's the news, Ms. D.?" they ask, each and every one, as soon as they arrive. "I have a headache," she replies, "and I didn't get it done." One student responds, "We'll do it," and she scrawls a quick note on the board:

> Daily News, January 17,
> Be good. Ms. D. has a headache today.
> Sabrina.

Now the students enter, read the news, and quietly go to their seats.

Offer daily news to your advisory students every day. It provides a constructive, inclusive routine that uses their reading, writing, and thinking skills, and it sets a friendly tone for the day that eases the transition into school.

CIRCLING UP

Purposes:

- To bring the community together, face-to-face
- To include everyone

> A group of 21 students and one teacher sit in their circle of chairs. Like the Knights of the Round Table, they sit as equals—no one at the head and no one at the foot. Each of them is open to the rest of the circle.
>
> —middle school advisory student, Cambridge MA

The circle is one of the best arrangements possible for gathering students together. In it, everyone can see everyone, and exclusion is less likely. The teacher can easily watch for put-downs or other rule-breaking, as well as for supportive moves that need to be acknowledged. In the circle, all voices are much more likely to be heard. Students are fully visible when they speak and can have all eyes on them, instead of speaking to people they can't see or, worse, the backs of heads.

The circle needs to be explained to the group on the first day. Announce your objective that everyone in the room will be respected by the group. Everyone will be welcomed. Everyone will be invited to have fun. You accept the people in your group and find ways to work well with them. Our school is an "Equal Opportunity" environment.

The Basics

Setting up the circle

Have the circle set up before students enter the room, or, if that is not possible, train students to move furniture in a careful, quiet, safe, and efficient way. Model moving a chair yourself, and then have one or two students model the same thing. Ask students what they saw, to make sure they paid attention. Then have a few at a time bring their chairs to the circle.

Essential

- Round circle
- Inclusive seating

Optional

- Sit on chairs or floor, but everyone at the same level
- Assigned seating

Students can generate their own look/sound/feel Y-chart to remind themselves of the standards for circling up. Post the chart on the wall. Then students can model the routines, following the Y-chart ideas, and afterwards, they can check the chart to see how well they did. The following chart example assumes that the chairs are already in place, and students merely need to find a seat.

Sample Y-Chart for Sitting in Circle Routine

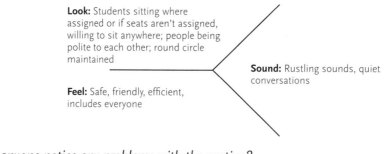

Look: Students sitting where assigned or if seats aren't assigned, willing to sit anywhere; people being polite to each other; round circle maintained

Sound: Rustling sounds, quiet conversations

Feel: Safe, friendly, efficient, includes everyone

Did anyone notice any problems with the seating?
Are there suggestions for improving our speed or courtesy?

Make it round

As best you can, keep the circle truly round—not an oval or square or rectangle or other polygon. Only the circular configuration allows all to see and be seen. Participation will decrease if the equality of the circle is missing, and you will miss small infractions if students block each other from your sight.

Assigned seats

To prevent the circle from mirroring the cliques of the moment in the class or in school, assign seats to everyone to set the tone for inclusivity. The inclusive nature of the circle immediately presents issues for students who tend towards exclusive friendship groups. In the circle, you must be willing to sit alongside any member of the group. Although eventually seating may be by choice at least some of the time, it is a good idea to begin with assigned seats to get the message across that this is an accepting and inclusive class. Everyone counts. Everyone is okay. If you secretly disagree, you must still act in a way appropriate to the routine and sit beside anyone.

One simple way to assign seats is to place nametags on chairs if the circle is made before students arrive. If students set up the circle, they can stand until seating is designated.

On the first day, if you know the students well enough, arrange the seating so that friendship groups are not clustered together. If you don't know the students well enough yet, seating will have to be randomly assigned, but that is bound to be less exclusive than allowing students to select their own places. If some students switch chairs to be near friends, it's best to redirect them to take the seat assigned in order to underline the importance of everyone mixing with everyone else.

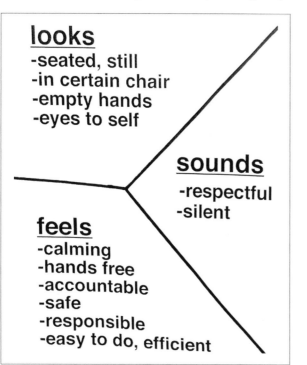

looks
-seated, still
-in certain chair
-empty hands
-eyes to self

sounds
-respectful
-silent

feels
-calming
-hands free
-accountable
-safe
-responsible
-easy to do, efficient

Y-chart for an advisory's circle

Random seating works well to mix things up, and there are lots of fun ways to direct students to sit randomly.

Sit next to someone of the opposite gender.

Get into birthday order and take seats in that order.

Pick a number and go to the chair with that number. (You can attach number tabs on the backs of the chairs.)

Sit next to someone with whom you haven't spoken yet today.

Plan for Success

The teacher is a member of the circle. He definitely has the most power to control what goes on. However, sitting in a way that is equal to everyone else in the room, instead of standing up and over everyone else, reduces the students' sense of being dominated by an adult. The adult's control and observation are tempered by body language.

When students mess up

If anyone tries to move a chair his own way, and that way is not acceptable, stop the action, ask for a reminder of the right way from the student, and then have him proceed. If the violation of protocol persists, have the student put the chair down and come stand next to you to watch while others continue. At the end, the wayward student can try again. Nothing but the agreed-upon protocol for moving chairs is acceptable. The moment you let slide one deviation, more will follow.

Challenge Them

Make the seating process transparent. Tell students that you are looking forward to the day when they are able to mix up their seating any old way and be just fine about it.

In a world where divisions between people are painfully apparent, and some fights are causing thousands to die, in a world where adults seem to cluster off into antagonistic groups of same class, same color, same lifestyle, in our class, and in our school, we can do better. We can create inclusive communities in which everyone is safe and cared for. If we do that in school, maybe it will begin to spill over into life outside school and be the beginning of a peaceful community, a peaceful country, a peaceful world. I believe you can begin the process right here in this room. You can make our room a place where people get along and have fun. In this class, everyone's okay, and we sit beside each other and talk in friendly ways. In this class, peace is possible.

Your own speech may be shorter and in different words, or it may contain a personal story. The purpose remains clear: to inspire young adolescents to walk the high road. You may not pull them all in this direction, but at least you point out the goal as one worth moving towards, to which you yourself are dedicated.

Here is where the advisory rules you made together (and perhaps the rules agreed upon by the whole school) will help keep everyone safe. For example, if you established a rule to respect each other, it is a sign of that respect that everyone is willing to sit beside everyone else. Once the rules have been established, reminders and reinforcements about them keep a protective fence around your community. We have limits, and the limits keep us safe.

Steady Progress

The formation of the circle presents an opportunity to keep stretching socially and emotionally. If you are transparent with students about your objectives in the seating process, they will understand the goal and the reasons for it, whether they like the process or not. You can set before them your wish that eventually, with no prompting or orchestrating from you, they will be willing to come into the room and take a seat next to anyone in the class. At that point they have new social power—the capacity to interact with each other in civil ways, whatever personal preferences they may have. The work world is waiting for people with this skill. It is a requirement for effective operations in any organization. Can they get there? How long will it take? When it does happen, stop everything and celebrate!

Q & A

Q. *What if a student refuses to sit in her assigned seat?*

Her decision means she refuses to follow the meeting guidelines, so she loses the privilege of being in the meeting. The meeting format promises the kind of relationship-building and fun that students need, so generally they are not happy about missing it. Even if the student acts as if she doesn't care, stay the course and have her sit out. The ticket into the meeting is the willingness to behave in a respectful way to everyone in the group.

Q. *What if things are going well, everyone is included, and I decide to let students start self-selecting their seating, but then—crash—they slip into old habits and start arranging to sit next to only their friends?*

Go back to assigned seating. The main goal is for the meeting to feel safe for everyone, and it doesn't feel that way when exclusive relationships start showing up. Tell them what you are doing and why, and challenge them to rise above their preferences.

Q. *If I don't have room or time to set up a circle, can we meet from our desks?*

The power of the circle shapes CPR. If you give up the circle arrangement, you're unlikely to get the effect of connectedness and equality the circle provides. Think as creatively as you can. Some teachers hold the meeting in a hallway or in another room available at advisory time. If all that you have to work with is desks with chairs attached, try arranging the desks in a circle, and have students sit on their desks so that nothing is between them and the space in the center of the circle. Some teachers hold a brief standing meeting—whatever it takes to pull the community together, face to face, and start the day with relationship, focused attention, and fun.

A Last Word of Encouragement

A sixth grade teacher, was having trouble with student behavior during CPR. He realized that one problem was that he couldn't see all his students, so he removed some furniture to form a true circle. Then everyone could see everyone else. He could see small things before they escalated, and the students seemed more relaxed and accepting. The circle had drawn them all together.

—6th grade advisory, St. Paul MN

The circle brings a connectedness that no other arrangement can, and along with that connection come better behavior, more inclusivity and civility, and a setup conducive to conversation and play—just what your middle level students want and need.

Students greet safely and with eye contact in a simple high five greeting

GREETING

Purposes:

- Students learn the skills of formal, friendly, and fun formats for social encounters
- Everyone relates to everyone in the community

In the beginning of the year, when we were asked to look the person sitting next to us in the eye and say good morning, no one could do it without bursting out laughing. Now we are mature young adults.

—middle school advisory student, Tabernacle NJ

As soon as the group has circled up—in chairs, on the floor, even standing or sitting on desks with chairs attached—everyone is greeted by someone. Format possibilities for this greeting are many, but the important thing is that it is done with a friendly, non-exclusive tone. Sometimes students go a whole day without hearing another student say their names in a friendly way. To say the least, this does not help build confidence. This is no way to create a safe community, and it is an impediment to learning.

What we have to realize to be willing to set aside time for greetings (however brief) and to overcome any early push-back to them is that even if only some of the students on a team or in the school feel left out, safety in the climate of the whole school is compromised. And it never stops at just a few students: exclusion breeds exclusion; cliques breed more cliques. The greeting is like a quiet, almost secret machine, building connections steadily, whatever else might be going on to pull people apart from one another.

Friendly, accepting greetings each day help us all become the people others *want* to include. It is difficult to feel important when nobody says your name. Nothing really begins between people until and unless they have acknowledged each other's presence. Although the structured greeting may begin as stilted and artificial, it will become important to students before long.

> In my 6th grade CPR meeting, after the greeting, a student reminded me that we hadn't yet greeted students who were absent. "Thanks for reminding us, Maria. Who can tell us who is missing?" Monty named three absent students, and we greeted each of them in turn. At that moment and every time we greet absent people, all the students who are present in the room know that in this community everyone counts. Whether students are at school or not, their community wishes them well with a greeting. Maria wasn't willing for us to skip that part, and if she hadn't reminded me, someone else would have.
>
> —6th grade advisory, Woodbury MN

> We wanted all the students in our advisory to feel that they were connected, even when they were absent, so we decided to make a quick call to those not there to wish them well, discover why they were not at school and say hello. Parents were amazed at how much this did to make their children feel connected to school and significant in the eyes of their peers.
>
> —6th through 8th grade advisories, LaCrosse WI

The Basics

Essential

- Greeting is the first thing that happens in the meeting, and it sets a positive tone
- Everyone is included and everyone's name is said
- Greetings are respectful and friendly; eyes make contact
- Time frame is 2 to 5 minutes

Optional

- Include gestures, voices, movement to add variety
- Include choice of person to greet (after CPR is well established)
- Include a brief share

Setting up the greeting

Start with a simple, universal greeting: "Good morning, Charles." "Good morning, Maria." The greeting is made person-to-person, around the circle, everyone being greeted and greeting someone else one time. From the most popular student to the least popular—everyone gets and gives the same or similar greeting.

Plan for Success

Model and practice

Greetings, like any other behavior that you wish to formalize, need to be modeled by the teacher and perhaps by a student or two, before the class as a whole tries them out. There is no substitute for a concrete, physical display of the behavior you are seeking. Every time you introduce a new greeting, use modeling to help students get it right.

Students can generate their own look/sound/feel Y-chart to remind themselves of the quality of greeting towards which they are aiming. Post the chart on the wall; then students can model the routines, following the Y-chart ideas.

Sample Y-Chart for Greeting Routine

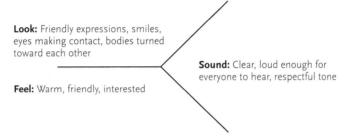

Look: Friendly expressions, smiles, eyes making contact, bodies turned toward each other

Sound: Clear, loud enough for everyone to hear, respectful tone

Feel: Warm, friendly, interested

Example: Introduction of the Name Card Greeting in which each student randomly picks the name of someone to greet

What did Sam do first? Where did he put the card that he turned over on the pile? What did he do next? What did you notice when Sam and Lola greeted each other? That respectful tone is what we want—nothing less is acceptable. Has everyone got it now, or should we model it one more time?

It takes time to be this proactive about a greeting, but it pays off in time saved and aggravation avoided when students get it wrong because they weren't clear in the first place. They need to hear it, see it, and ultimately feel it themselves. Once guidelines are established, you can link the performance of the greeting to them.

If we greeted each other in the spirit of our rule, "Respect everyone," how would we be behaving? What would be our tone of voice? How would the person greeted feel?

After everyone has participated in the greeting, reflect together on how well you did.

Thumbs up if you think we did pretty well on this greeting, sideways if you think we could improve. Sharon, what could we do better next time?

Keep it simple at first—nothing fancy, no personal spins

To build student capacity to do a variety of greetings well, keep it really simple at first—no handshake, no high five, no standing up. When you first introduce the greeting, for many, it is challenging enough to do the basic version of "Good morning, Jason" with respect. You have to turn your body towards the person, look him in the eyes, and have a friendly look on your face, even if your expression is serious. And you have to try to keep eye contact long enough to receive a response greeting.

The biggest challenge for many adolescents is maintaining this level of respect and friendliness when greeting classmates they may not know or, worse yet, have decided they do not like. Sometimes the issue is that the cool kids think this person is a loser. Sometimes the issue is a recent quarrel with the very person you must greet. No matter what, you use the same format with the same friendly tone. The standardization helps remove the opportunity to greet friends one way and other people another way.

Once the greeting is modeled and practiced, your job is to maintain the format as demonstrated, no matter who is greeting whom. As the leader, you keep asking students to notice the tone and attitude of the greetings—neutral or warmer is the goal, and everyone knows it.

How did our greeting go today? Did everyone give and receive a friendly welcome?

Day after day you greet around the circle, and soon it becomes a natural, ordinary ritual, as ordinary as saying hi to someone in the halls or greeting a friend outside of school. The difference in the CPR circle is that everybody gets a greeting—the same greeting—something that would never happen if you didn't orchestrate it. As a result, the chances of everyone having a productive day at school increase.

When Students Mess Up

The CPR meeting was about to begin. Students were gathered together in a circle, and before the greeting began the teacher reminded them, "Remember, one voice at a time. For any side talk or interrupting, I'll have the person sit out for a while until he or she regains self-control." Heads nodded, except for two students who looked down at the floor. As soon as the teacher began to introduce the day's greeting, one of those students whispered something to the person sitting next to him. "Brandon, take a break," the teacher said immediately, and continued with the greeting, watching Brandon out of the corner of her eye. Brandon sat still for a few seconds, then rose and walked slowly to a chair just outside the circle. The greeting began, and in a moment, Brandon returned and participated in it. Everyone was greeted without further ado. The teacher had set the tone for a respectful greeting and reinforced the safety of the circle.

—8th grade advisory, Minneapolis MN

Maintain rigor: protect the rules, and the rules will protect the group

When students break the rules, an immediate response from the teacher can keep the ship moving steadily through the waters—as long as that response in no way demeans the rule-breaker. When the rules are decided by teacher and students together, when the routines and protocols have been carefully modeled and practiced, and even so, a student violates them in any way, big or small, what is called for is a quick response that is respectful in tone, preserves the dignity of the student, and enforces the rules. The integrity of the social agreements and the credibility of the social fabric depend upon the teacher demonstrating that she means what she says and she says what she means.

After a class has modeled and practiced democratically made rules, the eyes of everyone in the circle will be on the teacher, to see if she follows through. It doesn't matter that it was a small thing like a quick whisper. It doesn't matter that the whisper happened to come from a student who rarely disrupts and is doing very well in school. The follow-through of the teacher, upholding the agreed-upon guidelines for behavior, is what counts.

CPR is an enjoyable experience from which students can learn a lot, both socially and academically, and its atmosphere needs to be a combination of playfulness and consistent rigor. In fact, it can be said that that combination is one of CPR's great strengths. When implemented as designed, it demands the highest levels of self-control from students at the same time as it provides them an outlet for fun and relationship.

The challenge for the advisory teacher is to maintain the rigor, watching carefully for rule infractions and inserting prompt and respectful redirecting when they occur. If a teacher notices a misbehavior, he has to address it, or the integrity of the rules begins to slip away. In the end, everyone benefits. If we address small problems, they don't become big.

Nowhere is this more important than during the greeting, where the smallest anti-social moves (rolled eyes, sarcastic looks, sounds of disparagement) can undo not only the feeling of welcome and belonging of the student who was greeting or being greeted at that moment, but of the whole group. If it can happen to one, it can happen to any and all.

Maintain rigor: watch over the general tone of the greeting

Gestures, facial expressions, tones of voice, and body language express feelings. But feeling angry or sad is not an acceptable reason for showing less than respect when students give and receive greetings. Nothing other than following the greeting protocol is acceptable. If you don't keep the standard uniformly high, somebody will soon use the greeting as a way to indicate who really counts with them and who doesn't. The power of the greeting to build community depends upon the teacher's maintaining the standard.

After the greeting has been modeled and practiced, when someone purposely shows disrespect to a classmate by refusing to look at the other person or by mumbling a half-hearted greeting, the leader must interrupt, ask for a repeat using the protocol as practiced (if it seems that might improve the situation), and ultimately, if the second try is still unacceptable or if the student refuses, direct the failed greeter to sit outside the circle during the rest of the meeting. The circle must be kept safe, or the meeting will not be effective.

Challenge Them

In civil societies, people greet one another. First they acknowledge each other's presence with a greeting, and then they proceed to conversation or activities together. A greeting is the mark of a civilized encounter, an acknowledgment of respect for each member of the community greeted. People need to have their presence acknowledged.

Greetings have become ritualized partly because the repetition of them makes them easier, more automatic, and as such they grease the gears of relationship. Either we learn to meet and greet each other in hospitable ways, or we steer clear of each other and build ... nothing. The good life and greetings go hand in hand.

What does it feel like to join a group and have no one look at you directly and no one greet you? We don't want that feeling in this advisory, ever. That's why we have a group greeting.

Students mingle and greet as a whole group.

Steady Progress

The directions for many greetings are provided in Appendix B. They are arranged by levels, the first ones being the easiest to manage socially and physically. At Levels 2 and 3, the greetings require more self-control, more acceptance of each other, and a higher social risk of embarrassment or showing feelings. Choose your greetings carefully, and don't move to more challenging levels until students have mastered the easier greetings. Each one, of course, is modeled when it is introduced, and practiced. When it has been mastered, it can become part of the class repertoire of greetings.

Sample Progression

See Appendix A to find greetings with levels indicated.

Level 1 (simple, low risk, low level of self-control, minimal autonomy)
Everyone uses the same simple greeting; teacher-controlled. Examples:

- All Group Greeting (each person greets the group and the group greets back)
- Basic Greeting (each person greets his/her neighbor in the circle with, "Good morning, _____.")

Level 2 (more complex, some risk, more self-control, some autonomy)
Everyone uses the same greeting; greeting may have a physical component or an additional phrase; teacher-controlled. Examples:

- Formal Greeting ("Good morning, Mr./Ms. _____.") with a handshake
- Informal greetings like High Five and other Hand Jive Greeting variations
- Name Card Greeting (students greet at random whoever's name they pick)

Level 3 (complex, greatest risk, need for high self-control, more autonomy, less supervision) Students are given the choice of whom to greet, and sometimes how to greet; teacher-supervised at first, eventually minimal teacher supervision. Examples:

- Choice Greeting (students decide whom to greet—one greeting per person; one greeting at a time)
- Ball Toss Greeting (students decide whom to greet and toss a ball with the greeting—one greeting per person, one greeting at a time)
- Theatrical Greeting (students assume a special voice or action while they greet)
- Greetings with minimal teacher control (e.g., One-Minute Greeting and Snake Greeting, or Gift Greeting, where students improvise)

There are many more active greetings that challenge students' ability to maintain self-control while they are moving fast in a small space, but the above list gives the idea of gradual movement toward increasing challenge. Because of the selective nature of many middle school relationships, the greetings in which one can greet someone by choice are risky. It may take a good deal of modeling and reflecting together to master a choice greeting. Unless it is done within the standards of including everyone and disrespecting no one, it endangers the group. It may help to challenge students to demonstrate that they have an adult finesse with greetings. Whatever you do, hold firm on inclusion and respect.

In this class, we are committed to everyone feeling accepted. How can we do the Choice Greeting in such a way that all of us feel good about it at the end?

Adding variations

The end goal with greetings is to launch the relationship-building of the meeting. Once students have mastered the Basic Greeting of "Good morning, Sam," you can begin to add variations.

My students last year liked pretty simple greetings, or ball toss. But this year, my group is really into drama. Their favorite kind of greeting now is when they assume voices: Greet your person with a Santa voice ("Ho, ho, ho! Good morning, Cecille.") Greet your person with an Australian hello ("G'day mate!"); Greet like Fat Albert ("Hey, hey, hey—I'm silly Sarah," and the group responds, "Good morning, Silly Sarah!")

— 7th-8th grade advisory, Minneapolis MN

Not all 8th graders would like this kind of silly flamboyance. But if some of the group want to be dramatic, the more reserved will have to learn to go along once in awhile, and so will the Fat Albert lovers when greetings are done that are not their favorites. Students learn to compromise, to be good sports, to let go of coolness enough to have some foolish fun. Slowly, the greetings become natural to them, and as they do, other possibilities open up.

Scaffolding greetings from simple to complex

The greetings described in Appendix B range within a continuum from simple and low-risk to more complex, more active, and more risky. Move along the continuum only as far and as fast as the students show they are able to manage with good social skills. When they slip, move back to a less challenging greeting format, and move forward again when they seem ready. Appendix A indicates greetings at Levels 1, 2, and 3.

Let them in on this growth process. Tell them there are lots of playful greetings you could try, and you'll introduce them as they demonstrate their readiness. Readiness means they have the self-control and confidence they will need for the more challenging greetings. Ask them if they think they are ready, and ask them to remind you and each other what readiness looks like. Then go for it! If you have to back up to easier greetings, let them know that you have faith in their ability to rise to the more challenging ones—if not today, then maybe next week, when you try again.

This new greeting calls for everyone to be moving at the same time inside the circle. Do you think you can handle this with courtesy? It will require that you be aware of the space and avoid bumping into people. Let's try it with just a few people to see what it will look like (greeting is modeled by 3 or 4 students). *Let's all try it now. If we can't handle it, we'll stop, do a simpler greeting instead, and try this one later.*

Now the challenge is out there, and the students will likely strive to rise to it. Eventually, the process of greeting can become truly their own when they choose which greeting to do, and when they begin to collect and invent new greetings for the group to try. The opportunities for autonomy and leadership are limited only by their capacity to handle themselves well.

Ultimately you want to be able to do what one group of 7th and 8th graders in Minneapolis was able to do: on cue, to have many students in the middle of the circle greeting as many other people as possible, with no one left out, and everyone greeting each and every person. The vigor and inclusiveness of the greeting is a good barometer of the health of the advisory community.

Q & A

Q. *What do I do when someone is told to sit out the greeting, but then wants to come back for sharing or the activity?*

Because the greeting acknowledges the welcome and welcoming presence of everyone in the circle, a student cannot be in the circle without giving and receiving a courteous greeting; otherwise, the circle feels—and is—unsafe. Other sit-outs from the circle because of behavior, for example during sharing or an activity, can be quick, with the student returning when s/he is back in control, but a sit-out during the greeting can last through the whole meeting. The best policy is "No greet—no meet." Only when a student is willing to greet all others respectfully (which s/he may choose to *return* to the meeting and do) does s/he get to participate in the meeting.

Students engage in a more complex greeting

Q. *What if the students say that the greeting is stupid, a kindergarten kind of thing?*

Try using anthropology and sociology to explain the function of greetings around the world: greetings are the hallmark of hospitality. In every culture, they express welcome and acceptance to friends and strangers. Lightheartedness is not childish – it expresses trust and ease, and enhances the atmosphere of welcome and safety.

Use practical work examples. In an interview, the initial greeting reveals much. A confident handshake, a friendly smile, and a warm voice set a confident, respectful tone for the first encounter with a prospective employer. Because future employment may depend in part on your ability to make a formal greeting with ease and grace, start practicing now!

Speak to their hunger for autonomy:

Once we master the basics of greetings and demonstrate some grace with them, you can begin to suggest and even invent greetings. The greater your power of self-control, and the more you show care for one another, the more freedom you'll have to design your own greetings.

Q. *Sometimes a student's cultural norm does not include a handshake or looking eye-to-eye during a greeting. Do you allow students to greet along the lines of their own culture whatever others are doing?*

Usually, no. The norm of the school shapes greetings within the school, just as the norms at home or on the street shape those encounters. Students can learn to adapt and do things more than one way, adjusting their behavior to circumstances. Adaptation is a life skill that invests an individual with a good deal of personal power. Young people have always created their own culture, in large part to distinguish themselves from adults, and they have moved back and forth between their own culture and the adult one. Today they must be even more multi-cultural, adept at changing from one operating mode to another as the complex situations of modern life demand. School, our advisory room, is one such situation.

If religious or cultural restrictions limit participation in the greeting, work out privately with the student (with help from parents if possible) what he can and cannot do, and adapt his participation so that it remains friendly and inclusive, even if it takes another form. This will probably require a conversation with the class about the student's special situation, and the need to extend full welcome and acceptance to him/her within the boundaries of his/her restriction(s).

Q. *How do you get kids to be sincere in their greetings instead of just going through the motions?*

Talk about how to do greetings in a friendly manner; ask students to describe the way a friendly greeting looks, sounds, and feels; model and have students practice the elements of a good greeting; and then reflect on how they did.

Still, some students may refuse to look at each other, or they may give a half-hearted handshake, or use a bored or sarcastic tone. They need to try it again, following the guidelines the group has set. If they still choose to be unfriendly, they need to sit out—not only the greeting, but the whole meeting. Remember, no greet, no meet. If a student cannot or will not give a respectful, friendly greeting, he or she forfeits the right to be in the caring society the advisory is designed to be. They need it too much to allow some to spoil it for all. Talk to the spoiler, and try to help him get past whatever is keeping him away from connecting.

Q. *How can I justify spending time on teaching kids to greet one another when so many of my students are failing in their core subjects?*

You can't have one without the other. You can't get focus and hard work from adolescents when they feel isolated and depressed. The greeting helps counteract those feelings. Happily, there are also some direct academic benefits that occur through this social interaction—it is the best way to build cognitive skills.

Academic learning skills developed in greetings

Focus: Greeters must pay attention at all times—when they are greeting, when they are being greeted, when others are greeting, and when the greeting involves changing seats or counting or using special designations or language. It all requires concentration to be successful.

Public speaking: Students practice the fundamentals of effective public speaking every day as they make eye contact and modulate their voices to be loud enough to be heard and warm enough to communicate civility and friendliness. They also get experience with the distinction between formal and informal speech, and learn to use both.

Languages: Students can greet each other in different languages, learning to take the risk of speaking as others speak in cultures not their own.

Listening: Listening to and respecting others is critical in academic disciplines, for forming and maintaining friendships, and in many other situations in life.

Q. *Doesn't it get boring to do the same greeting over and over each day?*

You can vary the greetings and you can allow students to choose the greeting, once a repertoire of good greetings has been established through modeling and practicing. Nobody complains about the boredom of the same old greeting when they encounter friends on the street or at the mall! It's just something we do. Keep it quick and friendly, vary the greetings somewhat, and it will come to seem as natural as greeting rituals everywhere. In fact, if you skip it, students are likely to ask why you left out the greeting. The greeting ritual, like all rituals, provides certainty and safety.

A Last Word of Encouragement

Angel walked in the room late and took a seat in the circle. Conversation stopped for a moment, and the student leading the group said, "Good Morning, Angel." "Hi, everyone," Angel responded with a little smile, and settled into the meeting.

It's not always easy to get students to greet one another with grace. The payoff for making the effort is that when a friendly greeting is in place as a daily ritual, you have a space where other connections, emotional, social, and intellectual, are much more likely to occur. It's definitely worth it!

SHARING

Purposes:

- Build relationships among students
- Create connections between school and home life
- Develop the skills of conversation, inquiry, and public speaking
- Help students see the world from multiple points of view

> We rarely have a student turn down an opportunity to share because she doesn't feel comfortable. We welcome everyone's thoughts and show them empathy. We comfort them when they get upset or when it is a sensitive issue, and let them know that we are there for them if they need someone to talk to, and we assure them that what they share will not leave the room.
>
> —middle school advisory student, Hudson MA

When we talk about sharing, what we mean is sharing *self*. The main purpose of this portion of CPR is to help make connections. Life outside school as told through personal stories connects with life in school. The life within our students' minds and hearts connects with their public existence. The advisory is the place where this integration is practiced regularly in school.

CPR provides a structure for making personal connections that create the heartbeat of true community. When a student feels safe enough to tell other students about something happening at home or at work or in his neighborhood, when those other students feel safe enough to connect to his story, to empathize and show a caring interest in his life, they can have good public conversations that forge the bonds of relationship. When students express opinions that challenge or disagree with others, the others are called upon to listen and try to understand a point of view different from their own.

It isn't easy to teach all this! Depending on a student's development, what happened over the weekend, or the weather or time of day, they might feel awkward, afraid, nervous, angry, or tired—too tired to try, too mad to care. The wonderful thing about routines is that they can carry the group along on habit, and in the midst of the sharing, the art of conversation can begin to emerge.

Young adolescents long to talk to each other, but to do so openly and inclusively is often harder than they can manage. They need adult guidance. In the sharing portion of CPR they have the safety parameters, constructed by savvy adults, within which risk-taking is possible. One by one, as they share bits about themselves, their thoughts, and their opinions, the environment begins to feel safer. Outside of school, conversation can be a minefield. At any moment you might say something that others judge to be stupid or lame. Inside CPR, it's safe, because there are rules. Over time, the stories emerge.

Marcus sat in the circle with his dark, wavy hair down almost to his shoulders, and shared that his mom was pushing him hard to get a haircut. "She says it's been three years since I've been to the barber, but I say so what! I'm open to ideas about how I can talk her out of this idea."

Marcus's peers had ideas for ways he could avoid the conversation, things he could say about his right to decide about his own hair, and suggestions about how he could keep it clean and well-groomed so his mom wouldn't have anything to complain about in that department. "It does get pretty grubby sometimes, Marcus."

A week later, Marcus reported back in another share during CPR meeting. "She said I don't have to get it cut if I keep washing it and keeping it neat."

The group asked how the conversation had gone, and in a closing comment, someone said that it looked good now—shiny and clean.

The following Monday, Marcus arrived with a short haircut. Everyone wanted to hear what had happened, so Marcus shared again. "I had lice, so we had to cut it off to get the eggs and stuff out."

The teacher was nervous, and prepared to shut things down if the conversation turned towards disgust for Marcus and his situation. It did not—his peers knew him and respected him. They did what adults do, and asked polite questions. "What does it feel like?" "What do the lice look like?" "What did you do to get rid of them?" "Did it hurt?" There were no "yuk's"—just curiosity. Marcus answered all the questions, and someone made a closing comment: "Well, Marcus, you tried your best, but what can you do when you have bad luck? You can grow it again if you want to."

Marcus nodded, and the pain of the haircut was clearly compensated for by the pleasure of being known and accepted by his peers.

—7th/8th grade advisory, Minneapolis MN

The Basics

Sharing is basically a structure for conversations that might not take place if we didn't create a format for them. Left to their own devices, adolescent conversation often happens in cliques, and often includes jockeying for favor and position. The cool kids get center stage. The shy and less popular ones hang around the edges or separate entirely.

Sharing in CPR includes everyone, is consistently respectful, and models for middle level students what caring conversations look, sound, and feel like. Even the simplest kind of share—the one we call Whip Share, in which each person around the circle responds to a question with a word or phrase—can be the beginning of a dialogue, if the process opens up for questions, which may be addressed to anyone in the circle. In its most conversational version, sharing sounds like a group of people interested in a topic and in each other, asking, commenting, and responding to each other in an inclusive way. Through such conversations, week after week, students come to know and care about one another.

Essential

- Everyone (including the teacher) gets a chance to share, but not necessarily every day
- Use a share format; the formats can vary: individual, whip, partner, etc.
- Whatever the format, there are responsibilities for those sharing (clarity, volume, detailed information, calling on responders) and for those listening and responding (attention, respect, empathy, clarity, volume, interesting questions and friendly comments)
- The teacher's job is to monitor the time, student behavior, appropriateness of topic and language, quality of communication
- Time frame is about 5 minutes

Optional

Sharing may also

- be in response to a focus question or open to self-selection of topic
- be done by everyone, some, or only one person per meeting
- be on personal, social, or academically-related topics

Individual Share format

The basic format for sharing personal news is the Individual Share. It's called Individual not because only one person speaks, but because one person is the focus of the conversation. Students share about what is going on in their lives either on an assigned topic or on a topic of their own choosing. Usually students tell about things that are going on in their lives and how they feel about them.

Sharer's job: to tell a little about the topic: a lead sentence followed by a couple of supporting details, just enough so the other students can get interested in what the sharer has to say. Then the sharer invites others into the conversation by saying, "I'm open for questions or comments."

Next week we're getting a dog. My uncle's dog had puppies, and as soon as they are old enough to leave their mother, we get to bring one home. The mother dog is a black Lab. I'm open for questions or comments.

Other students' job: to participate in a conversation with the sharer on his chosen topic. The students participate by asking relevant, interesting questions of the sharer, and by making relevant, friendly comments.

How old do the pups have to be before they can leave their mom?

Do you think they will really miss their mom and the other pups, and if so what will you do to comfort your dog?

Who is going to train the dog, and how will you train it?
I trained my dog at the Humane Society, and I think they're good. Are you going to take your dog to classes? If so, where?

What eventually emerges from this somewhat rigid structure are genuine conversations about topics that interest the students. They are opportunities open to anyone to give and take ideas, opinions, and life experiences.

Plan for Success

Model and practice

The Individual Share, introduced for the first time, needs to be modeled and practiced so that the wheels are greased for success. The teacher takes the leap first, to talk a little about her life outside school, and this risk-taking helps establish safety for others. The teacher starts by explaining:

I'm going to demonstrate a way of having conversations that we'll use in CPR. I'll share a little about something that happened in my life outside of school, and then I'll invite you to ask me questions about what I've shared. By the time I finish answering your questions, you'll know some details of my story. Here are the basics: Sunday was my birthday, and my kids and husband served me breakfast in bed. It was a complete surprise and I loved it! I'm open now for your questions.

Students ask questions:
What was in the breakfast? Was it good?
Who did the cooking?
Did they serve it on a tray in your bedroom?
Were you sleeping when they brought it in?
Did your husband and kids eat with you?

The teacher answers each question. Over time, as you work with your students on the skills of questioning, they will become more and more adept at asking interesting, open-ended questions.

After the questions and answers, the teacher invites students to reflect on the process of sharing.

Teacher: *Who can describe how I started the share? What did you notice about my comments about the breakfast?*
Student: *You started by telling us that your family made breakfast and served it to you in bed for your birthday. You said you liked it a lot, but you didn't give many details about it.*
Teacher: *How did the details come out?*
Student: *We asked you questions and you answered.*
Teacher: *Yes, and I noticed that all of the questions were interesting and respectful. I appreciated being asked those questions. It made me feel good that you were interested in my birthday. Thank you.*

The teacher invites a student or two to share something from life outside school so students can get more practice with the Individual Share format:

Now that you know the format we'll be using to do these Individual Shares about our lives, would someone else be willing to share something that happened to them or is going to happen?

This Individual Share will be followed by questions and comments from the group

One or two shares with questions serve as additional models. The teacher concludes:

At our next CPR, we'll have time for two or three Individual Shares. Be thinking over the weekend about your birthday and how you celebrate it or would like to celebrate it. Be ready to tell us on Monday. For now, let's review what would make this kind of conversation effective within our advisory guidelines. What should it look, sound, and feel like when we are sharing our lives with each other?

Students can generate their own look/sound/feel Y-chart to remind themselves of the qualities of successful sharing. Post the chart on the wall so students can model the routines, referring to the Y-chart as necessary.

Sample Y-Chart for Sharing Routine

Look: Speaker focused on topic; listeners focused on speaker; sometimes serious and sometimes laughing faces

Sound: One person speaking at a time; people asking and answering questions; sharer calling on people

Feel: Respectful, interesting, friendly, caring, fun, sad or serious as appropriate

Declare your support.

I think these guidelines for sharing are important for our community, and I will protect them by reminding anyone who slips, and sometimes by asking a person to sit out for a while. If we maintain the standards we've set, I think we'll all feel comfortable enough to share.

To maintain these high standards, lead students in a quick reflection after the sharing component.

Looking at our Y-chart on sharing, how did we do today?

What could we improve?

How are we doing at asking interesting questions?

How are the sharers doing at answering in full sentences?

When Students Mess Up

There are lots of things that can go wrong in the sharing portion of CPR. Students may be reluctant to share. Eighth graders, especially, are often self-conscious to the point of silence and may need to proceed more slowly than the more socially comfortable sixth or seventh graders. In addition to slowly going through the challenges of sharing, watch the classroom climate closely, just as you do during the greeting. Small things can sabotage safety. A dirty look, rolled eyes, a demeaning gesture, a "whatever" shrug, avoiding looking at the sharer, or reluctance to ask questions after the share can paralyze a thirteen-year-old speaker.

We have special rules, and we have a say in creating them. We discuss what proper behavior looks like, sounds like, and feels like. When we behave in ways that follow [these rules], we open up to each other and express our true selves.

—middle school student, Tabernacle NJ

Establish the rules for good listening at the beginning, and indicate that no violations of the respect guidelines are acceptable. Demonstrate that you mean what you say by redirecting any student who interrupts or puts down another.

Because verbal reminders interrupt sharing, the best teacher response is often a quiet signal to the rule-breaker that he or she needs to step out of the circle, and return with better self-controls. The atmosphere needs to be free of demonstrations of negativity that go unchallenged. No matter whether the teacher or a student is leading CPR, it is the teacher's job to pay constant attention to the atmosphere in the room, correcting any behavior that threatens to damage it.

Challenge Them

Put it to the students directly.

How do we want our advisory to be? We agreed that we wanted an advisory where everyone would feel safe and included. We have to decide whether we will really be together or whether we'll just sit here, each person alone. When people share, they put themselves out there, and our job is to send the message back that we are listening and we wish them well. Think about the look on your face, the body language you are using, and ask yourself if you are part of that message. And when it's time to volunteer to share, know that here you are safe—step out and talk to us.

Students enoy a Whip Share

Steady Progress

Setting up the Sharing: Start with a simple Whip Share

Begin, as always, with the easy pieces. The tight structure makes it easy. For example, in a Whip Share, each person has a turn to respond briefly, with a word or phrase, to a direct question asked by the teacher.

What is something you enjoyed during summer vacation?

Name a favorite movie (or food or song).

The idea is for everyone to participate in the order of their seating around the circle. The teacher is watching for the respectful listening and speaking described in the sharing Y-chart, and for full participation.

In a Whip Share, attention is on the sharer for just a moment, so self-consciousness is minimized. It feels like a game going around the circle. In a Whip Share, we want to hear a personal opinion, but it's quick and fairly painless to say a word or two—and then you are out of the spotlight. Introverts might speak very softly at first; extraverts may say something dramatic or silly. The Whip Share is simple and easy, and most students go along with it. In spite of posturing to the contrary, they are interested—very interested—in each other's answers to the question.

Introduced for the first time, the Whip Share needs to be modeled and practiced, like any other new format or routine. The teacher demonstrates by giving her answer to the question:

What is something you enjoyed during summer vacation?

I took my kids and some of their friends swimming every week.

A discussion of some finer points follows.

Teacher: *What did you notice about my answer?*

Student: *It was short. You said a complete sentence.*

Teacher: *Yes, I did answer in a full sentence, but in this first round that's not a requirement. What else did you notice?*

Student: *You looked at us when you talked.*

Student: *You used a pretty loud voice so everyone heard you.*

Teacher: *One reason you could hear me is that I was looking at people, so my voice didn't go down into the floor. When your head is down, your voice is muffled. One of the things we'll work on is looking at your audience whenever you are speaking. Sometimes you find one person to look at while you speak, but better speakers look at many of the people they're speaking to so people feel included. It's a skill of good speaking. If you learn it here, you'll have a skill that will help you the rest of your life.*

Let's try a go-round with your answers. I'll ask the question again, give you a minute to think, and then we'll each answer. I'll go first with my answer, and next will be James. If someone gets mixed up or forgets what to do or doesn't follow the protocol, we'll stop and he or she can try it again. Any questions?

At first, there may be uncomfortable posturing, and students may say something is their favorite even when it isn't ("watch TV" or "pizza") because they know it's typical. It takes a certain amount of safety to admit that you really like baklava best, or you love to play the piano! A marker of the beginning of true community is when students begin speaking honestly, and are not afraid to reveal that they are a little different.

Whip Share variations

As students get adept at a particular kind of sharing, you can introduce variations. The simple Whip Share can be made more dynamic and interesting to students with these variations.

Who remembers: after everyone has shared a quick answer to the question, ask for recall of the answers.
Who remembers some of the things people said they did on their vacations? Who remembers who said she went to a friend's cabin for a week? Who remembers the places people said they visited during the summer?
The questions help students practice good listening and accurate recall, and they highlight each individual's experience and show each sharer that the group heard what they said and remembered—an important link in forging relationships.

Student questions: invite students to contribute questions for the group to answer (you review them first), and choose students to ask Whip Share questions.

Follow-up questions: an extension of the simple Whip Share is to open up for questions after everyone has shared an answer. For example:
After everyone has said something he/she plans to do this weekend, we'll open up for questions. Each person may ask a question of someone else. For example, someone might ask me whether I swam too when I took the kids swimming.

Collecting data: scribe the answers (without names attached), then graph the responses. Over time you may create an "almanac" of information about the class based on their responses to various Whip Share questions, such as birthdays, favorites, pet peeves, size of family, birth order, hobbies, etc.

These variations extend and enrich the Whip Share by adding to our knowledge of each other.

As students become comfortable with the short responses of the Whip Share format, introduce other formats for sharing that call for more information or a longer presentation or more opportunities to recall information, ask each other questions, and make comments. Move along slowly enough to build a scaffold for students to take more risks and manage formats that require more self-control and skill. Here is a continuum of sharing formats that you can use as students show increasing competence and confidence.

Sample Progression for Sharing

See Appendix A to find sharing ideas with levels indicated.

Level 1 (simple, low risk, low need for self-control, minimal autonomy

- Whip Share with teacher-designed questions
- Whip Share with student- and teacher-designed questions
- Partner Share with a low-risk topic—favorite foods, colors, etc.
- Post-it Share (students read posted responses to a topic)
- Whip Share followed by "Who remembers...."

Level 2 (more complex, some risk, moderate need for self-control, some autonomy

- Partner Share with a more challenging topic, e.g. favorite music/sport, school goal, etc.
- Inside-Outside Share (students rotate in two circles, sharing on a topic for a given time with each person they meet)
- Whip Share with follow-up questions from listeners
- Popcorn Share (students volunteer to share on a topic when they are ready, out of the circle order, without raising hands)
- Individual Share on a teacher-designed topic or any topic; brief, followed by questions. Sample topics: a time when you were injured or very sick; a favorite cousin; how you like to celebrate your birthday; a favorite place; something you're good at.

Level 3 (complex, greatest risk, need for high self-control, more autonomy, less supervision)

- Individual Share on student-designed topic; a few students share briefly on the same topic or open to any topic; each is followed by questions and comments from the group
- Brown Bag Share (students share about objects of personal importance placed ahead of time in a bag)

- Individual Share with student talking on a chosen topic for one minute, followed by questions and comments from the group. Lengthen to 2 or even 3 minutes to challenge students.

- Open conversation on a topic brought up by the teacher or by students (with approval of the teacher); everyone must contribute. Teacher facilitates and keeps track of participation

- Open conversation on a topic brought up by the teacher or by students (with approval of the teacher) without raised hands; everyone must say something. Teacher facilitates and keeps track of participation.

- Open conversation on a topic brought up by the teacher or by students (with approval of the teacher) without raised hands; everyone must say something. Student facilitates and keeps track of participation.

Scaffolding

Students need help to learn good sharing. A carefully planned sequence of steps is fundamental to success. Students need support in choosing topics, responding in complete sentences, telling the basic facts of an event, listening to others, asking interesting questions, and making friendly comments. All of these skills need to be modeled first and practiced; none comes automatically or intuitively.

The best way to support students in acquisition of these skills is to build a "skills stairway" to get them to the point where they can engage in an open discourse effectively. The following steps can scaffold their way.

Scaffolding Topics

After a few weeks of whip sharing on topics the teacher has chosen, students may be ready to contribute to the list of topics they would find interesting to discuss. Brainstorm ideas together, and make a list from which the teacher will choose. After a while, students can make the choice themselves, for Whip Shares (everyone answers the same question) or for Individual Shares. Naturally, students want to choose the topics they talk about. A good menu will stimulate their thinking and encourage participation.

<u>Examples of share topics</u>

Share about a time when you were brave.
What is the best gift you ever gave to someone? To whom did you give it?
Describe the qualities of a good friend.
Name something that stresses you in life and tell how you handle it.
Describe the kind of person you would like to be when you are an adult.
What is your favorite season, and why do you like it?
What do you do to stay healthy?
(See Appendix E for more share topics)

<u>Examples of student connection to academic topics</u>

If you were a woman in 19th-century America, what jobs would not be available to you?

What are ways to reduce waste that you personally use or could use?
Describe extreme weather you have experienced.

When CPR is organized around themes, academic connections are particularly easy to make. See Chapter Five: 170 Thematic Advisories for many examples. However, CPR is always about the *integration* of social and emotional and academic experiences. Working with thematic topics, the focus in sharing needs to be on making personal connections to ideas and information. Don't turn CPR into just another lesson! Use it to help students create deeper connections to learning, and it will leverage all their learning.

Some of these topics are best for a quick Whip Share, and others invite more conversation. Some will work well for both if you add *why* to the topic or question. Some topics are perennial favorites— for example, a group of 7th and 8th graders took on the topic of Our Names. They researched the meanings and origins of their names as part of a unit on rites of passage. They consulted their parents and the Internet for information, and were excited and eager to share what they learned and to hear about what others found out.

At first the teacher selects all the topics for sharing, but soon students can have input, either by ranking the questions on a poll, contributing their own questions on index cards from which the class can select during the year, or by assuming the responsibility of selecting the topic for sharing during a CPR. What is important is that the topics interest them. There is always the academic payoff of improving presentation skills.

Scaffolding Speaking Skills

The first time you do a Whip Share, you'll probably get words or short phases for answers: "What is your favorite food?" Replies: "Chocolate." "Pizza." "French fries." After you've done a few Whip Shares, and students understand and accept that they must give a response, you can begin working on the following qualities of the response.

Volume: insist that the response be loud enough to be heard by everyone.
Raise your hand if you couldn't hear what Nathan said.
Nathan, please repeat your answer so that everyone can hear it.

Sentence structure: require that answers be given in complete sentences.
When you give your response to the Whip Share question, I want you to answer with a complete sentence. I'll show you what I mean: My favorite time of the year is spring.

Extended thought: some of the time, require students to tell *why* they responded as they did.
When you answer today's Whip Share question, tell us not only one of your favorite things to do but also why it's your favorite. For example: Something I enjoy a lot is having dinner with friends because we eat and talk and get to know each other better.

Summarizing: as students move from simple Whip Shares to Individual Shares that invite responses, they need help in learning how to tell the gist of a story succinctly. Model the process of making a summary statement about a topic, and then fill in with a couple of important details.

The highlight of my weekend was a dinner with friends at Mario's. I love Italian food, and I enjoyed being with friends I hadn't seen for awhile. I'm open for questions and comments.

Scaffolding Listening Skills

When someone is talking, others have the job of listening. During Whip Shares, encourage careful listening by asking after the round, "Who can remember something that someone else shared?" See how many shares the group can recall. Ask those whose answers were not mentioned to raise their hands and repeat them. With time, the group will get better and better at remembering what they heard.

During individual sharing, after a person is finished with her opening statement you can ask the group what they remember from her opening before the sharer invites questions. You can also ask what people remember after the group has asked questions of the sharer. The sharer can confirm what is correctly remembered and fill in what was forgotten. Usually the group as a whole can remember every detail. You could have

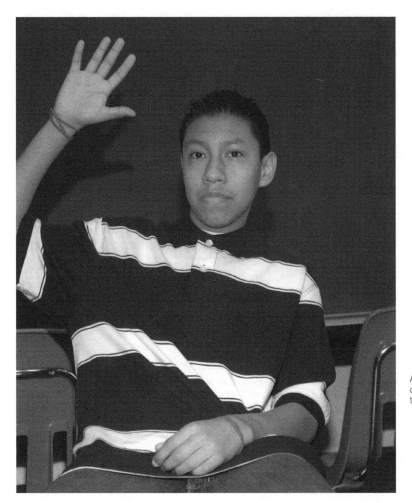

An eighth grader has a question or comment for the sharer

students jot down what they remember, and see how many details they can recall. The ultimate test would be to wait until after two or three people have shared individually, and then see how much of all three shares the group can remember!

All of these remembering games hone listening and recall skills. You can keep a running record of the group's success, and report back to them in March how much better they are at remembering than they were in October.

Scaffolding Questioning Skills

The best conversations are rich in information and feelings, contain humor and surprises, and are often moving. A hallmark of good conversation is questions that bring out all these dimensions in interesting answers. Young adolescents don't ask such questions automatically. The first questions that come from them are usually simple yes-or-no or short-answer questions such as:

Where did you go?

Did you have fun?

Who was there?

Did you win?

What was the score?

These questions ask for information in a minimal way. If the sharer extends her answers, more interesting information will emerge. What makes good conversations more likely is skill-building with students on questioning that invites a variety of interesting answers. Asking interesting questions is a high-level thinking skill, and it doesn't come without work. There are several ways to teach questioning skills.

Brainstorming

Brainstorm questions to ask about a topic ahead of time. List the questions, and have them visible when students begin to share on the topic.

We're going to have a round-robin or Whip Share response on the topic of special interests. I'll tell you a little bit about my quilting hobby and then invite you to ask me questions about it. First, let's brainstorm some questions you might ask about someone's hobby or special interest.

Write the questions on a chart or board so they are in plain sight. With those prompts visible, share something you like to do. Going around the circle, three or four students ask one of the questions on the list. Finally, invite someone else to share on the topic, and direct the group to use the questions as a prompt as you go around the circle during the response time.

- Brainstormed questions on the topic of birthdays:
  What did you enjoy about your birthday? Why?
  What would you like to do for your next birthday?
  What foods did you eat? Which was your favorite?
  What was your favorite present, and why did you like it?
  What would be your perfect birthday celebration?
  (See page 63 for more on this subject.)

- Brainstormed questions on the topic of cousins:
  How old is he?
  Where does he live?
  How often do you see each other?

- More open-ended questions on the topic of cousins:
  What's your favorite thing about him?
  Tell about something fun you've done together.
  What interests does he have?

Boosting participation

Another way to prompt questions is to begin the questioning process with partners brainstorming to develop one good question, which one of them asks the sharer. Still another strategy is to give each student two "chits," represented by sticks or pieces of paper. Each time a person asks a question, he or she turns in a chit. Students may use a maximum of two and must use at least one chit by the end of the meeting.

Higher-level questions

Here are some ways to teach students to ask higher-level questions.

- Teach the difference between "skinny" questions (evoking a very brief answer) and "fat" questions (those that stimulate the sharer to speak at length to explain or describe). Who, what, when, and where questions are generally skinny, while how and why questions are fatter, and prompt richer answers. Challenge students to ask more questions that begin with how and why.
  How did you manage to do that?
  Why is that important to you?
  How did that happen?
  Why did your family decide to go to North Dakota?
  How will you explain to your mom that you don't want to go?

- Teach and practice different kinds of "fat" questions, such as compare-and-contrast or wondering questions. A list of questions that are open-ended and wide-ranging can improve conversations and teach questioning skills at the same time.
  How does your new dog compare to the dog you used to have?
  What do you think would have happened if you had told your parents you didn't want to go on the trip with them?
  What's it going to take to make your basketball team a winner this year?
  See Appendix E for Asking Quality Questions, including questions that prompt interesting answers.

You can work on these questions by sharing something yourself, and then giving the list of higher-level questions to students who ask them round-robin style around the circle. Continue to use the list until the higher-level questions become familiar and more natural for your students. Post some favorites on a chart and hang it near the meeting area.

Connections to writing

Interesting questions bring out lots of concrete details about the sharing topic. You can make a rich parallel to good writing by diagramming the share. The topic sentence will now have not only the specific details which the sharer gave in her initial statement, but also the details that came out in response to questions.

Any of these strategies will improve questioning skills. With interesting, varied, open-ended questions, you have the makings of good dialogue. Watch one-word answers turn into more fully developed commentaries, and watch the spill-over into academics! The better a student's questioning skills are, the deeper the learning.

Scaffolding Comments

One of the best places for comments is at the end of an Individual Share. For example, the conversation has gone on for a couple of minutes, everyone has heard the information, and it's time for a closing comment that rounds off the conversation and wishes the sharer well:

Bella, I hope your birthday is really fun!
Richard, it sounds as if you're going to have a great time on your trip.
Simon, I hope your mom feels better.
Neela, congratulations on your new baby sister!

There are other occasions where a comment is appropriate and enjoyable. One is to express a connection with the experience:

I saw that movie, too, and I thought it was cool.
I had the same problem with my sister, but we worked it out. I hope you and your sister can.

A good comment enlarges the discussion with the listener's point of view. Such comments are best if the speaker turns the attention back to the sharer by following the end of the comment with a question:

What was your favorite part of the movie?
Do you think she'd be willing to talk it out?

Q & A

Q. Some kids always want to share, and tend to monopolize. What should I do?

You are the one who decides who talks and for how long. Be direct about when it's time to move on: "You can take one more question, Gabe." "Does anyone have a closing comment for Gabe?" You are the one who decides about taking turns sharing. What often creates imbalances is that some students don't volunteer to share at all. Establishing a high level of safety in the room helps, as does providing the scaffolding students need to be successful at sharing. The best balance to the domination of some is the push-back of others who have something to say as well.

Q. Some students never seem to want to share. Should I make it mandatory?

Insist that everyone share in a Whip Share, in which full participation is an expectation. Sharing news about one's life outside of school needs to be a student's choice. However, there are lots of things you can do to encourage full participation in all kinds of sharing.

A crucial step is the careful, leveled introduction of sharing starting with the most comfortable, least risky Level 1 formats, and gradually moving to more challenging formats, with lots of modeling and a variety of topics along the way. Willingness to share your life is directly correlated to the degree of safety you feel in a social setting.

Look at other elements in your classroom, such as student ownership of the class rules; ample opportunities to see routines modeled; respectful, realistic, and relevant consequences that follow rule-breaking; and perhaps most important, respectful teacher language that shows confidence in students and is delivered in a neutral or warm tone. All of these elements affect the climate of the room and, as a direct corollary, the performance of the students.

Work with individual students to help them feel confident enough to participate in sharing. Get to know them well, so you are able to make specific suggestions and requests for them to share something. Offer a shy student an opportunity to simply take questions from the group when it's his turn to share—no opening statement other than "I'm open for questions."

Ask a couple of students ahead of time to share. Some teachers use a rotation system, and remind students a day ahead whose turn it is to share and help them get ready.

Having a topic for sharing that is attractive ensures a higher level of participation than sharing that is open to any topic. Some easy favorites with which you can begin are hobbies, afterschool activities, families, and sports. You can also help students work their way up to a conversation with questions and comments, by asking for a simple Whip Share on a topic, and following it with a few questions asked of any person in the circle. *Anthony, you said your favorite food is haggis. What is it? How does it taste? Genevieve, what was your favorite thing you did or saw on your trip to California?*

If you've done everything you can to set up a successful individual sharing, and many are still reluctant, try a simple Partner Share. Have students make "high five partners" with a person next to them and then invite them to share with their partners one thing they did over the weekend. Most people feel freer to share one-to-one than in front of a group. At the end, invite volunteers to share what they said or heard with the whole group. With a generally reluctant group, you can use Post-it Shares, in which everyone shares on paper, but the teacher reads the comments, making it an easy and safe way to share. After a few low-risk sharing days, start working up to Individual Shares.

Q. Some kids get a lot of response when they share, and others get very little. Should I ask questions to help out?

If you're going to participate, do so at random with all students. Otherwise, it will seem like a rescue for you to ask a question of someone. Students can sign up in advance to share, which allows time for you to discuss a student's share with him ahead of time, to help make the share interesting to the group. You can do round-robin (around the circle) questions and comments some days, which guarantees response to a share. Again, you have to do this with *everyone's* share that day, and not single out a student because he usually gets few responses. To facilitate good questions and full participation, brainstorm the questions ahead of time.

You can also talk directly about some sharers getting very few questions as a form of exclusion. Tell students it is their job to listen carefully and ask interesting questions of the sharer—any and all sharers, with no one left out. The more practice in questioning, the more comfortable students are with it. The more work you do with the group building name recognition and knowledge about everyone, the more everyone is included.

If you still see exclusion, go back to simple Whip Shares for a while. Work on team-building through the activity portion of the meeting, and return to individual sharing when you think your students are ready for full inclusion.

A Last Word of Encouragement

Stephen was sharing. "There was a shooting in my neighborhood last night. The guy next door had a bullet go through his living room window. My ma says I can't go out after 6 anymore, and I'm bummed. I'm open for questions and comments." Some students asked questions; most just nodded and offered sympathy. A closing comment came from Angela: "I'm really sorry, Stephen. I hope things settle down in your neighborhood so you can go out at night again soon."

—6th grade advisory, St. Paul MN

Sharing is an opportunity to teach the art of conversation to young people. Carefully orchestrated to prevent put-downs and exclusion, sharing is a time to speak about what matters to you, and others will listen and respond respectfully. It may not be happening for our students elsewhere, but they can experience it in advisory regularly through the Circle of Power and Respect.

CPR gives students power and control, which allows us to share ideas with each other. I get to tell the class what's going on in my life, good or bad.

—middle school advisory student, La Crosse WI

Seventh graders demonstrate a new dance, then all practice it during the activity component of CPR

ACTIVITY

Purposes:

- Build relationships
- Develop academic and social skills
- Have fun

> I woke up one morning. I was so tired! I went to school. The game during circle time woke me up because of the movement we had to do. Oh, yeah!
>
> —middle school advisory student, Red Lake MN

Young adolescents love to play. All human beings *need* to play—it's one of the basic ingredients of psychological health, according to psychologist William Glasser (Glasser 1998). They will find a way to get it into their day, no matter what, but their strategies for fun may be disruptive to the school community or its purposes. By building appropriate opportunities for fun into the school day, we provide the experience of enjoyment and learning combined.

CPR's third component is designed to achieve this result. After students have greeted each other and shared about themselves, CPR offers a chance to play a game, do a dramatic choral reading, sing, or learn a dance together. These activities serve both academic and social ends, since all of them require cooperation, responsibility, self-control, and graceful recovery from mistakes—your own and others'.

Young bodies confined to seats for 50 or more minutes at a time fatigue and grow very restless. A game can loosen up both the bodies and the minds of students because of the increase in oxygen levels to the brain from movement. Watch the attention level rise after a few playful moments! In addition, activities can bring academic benefit when they include a review of content or skills, since they draw from student memory or call on students to problem-solve. Game-playing activities can require intense concentration, the kind of focus we try to cultivate in academics. Students can learn what concentration looks and feels like from playing, especially with a few minutes to process afterwards.

Teacher: *What did it take to be successful in that game?*

Student: *Paying attention.*

Teacher: *Remember what that felt like. When we talk about focus and concentration on schoolwork, we're talking about that same feeling of intense concentration you had during the game. It makes all the difference in being successful in school.*

The Basics

Activities offer a moment of fun and freedom, but in a school context they are followed by a call to serious focus on content. What makes the switching process successful is building a structure for self-control and consideration of others into the playing. Structured activities facilitated by a watchful teacher result in pleasure for everyone and in strengthened social skills. Everyone participates with a sense of safety, and no one interferes with anyone else's enjoyment. When the game is over, we focus on our work.

- Activities are cooperative
- Everyone is included, but students may opt to just watch
- Each activity is introduced carefully and revisited when necessary so everyone knows the rules
- Activities are played with fairness, safety, and caring, or they are halted

Optional

- Some activities are competitive, once community has been well established
- Students can create variations on games and introduce new ones
- Activities are repeated many times if they are popular
- Each activity has its own set of rules and its own flow. To be successful, students must be introduced to each activity carefully through modeling and practicing.

Plan for Success

Model and practice

The success of the activity component involves modeling and practicing the steps of the activity before you engage in it. Any aspects that might be unclear or especially challenging, or that might require extra self-control, must be introduced, carefully modeled by the teacher and/or a student, and sometimes practiced by everyone before the game is launched.

This game involves chair-changing. Sometimes all of us will be out of our chairs at once, and finding other places to sit as quickly as we can. Who can demonstrate what changing chairs might look like? (Two people switch seats). *What did you notice about the way Glenn and Marie changed seats?*

Now let's have two people aim to sit in the same seat at the same time. This is a problem that must be solved on the spot. What will the two people have to watch out for in order for their actions to be safe, fast, and successful, to keep within our advisory guidelines (chart the reminders)? *Who is willing to try it? We need two volunteers. Good, now everyone watch as they head for the same seat, but somehow quickly resolve the situation so that no one is hurt.*

(Demonstration by the two students)

What did you notice about how Sigrid and Dan handled this? What did they do to succeed? Now we'll try playing the game, watching for any problems, and stopping if any show up. I think we can do this. Let's give it a try!

If something goes wrong in the demonstration, go back to the modeling, review, and identify what went wrong. Then have two students try it again. The message is that there is only one way we're going to play this game, and that's the safe way, both physically and emotionally. If the group as a whole isn't cooperative, the game is set aside until sometime in the future when the group is able to handle it. If there is time, play a simpler, more familiar game that they already know how to handle.

Elements of activities to model

Body control

Voice level control

Teamwork

Problem-solving

Handling mistakes

Students can generate their own look/sound/feel Y-chart to remind themselves of the standards for the activity. Post the chart on the wall. Students can model the routines, following the Y-chart ideas.

Sample Y-Chart for Activity Routines

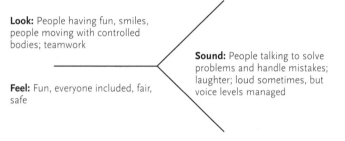

Look: People having fun, smiles, people moving with controlled bodies; teamwork

Sound: People talking to solve problems and handle mistakes; laughter; loud sometimes, but voice levels managed

Feel: Fun, everyone included, fair, safe

Follow each activity with reflection

If you want your students to get better and better at something, lead them in a quick reflection after every experience of it:

What did you enjoy?

What could we improve?

How can we make the game more safe, fun, or fair?

Young people love to play, but they aren't always good at it. They quarrel, they get confused, and they break the rules at times. But because they want to continue to play, they are interested in reflecting on how things went and on fixing what went wrong. Use the reflective loop to review the game and improve it for next time.

Create a caring climate for play

The tone of the group and the atmosphere in the room determine how much fun everyone has. Games by themselves do not make fun for all. When exclusion or put-downs creep in, the playfulness disappears, and in its place are social one-upmanship and pain. All it takes is sarcasm or a roll of the eyes or a comment like "Jeez!" when someone messes up, and the safety level for *everyone* plummets. Clear away all such impediments to community.

Sample Activities

See Appendix A to find activities with levels and activity types indicated.

Getting-to-know-you activities

Because students may not know everyone in the room, getting-to-know-you activities are a good way to start the year.

Name with Gesture: Do the Choice of Gesture Greeting and afterwards, in the activity, ask for volunteers to name as many students as possible, and repeat their identifying gesture (the gesture helps you remember the name).

Concentration variation: The next day, after everyone is familiar with the names and/or gestures, do a Concentration-like game in which the first person says his own name and makes his gesture and then says someone else's name and makes their gesture. The person named does the same for a third person. The object is to move quickly from one person to another without pausing. The same person can be named more than one time, so everyone has to stay alert throughout the game.

Concentration variation: Only the gestures are passed from one to another, and no names are used. This requires careful observation.

Easy games

When you introduce game-playing, keep the risk and skill levels low. Inclusion and participation are our goals at this initial stage. Games that require no particular skill or knowledge are good at the start because they avoid embarrassment. Students who are honing their "cool" identities are not ready for higher-risk activities that might make them appear foolish to their peers.

Zoom: This game is almost fool-proof. Pass a sound that imitates a racing car ("Zoom!") from person to person around the circle as fast as possible. A stopwatch tells the group how fast they were, and the group can repeat the circuit to improve their time.

Students participate in a team-building game, maintaining cooperation and safety

Zoom Variations (add interest): Add the power of reversing the direction of the car with an accompanying sound ("Screech!"), or turn the corner onto another street (call out the name of a person in the circle—"Natalie Street") or call out a bad driving move ("Cell phone!"); the next person must continue with "Zoom" without faltering. A mistake means that the group starts over. The object is to see how long the group can keep it going without a mishap. Later in the year, the group might choose to eliminate players when they make mistakes, but at this point avoiding competition builds better group connections.

Academic games

Lots of activities, especially those that involve memory, lend themselves to academic content. When an activity involves using topics, you can have students recall facts within an academic topic. For example, in Around the World, the topic might be numbers evenly divisible by 3; "It" says as many numbers evenly divisible by 3 as she can within the time allowed. It's a playful way to review. See Appendix A to find activities with topics indicated.

Challenge Them

Name what you're up to. Build tolerance and inclusivity.

This advisory is a place where everyone is accepted, even when he/she makes mistakes, big or small. We can create a community in which nobody gets put down. What it takes is a commitment from all of us that we're going to create a space where everyone is welcome. I'm going to support that commitment every moment we're here together. If you forget, I'll remind you. If you're mad and want to take it out on someone, I'll ask you to sit out until you can get yourself together to live by our community guidelines.

Students enjoy an active chair-changing game

When Students Mess Up

Careful scaffolding of playful or performance activities from low risk or skill to higher pays off in respectful participation. So will proactive modeling of protocols and skills needed for the activity before launching into it. But sometimes students break rules and disrupt the group, no matter how pro-active you have been. These are moments for reactive strategies.

A group of 7th and 8th graders were playing the game "Keep It Up," in which the object is to keep a light ball in the air as long as possible (rallies are timed). The game required teamwork. In the first try, something went wrong. There was pushing, and some were taking advantage of a somewhat reticent boy who had a tendency to shy away from the ball. They slammed it at him to make him participate, and he repeatedly yelled "Ouch!" whenever the ball was pushed towards him, until finally he walked away. The teacher stopped the game, brought the group back to circle, and asked, "What are we looking for here? What's the purpose of the game? Can someone remind us?"

After the reminder, the teacher continued, "If one of us is not having fun, we're all not having fun. Fun at the expense of someone is not who we are. Think about our conversations about the kind of advisory we want. How does one person feeling uncomfortable affect all of us? At the beginning of this year, what kind of an environment did we say we wanted?"

After the conversation, they tried the game again. Then and thereafter, they played with the intent to keep the ball in the air. There was no sabotage, and any wildness was unintended. Now "Keep It Up" is a favorite with everyone!

—7th/8th grade advisory, Minneapolis MN

The purpose of teacher responses to rule-breaking is to stop the negative behavior and to teach the students who erred how to better manage themselves in the future. The objective is not punishment, but setting things right, and building the capacity for self-control and self-discipline.

Sweat the small stuff

It is much easier to right wrongs when the break in the rules is small. If you overlook small problems, they will grow into bigger, much more difficult infractions. It's much harder to restore students to self-control after they have shouted an expletive or thrown their bodies or some object around than after a whispered aside or a blurted comment. We watch for the *beginnings* of loss of self-control so that we can help students reverse the behavior quickly and center themselves. This takes careful watching from the teacher at all times. No matter how much fun you may be having with students during an activity, no matter how well things are going, any slip by any student calls for quick action from you.

Getting students back on the path to self-control may require no more than a verbal reminder or a look, or just moving close to the student as a reminder. However, if you do many such redirections one after another, the community atmosphere starts to fray and the game begins to fall apart. A quick direction to a student to sit out for a few minutes to regain self-control is often more helpful than a chain of verbal reminders. Taking a break gives the student a chance to change his vantage point for a few minutes by staying away from the flow of the activity. It can interrupt a slide in the wrong direction and preserve not only the student, but the centeredness of the whole group.

The game is in full progress. Everyone is changing chairs, laughing, and concentrating on the game. Anthony stealthily grabs the edge of Maria's sweatshirt, so she can't get a quick start in the next round. She laughs as she ends up in the middle because she didn't get a chair. The teacher says quietly, "Take a break, Anthony." "But she likes being in the middle!" protests Anthony. "Take a break, Anthony." Anthony walks to the break chair and sits. He returns in a minute. The game continues with no disruptions.

Steady Progress

In the beginning, use activities that require a minimum of social, emotional, and physical risk-taking. After several experiences of fun without embarrassment, oneupmanship, exclusion, and poor self-control, students are showing you that they may be ready for more challenge. At first, make it easy to play and easy to succeed. Keep the demands to work together cooperatively and effectively at an easy level. A wise teacher saves games that require higher levels of teamwork, skill, and trust for when students show stronger connectedness.

<u>Sample progression of activities</u>

The activities described in this book are ranked according to their level of challenge—a combination of emotional, physical, and intellectual demands made by the activity. See Appendix A to find activities with levels indicated.

Level 1 (simple, low risk, low level of self-control, minimal autonomy)

- Something's Changed: students identify small changes in a classmate's appearance

- Twenty Questions: students use up to twenty questions to identify a category

- Me Too: students share and discover things in common with each other

Level 2 (more complex, some risk, more self-control required, some autonomy)

- Frogger: a game involving silly gestures and dramatic reactions

- Mrs. Mumble: students pass a mumbled question and answer around the circle

- No, No, No... students tell an outrageous story, changing it as it moves around the circle

Level 3 (complex, higher risk, high self-control required, more autonomy, less supervision)

- What Are You Doing?: a mixed-up pantomime game passed from student to student

- Line or group dance: student or teacher leads the group in a dance

- Ra-di-o: students pass a series of words and gestures around the circle with considerable confusion

Choose Level 1 and 2 activities early in the advisory year. Later, when you and the students sense strong trust and relationship in the group, introduce Level 3. As you build the repertoire, you can always play the Levels 1 and 2 games as well as the higher levels. As the students grow in their social capacity, you have a wider range from which to choose.

<u>Sample progression of name games</u>

You can scaffold the risk level even in a set of similar games, for example games that use classmates' names. See Appendix A to find activities with levels indicated.

Level 1 (simple, low risk, low level of self-control, minimal autonomy)
- Name with Gesture: students volunteer to recall student names and a corresponding gesture

Level 2 (more complex, some risk, more self-control required, some autonomy)
- Concentration with names and/or gestures: students recall names and gestures on cue

Level 3 (complex, higher risk, high self-control required, more autonomy, less supervision)
- Name Us All: students volunteer to name everyone in the group without looking

Resources for Activities

See Appendix D for descriptions of a variety of games and other activities. Use the Appendix A index to guide you in choosing low-risk, easy games for early in the year to help your group get to know each other and play together without friction or reluctance. If you've got a group of students who like to talk and be the center of attention, try some drama activities that give them a chance to perform—poetry or choral readings or a scene with dialogue from a play or novel. Some teachers are successful with group singing, and create a repertoire of songs that range from funny or silly to folk music from the sixties or other eras.

Challenge Them

Introduce students to the organization of activities by levels. Tell them that as they grow in social skills, like learning to maintain self-control even when the games get very active or silly, they will be able to play games at higher levels. The activity portion of CPR is ideal for teaching social skills because student investment is high. They want the harder, riskier, edgier games. Their love of risk gets a healthy outlet and they learn self-control at the same time.

Today is our first chance to play a Level 3 game. We have been working up to this for a long time. This game requires us to use all of the skills and self-control we have learned so far. If it goes well, we'll play others from Level 3.

There are many great games that are more challenging to our ability to manage ourselves—I hope we get to play them.

Q & A

Q. *My class gets out of control when we play some games even after we've modeled and practiced them!*

Here's where the game levels help. Students usually know when they have messed up, and they know when you're not happy with their behavior. Don't lecture them about it: just tell them.

I can see that you're not able to handle a Level 3 game yet, so we'll drop back to Level 2 for a while, starting with the next CPR. That way we can continue to have fun and keep to the guidelines for our class at the same time. When we're ready to move back to Level 3 we can try this game again. We'll get there!

Q. *My students quarrel during a game about the rules or about what someone did or didn't do wrong. Should I stop the activity and talk about it?*

Not unless it has become a safety issue. Teach your students to keep on playing and wait until the end of the game to reflect on how it went. Follow games with a quick reflection:

What went well in that activity? How could we make it more fun? More fair? More safe?

Once your students get used to the routine of play first, talk about it afterwards, they won't dissolve into arguing during the game. They'll know that there will soon be a chance for them to process how the game might be played in the future.

Q. *Sometimes, some students don't want to play the games. Sometimes they think it's cool to scoff at "kid" games. Should there be a consequence for sitting out? Should I insist on full participation?*

Participation in games is optional, but the goal is full participation. See to it that full participation gets into the advisory guidelines, and then you can refer to it throughout the year.

We agreed that we would all work to participate in everything—it's in our guidelines: Participate in advisory activities. What might make a person not want to participate in some part of CPR, and what could he or she do to follow our rule?

Brainstorm with students to generate a list to which you can refer if someone seems to make a habit of sitting out.

The natural consequence of sitting out is that you miss the fun. Make sure that your games are enjoyed by most of the students. Sitting out while everyone else is laughing and enjoying themselves loses its appeal quickly. Do not switch to competitive games as a regular diet. Cooperative fun builds community best, although adding mild competition when they are ready is a healthy way to teach the skills of winning and losing.

When the students select the games and lead the meetings (see page 93 for more about student-led CPR's), you'll notice an increase in enthusiasm. The opportunity to run the show is appealing to most adolescents, who crave opportunities for autonomy. Different people enjoy different sorts of activities, so having the power to choose an activity can help energize game-players: "It's my day to lead, so we're going to play Green Door!" Students also discover that if they are enthusiastic in playing the games others choose, others are more willing to return the favor.

Q. *Help! I'm running out of games ideas.*

Many games are described in this book, and there are countless games books for sale. A free, extensive, and ever-growing source of games (and greetings) is the Origins website, www.OriginsOnline.org. Remember that you can do fun things besides playing games for the activity portion of the meeting—rhythms, singing, yoga, exercises, community dances, skits—all provide variety, movement, and fun.

A Last Word of Encouragement

The sixth grade students trooped in angrily. Something had gone wrong outside during lunch-recess, and some were too mad to focus on the scheduled lesson. "Time for I Sit in the Grass with my Friend," the teacher said. The kids paused, looked up, and smiled. For five minutes the group switched chairs in a tricky little game that requires constant attention or you might mess up. At the end, tension was gone and reading could begin.

Activities clear the air and bring fun into the school day. They bond those who share them, and lighten the tone for students and teacher. They offer fun ways to remember facts, learn how to solve problems, and get to know one another. A quick game can change a sluggish climate to one that is open and eager.

A teacher leads a discussion of responses to the daily news message

CLASS READS AND PROCESSES THE DAILY NEWS

Purposes:

- Inform the community about the day and/or the advisory
- Ease the transition into the day
- Practice social and academic skills

The Basics

After the activity, it's time to read aloud the news as a class. Students have already read it to themselves silently, but the group re-reading provides an opportunity for students to work on their oral reading skills. Like everything else we want students to do well, first we model and practice the read-aloud.

To model, the teacher might read the news for a time or two, using an expressive voice loud enough for everyone to hear. The reading can be followed by a noticing question: "What did you notice about the way I read the news?" Students might remark on the volume, expression, pauses, fluency. The next day, after asking students to remember what stood out for them from yesterday's reading, the teacher calls on a student to read the entire message or just a paragraph. Several students may read, each taking a paragraph.

Essential

- Take turns reading the news aloud so everyone gets a chance over time
- Clarify information about the day
- Process student responses to questions and directions

Optional

- Work on vocabulary words (one or two) in the message
- Work on grammar, spelling, math, and other academics

Students can brainstorm standards for reading the news which you can record in a Y-chart that labels how the class processing of the news looks, sounds, and feels. Post the chart on the wall. Then students can model the routines, following the Y-chart ideas.

Sample Y-Chart for Daily News Reading/Responding Routine

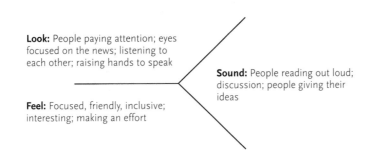

Look: People paying attention; eyes focused on the news; listening to each other; raising hands to speak

Sound: People reading out loud; discussion; people giving their ideas

Feel: Focused, friendly, inclusive; interesting; making an effort

Reflective loop: It is the job of the teacher to monitor the standards set by the group.

Now we can use this description to guide us during the last part of CPR, when we read and discuss the news. If someone forgets, we can remind each other by pointing to the Y-chart.

When a reader gets to the place where students have responded to a question or direction, she reads aloud the responses that students have given. Another option is to have each person read his or her own response aloud. Following is an example of how you can facilitate the group reading of the daily news message and process the responses to the question or direction for the day.

Sample Chart for Early in the Year

October 6, 20__

Welcome, Everyone!

Today is a B schedule day, and there will be a guest teacher for PE—Mr. Smith, who used to coach girls' softball, will be here today and tomorrow for Mrs. Munson, who will be back on Wednesday. Remember our previous discussions about helping out a guest teacher? We'll check back tomorrow to see how well you did in helping Mr. Smith be successful.

We're in the 5th week of school, so let's check in to see how everyone is doing with homework. Make a single check-mark under the category that best describes how often you've been completing your homework and getting it in on time so far this year. Be honest—this could really help you change any bad habits. We'll share in CPR about work habits.

Never get it in   Sometimes get it in   Usually get it in   Always get it in

Let's have a really successful day!

Mr. Morris

Discussing Student Responses

The group discusses the responses. Sometimes, when there is a wide variety of answers to a question, the group can analyze the trend of those answers and possibly quantify the results and even graph them. This is also the time for ethical discussions about, for example, the right thing to do in certain circumstances, or how to handle a social situation, or why politicians offer more than they can deliver.

In the sample message above, students could see at a glance that most of the check marks fell under "sometimes get homework in." What naturally follows is a discussion about how to move the class from sometimes to usually, and students could brainstorm ideas for becoming more responsible in the area of homework.

Examples of processing data from the daily news message

- Based on the responses to the question "Whom would you vote for if the election were held today?" students made a bar graph showing the candidates running for president and the number of student votes each received.

- Students made a pie chart of types of after-school activities in which students reported they engaged.

- A class noted the variety of geometric shapes drawn on the chart and named each one.

- A group compared some of the vocabulary-word definitions given by students to dictionary definitions.

The most important thing about processing the interactive news portion is to make sure that you do so! The processing shows respect for students' responses and provides an opportunity to make it meaningful.

Sample daily news message content: Learning geography day by day

A popular piece of content for the news is geography. Middle level students at New City School in Minneapolis often find place names mentioned in the message. Their job is to look up the places on a map or globe or in an atlas to determine their locations. The questions vary:

Name ten countries in Asia.

Name a major city in the world—one apiece, no repeats!

In what countries are the following cities located?

Put these cities in order from those closest to us to those farthest away. Write your list on a Post-it with the closest city on top. You may collaborate with someone on this.

Lots of discussion occurs in the process before the meeting begins.

That's somewhere in Asia, isn't it? Look in China first.

The Amazon? That's a river in South America.

Let's use a ruler to see how far away each city is from here.

But that doesn't tell us how many miles you'd have to travel to get there.

I know, but we'll get a rough idea, and then we can eyeball it.

Students in this middle school don't have a geography unit *per se*, but these quick challenges day by day have gradually familiarized them with the names and locations of many cities, bodies of water, mountains, etc. The news is helping them to become geographically literate.

"Working" the Daily News

You can work on writing skills in the daily news segment. You can work on punctuation or spelling, or any aspect of writing mechanics. Leave out some punctuation and have students come up to put it in, or do a little work with homonyms: have a student write "two" and "too" alongside "to," and then ask, "Does the message have the correct word for its meaning?"

You can provide a daily opportunity to build vocabulary by asking students for other ways to say something, or by highlighting a word or two in the message that will enrich students' speaking and writing vocabulary. See the vocabulary words highlighted in the daily news examples in Chapter 5.

The chart might read:

I hope everyone had a good vacation! What other adjectives besides "good" could we use to indicate the kind of vacation we hope everyone had?

An eighth grader prepares the daily news message before CPR begins

Students can brainstorm responses such as "fun," "great," "exciting," "inspiring," etc. Then after defining the words that are unfamiliar, re-read the sentence using all the adjectives, as fast as you can—the playfulness supports enjoyment of language, a pleasure that helps lead to reading and writing competence.

Some teachers extend this kind of activity into future advisories, especially when students have come up with interesting words that are less familiar (the teacher can add some, too). They ask students to look for ways to use words they have suggested.

Choose one of these words that's new for you or not part of your everyday speech, and find a way to use it this week. Whenever someone says one of these words, we can squeeze the rubber duck to make a loud squawk, and recognize that you've scored.

That adds to the fun, and provides an incentive to use new vocabulary right after you learn it, the best way to make it your own.

Plan for Success

Keep it simple

The news message doesn't have to be elaborate or long, just relevant so you can have a good discussion during CPR. You can reinforce notes about the day's schedule when the news is read aloud, and provide time to ask questions. Instead of asking you as they enter the room, students will know there will be time for questions during the group reading in CPR.

Use the opportunity of the group reading of the news to get students' minds activated by processing the question or quote or statement you've given them after the group has read it aloud. Because they've already been told to think about something or write a response, in this group processing of the news you can expect full participation.

To help students improve their work with the news message, lead them in a quick reflection after processing it together.

What did we do well in processing the news? What do you think we can improve?

When Students Mess Up

Reading aloud is something poor readers avoid, and some may balk at reading. To make the process feel safer, especially at the beginning, have students read just one sentence each. Give easier sentences to students who struggle with reading. If there is any disparagement about someone's reading, redirect the person who made the put-down to take a break and rejoin the group when he or she is settled enough to follow the rules.

Steady Progress

As students become more independent in running their CPR, they eventually can take over leading the group to read the news (calling on classmates), and even working the chart in the ways that their teacher has modeled. Rehearse a bit when you review the student plan or right before the meeting with the CPR leaders for the day, and make suggestions about reading and working the daily news message in ways that are fun and productive. The opportunity to teach peers by facilitating the daily news portion of the meeting is an opportunity for leadership, public speaking, and a chance to work on social skills, especially assertion, responsibility, empathy, and self-control. Chances to lead in real meetings with peers are among the best ways possible to build such skills.

Challenge Them

The best way to learn something is to teach it. You don't have to be perfect to read the news to us, just willing to work. We all make mistakes in reading, and we all need the daily practice. In this room, you can take a chance. Our job as listeners during the reading is to support the reader in every way we can.

Q & A

Q. *Reading the daily news message together comes at the end of CPR, and sometimes we run out of time. Is it all right to just skip the reading and processing part?*

The processing of the news underscores its importance, even when there's not much to process. It reinforces the need to read it as you enter the room and make your responses if necessary. What you're describing is really an issue of controlling the time, and that is a job a teacher has every minute of the day. If you find that your CPR components are running overtime, ask a student to give the group a signal when it's time to shift from one component to the next. The flow and the satisfaction will improve when you see to it that all the pieces are included.

Q. *Why can't we just read the news first when we gather in the circle? The students have just read and responded to it, so it's fresh in their minds.*

The first thing that a friendly group does when they get together is greet each other (greeting) and check in with each other on how things are going, what's new, and what they've been thinking (sharing). That's why the greeting and sharing components come first. Then, after ten minutes or so of sitting and talking, the activity refreshes everyone. Finally, students get daily experience in using their self-control to settle down after an activity, and read the news together. It focuses their minds, sparks their thinking, and provides a bridge into the academic day. Don't miss the opportunity to use it that way!

Q. *What do I do when students make mistakes reading the news?*

Be proactive about mistakes (see Challenge Them above). Set students up to *expect* mistakes, because they are a natural part of becoming a good reader—especially a good read-aloud reader. When mistakes occur, re-direct any negative comments, sounds, gestures, or body language immediately. Be rigorous regarding put-downs. No lectures (they just call more attention to the moment)—just a quick, low-key direction: "Take a break, Chris."

A Last Word of Encouragement

I've placed a few mistakes in today's news on purpose. Raise your hand if you can spot one, and tell us what change you suggest. This is a good way to work on our proof-reading skills.

Reading and discussing the message is a little like talking about the morning newspaper. It gives the group a chance to think together about what is said and the way it is said. It sharpens the eye and the mind, and helps smooth the transition from home and bus to the rigors of the school day. The first-hour class will benefit from the wake-up of daily news.

AFTER THE MEETING

After the daily news discussion, CPR is over, and you and your students will benefit greatly from a moment of reflection about the meeting.

What is something you enjoyed about today's meeting?

What is something you think we could improve?

Using 1-5 fingers, indicate how well we did in following our guidelines during this meeting (5 means we did a great job; 1 means we have a lot of work to do!)

The habit of reflecting on the meeting has several payoffs. You have a daily means by which you can improve your meetings. You are modeling for the day when students lead the meeting and they will need assessment and feedback on the quality of their meeting and their leadership. And finally, you are establishing the lifelong habit of the reflective loop, the means by which all competent people operate.

Leading CPR helps prepare students for future leadership roles

STUDENT-LED CPR: ONE OF THE MAIN PAYOFFS

I know many kids who do not like grown-ups telling them what to do, let alone one of their class-mates, but they do like kids running the meeting, because we are friends and we respect each other.

—middle school advisory student, Minneapolis MN

Throughout the discussion of the components of the Circle of Power and Respect, there are references to student leadership of CPR. Leadership is a big payoff of CPR. Students get chances to exercise the responsible independence that is essential for their success in school. Adolescents' craving for autonomy, their desire to demonstrate their competence in the world, their desire for good relationships with peers, and their constant search for ways to have fun—all these fundamental needs are satisfied in their leadership of CPR, a structure designed to boost them towards school and life success.

Sample Student-led CPR

Dejon raises his hand as a signal and the circle of 8th graders falls silent. "Our greeting today is Slapjack. I'll demonstrate with Alex." The two do a hand jive and greet each other: "S'up, Alex." "S'up, Dejon." The greeting moves around the circle. The students have done Slapjack many times before, so they are comfortable with it. Some smile, others look a little sleepy. Everyone looks at his or her partner, at least briefly.

The topic for individual shares today is the same as yesterday—tell about a place in the world you'd like to visit. Tell just a couple of things about the place, and then open it up to questions and comments. Sylvia, you're up.

Dejon leads the group through the sharing and then calls for a round of Frogger, a game that requires careful observation and focused attention, and ends with most of the group pretending to be asleep. It is both silly and challenging.

Finally, Dejon asks for someone to read the news message aloud, and facilitates a discussion of the famous people identification challenge in the news: "Nobody got Golda Meier or George Washington Carver. Anybody have an idea about either one of these?" After a couple of guesses, Dejon calls on Catherine to look up the names in the Famous People Biographies book.

Let's rate this meeting. Give a thumb up if you think it went well, thumb sideways for so-so, and thumb down if you think it wasn't a good CPR at all (then you've got to tell us why). OK, on the count of three—one, two, three, thumbs! (Looking around) *Everybody seems to think it went pretty well. Thanks. Anybody got an idea for a cheer to end with today? OK, let's try the Gorilla. Ready? Uhn. Uhn. Uhn. Meeting's over—have a good day.*

A student leader asks for silence

All that Dejon did in leading the meeting was planned ahead, had teacher approval, and was patterned after the CPR meeting routine that, as a member of this advisory, he had practiced since the first day of school that year. Now it was April, and the group no longer needed an adult to lead their meetings. Much to their satisfaction, they were able to do the leading independently and responsibly. The students took over single components of the meeting gradually. They began by choosing and leading an activity. By the second semester, groups of four led meetings, each person taking one part. By the end of March, one student could lead the entire meeting. CPR meetings were now giving these young people daily opportunities to satisfy their needs for feeling competent and autonomous, and for having fun with their peers as well as with their teacher.

Plan for Success

Timing is everything in a process of turning control over to students. If you give them independence and power before they are ready to use it responsibly, you get a disaster: they fail, and you have to pull the power away from them. If you wait too long to give over some of the control, students grow restless and resentful and eventually may balk at participation.

Look for these signs of self-control

- When students can greet each other cordially each day, without discrimination or a subtle sliding scale of friendliness, they are ready to lead greetings.

- When students listen carefully and without interruption to peer sharing, and when they ask interesting questions and make friendly comments in response to everyone's sharing, without slighting some with their silence, they are ready to lead sharing.

- When students participate enthusiastically in games and other activities without losing their self-control, when they can get rowdy and then calmed down and silent in response to the silence signal, they are ready to lead activities.

- When they participate in reading and discussing the daily news message and are willing to do a careful job planning and executing the chart or overhead, they are ready to start creating and leading the review of the news.

Careful planning is required for all the components of CPR, so student leaders must create a plan, present it to the teacher for review and revision if necessary, and follow the approved version. A CPR Plan Sheet will guide them through the steps they must take to create a good meeting. The plan will be reviewed by the teacher for an OK before the meeting takes place. See page 270 for a Student CPR Plan Sheet.

Challenge Them

Let students know that you are hoping they become skilled enough in CPR to lead it themselves. Tell them that what it takes is learning the routine and some greetings and games, and most important, learning self-control.

As time goes by I will introduce you to more challenging greetings, shares, and activities. As you learn to handle them, your skills will grow, and then we'll start talking about student leadership of the meeting. I know you can do it, and I'll do everything I can to show you how.

Steady Progress

Students generate ideas

Capacity-building for leadership of the meeting happens incrementally. It begins with students making suggestions: ideas for greetings, sharing, and activities, and interesting questions or tasks for the daily news. Greetings are easy to invent; students dream up creative handshakes and body movements and language all the time. The best sharing topics reflect the things students want to know about each other, and as long as the topics remain appropriate, a broad range of them will bring variety and energy to the sharing component. The activity component is usually easy for students to handle—they know lots of games already, and may ask to play them and/or teach them. Watch out for games that are too competitive that can damage the cooperative spirit of the advisory.

Setting the criteria

Student suggestions for CPR will steadily improve if you establish guidelines for what will and won't work in meetings. The guidelines can be brainstormed with the students, but the teacher has the final say. It is your job to keep the community close, safe, and caring, so you lead the guidelines process. Use the Y-charts already generated for the components to set the guidelines, adding content relevant to planning, not just participating in, the meeting. What follows are suggested guidelines; you may create your own or revise these.

Preparing the Daily News
- News is legible, accurate, and clearly written
- News contains useful information about the day
- News contains an interactive question or exercise

Greeting
- Everyone is included
- The greetings are respectful and friendly
- Time frame is 2 to 5 minutes

Sharing
- Everyone gets a chance to share, but not necessarily every day
- The format for the shares can vary: individual, whip, partner, etc.
- Students get a chance to ask questions and make comments with some of the shares
- The sharer's job is to start the story with the basic facts, to call on a variety of people, and to answer questions

- The group's job is to listen attentively, ask interesting questions, and make friendly comments
- Time frame is about 5 minutes

Activity

- Most of the games are cooperative, not competitive
- Everyone gets a chance to play
- Games are played with courtesy and self-control
- Time frame is about 5 minutes

Daily News

- Everyone responds to the interactive part
- Everyone gets a chance to read the news aloud, but not every day
- The interactive part which includes some form of learning, social or academic, is processed by the whole group
- Time frame is 3 to 5 minutes

Once the guidelines have been decided on, they can be posted so everyone who makes a suggestion about a greeting, share, or activity can use the guidelines to shape the suggestion. At this point, suggestions are welcome. Later, when student partners are planning entire meetings, they can use planning sheets that contain the guidelines. You may decide to add your criteria to a Student CPR Plan Sheet based on the sample on page 270.

Challenge Them: Cooperation, not competition

Students need to understand that the games, in order to build community, need to be mostly cooperative, not competitive, especially early in the year. That may take an explanation from you:

I have lots of activities for us to try, and I'm sure you have good ideas, too. One thing I want to make clear, though, is that we're going to mostly have games that are not about winning and losing. In other words, I want non-competitive games that will help us get to know each other and are enjoyable for all, including people who are just learning the game. Competitive games can be stressful and can pull groups apart rather than build them up. Later on in the year, when we're used to playing together, we might look at some of the competitive activities and add them to our repertoire. For now, let me know if you have an idea for a cooperative game we can play.

If students suggest a competitive game anyway, you might be able to lessen the competitive aspect by using revolving outs: as soon as the next player or team is out, the previous 'out' player or team returns, so there is never more than one player or team out at a time, and no one is out permanently.

To completely avoid the winner/loser aspect of a competitive game, you can often drop the elimination element and use a timing goal for the whole group, or an everybody-makes-it goal instead. Here's an example of such a conversion.

Sample Competitive to Cooperative Conversion: Key Punch Game

• **Key Punch** (page 246)

Original version of the game: Teams race against each other in an effort to touch all the numbers (1-10) in order, as they lie scattered on the floor. Each team member has a turn stepping or jumping from number to number, until the entire team has had a turn. Whichever team finishes first wins.

Revised version to build community: Teams race against the clock, and their times are recorded. Then the two teams combine and time how long it takes for everyone to make a run. The challenge is to see if the two teams combined can beat the times of the two individual teams added together. The combined teams are given time to strategize, and they have three tries. If they come up with good strategies in their combined brainstorming, make use of everyone's previous experience, provide coaches all around the circle and guide and cheer each other on ("Six, over here!" "Seven, in the back!"), they might beat the time of *either* of the individual teams alone!

Students lead one component

On any day, a student might lead one part of CPR. To do this well, the student will have prepared a plan and run it by the teacher for revisions, if necessary, and approval. Leadership of just one component is less demanding, and success is more easily achieved.

After a student or partners have led a component, they ask the group to reflect on the component.

What worked about our greeting today?

What could we improve next time?

Using fingers to indicate 5 (really liked it) to 1 (didn't like it), show with your hand how much you enjoyed today's greeting (or sharing or activity).

These questions will give the leader of the component feedback that will help him or her plan for next time.

Students take turns leading the meeting

Generally, at least half or more of the year is over before an advisory gets to this point. It usually takes that much steady work on social skills, inclusion, building a repertoire of greetings and games, and becoming clear about the criteria for students to be ready to steer the ship. At this point, students (usually partners or a small group) take on the responsibility of planning and leading a whole CPR meeting. It takes a series of steps to do this each time they lead.

1. The group is formed, and they come up with ideas for the meeting. These ideas are described on a Student CPR Plan Sheet (page 270).

2. Group submits their plan to the teacher.

3. Group conferences with the teacher, revisions are made as necessary, and a date is set.

4. Group leads the CPR meeting, followed by a brief class reflection (oral or written) on the meeting. The group is acknowledged by the class for their accomplishment.

5. Group members write their own reflection on the meeting process and hand it in to teacher.

The whole process is set up for success. By the time students step into the leadership role, they have experienced months of CPR meetings, know the criteria for each of the components, and have been guided in their planning by the teacher. The scaffolding is in place, and a good result is predictable. Successful leadership builds confidence, competence, and the satisfaction of autonomy: we did it ourselves! Student leadership of CPR prepares students for leadership in other arenas, and gives thrust forward to students' sense of connection to school—a feeling that their school really does belong to them and they to it. School attachment is a hallmark of student attitudes in healthy middle school climates.

Students participate in an extended silent reading

CHAPTER THREE

Activity Plus (A+) Advisories

Some days you want to use your advisory period to do an extended activity, and you don't have enough time in the CPR framework to do it. You need a structure that is consistent with CPR and continues to build your community. On these days, you can use the Activity Plus (A+) structure.

In A+, the advisory begins with daily news and a greeting, just as it does in CPR. These can be quick and still provide the comfort of familiarity and the rhythm of routine. Seeing the daily news message and beginning with a friendly greeting helps students transition into the school day and addresses their need for relationship, no matter what the main activity may be. Starting each day the same way heads off disruptions by providing a dependable structure which some students cannot do without. Routine is our friend, and routines that build community nourish all of us every day.

A+ Format

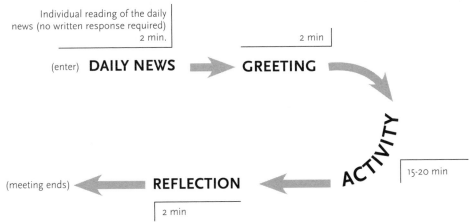

| Individual reading of the daily news (no written response required) 2 min. | 2 min |
| (enter) **DAILY NEWS** ➡ **GREETING** |

ACTIVITY 15-20 min

(meeting ends) ⬅ **REFLECTION** ⬅ 2 min

The advisory begins much the same as CPR, but most of the time is spent on the extended activity. The greeting, introduction of the activity, and final reflection are all well suited to the circle, the best way to gather for community-building. When you feel that the length of the activity doesn't allow time for a circle, make the necessary adaptations.

Daily News

The news announces the activity for the day in advisory, and anything unusual about the schedule. It doesn't usually include an interactive piece, so it's a quick read. Starting the day with the news lets everyone know immediately upon entering the room what will be happening in advisory that day. It indicates with its announcement of an activity that something is different, while it reassures with the familiar routine. See Chapter 2 for detailed information about writing the daily news.

homework buddies
at work

Greeting

If you have minimal instructions to give and no time to circle up, consider doing a standing circle around the edge of the room for the greeting. Another possibility is to have students do a One-Minute Mingle Greeting around the room and then sit at desks or form into groups or move to the gym for instructions.

The greeting ensures that everyone is acknowledged by someone, that everyone hears his name said in a friendly way every day. The greeting says, "Today, as always, we are a community." See Chapter 2 for detailed information about successful facilitation of the greeting.

Activity

The activity usually takes place away from the circle and uses most of the advisory time (15 - 20 minutes). It can be play (sometimes with other advisories), projects, art, writing, planning meetings, role plays—the list is long and interesting. This is how you fit into advisory enriching and diverse activities that your students may already enjoy. For detailed information about planning and orchestrating an activity, see Chapter 2 and the suggestions below for implementing specific activities.

A word about timing

Timing is crucial in facilitating A+ advisories, because the extended activities could easily take up more time than you have available. You might want to plan to devote more than one advisory to the activity. Watch the time closely, and start bringing things to a conclusion a minute or so before you need to stop for the reflection. A timer helps, and sometimes a student can assume the role of timekeeper. Even though you could let the activity keep going (especially when it's really successful) right up to the bell, there will be much more satisfaction for everyone if you stop in time to reflect, even if very briefly. It takes self-discipline, but the reward is a feeling of completion and order.

Reflection

Students share about the process or the results of the activity. The reflection works best in the circle, but students can reflect and/or share their work with partners, small groups, or individually, at their desks or tables. Perhaps only a couple of students share with the whole group. Another quick option is to have students write down an answer to a reflection question, signed if appropriate to the question. This becomes their "Exit Card," collected as they leave.

Was the book you read at the right level for you?

For how much of the 15 minutes did your attention focus on your book?

What did you enjoy about making the banner?

On a scale of 1-5 with 5 being the strongest support, how much do you agree with the decision our advisory made today?

In these couple of minutes of looking back at the end of advisory, students reinforce the habit of reflective thinking after an activity. It's a habit that provides lifelong payoffs. Also, instead of merely leaving after clean up, students and teacher get a minute to take a breath, think together, and experience the satisfaction of closure before hurrying off to something altogether different.

Weekly Schedule: Two possibilities

Mon.	Tues.	Weds.	Thurs.	Fri.
CPR	A+	CPR	A+	CPR

Mon.	Tues.	Weds.	Thurs.	Fri.
CPR	CPR	CPR	A+	CPR

The option of doing CPR every day is always a good one, and *imperative* at the beginning of the year to establish understanding of the components and safety within the group. You can easily provide enough variety in CPR to keep it interesting simply by varying the greetings, sharing topics and formats, and activities. But A+ advisories give you additional options.

Plan for Success

Remember that you can invite students to reflect on the *process* of the activity as well as its substance. Advisory is a good time to focus their attention on how they work with others, on how they solve problems, and on their work habits.

How well did you and your partner work together?

Do you feel that the work was done evenly by everyone in your group?

What's one thing you might do differently if we do this activity again?

How focused were you throughout the activity?

The reflection is also a time when you can encourage higher-level thinking about a topic. Invite students to evaluate, compare, integrate, and apply what they have learned during the activity.

On a scale of 1-5, how high would you rate the speaker in his understanding of adolescents?

How might the work you did with your partner help you in school?

In what ways might you use what you learned during this advisory in your life outside of school?

Q & A

Q. *What if I run out of time for students to reflect?*

Sometimes it's not easy to stop in time to reflect, but reflection needs to become a habit. Even if you stop just one minute before the bell rings, and have time for only one person to answer the question you pose, or a little time for students to talk with partners, even that little bit of reflection will support the routine, strengthen the habit, and give you and your students closure for your time together.

A+ ADVISORIES EXAMPLES

Here are examples of types of activities appropriate for and of interest to middle level students. Most can be repeated with different content or topics. Some will become favorites. All will quietly and effectively build skills and address adolescent needs for relationship, fun, competence, and autonomy. Each example shows how the daily news, greeting, and closing reflection integrate with the activity for the day.

SILENT READING

In general, the more students read, the better they read. Commit some advisory time each week to silent reading within the context of the community-building framework of an A+ advisory period.

Daily News

Monday, October 10, 20__

Greetings, Friends!

Today is silent reading day. Write the title of the book you are reading:

If you didn't bring a book, select one from the assortment on the table in the back. Check out what other students have said about the books on an index card inside of them. Write the name of the book you're reading and your name on a Post-it, and attach below.

We'll start with a greeting in the circle at 8:35.

It's a great day to read—enjoy your book.

Yours truly,

Mr. Flaherty

Greeting (1-2 minutes in circle)

Basic Greeting

Activity (15-20 minutes)

Everyone reads a book or article

Spark: (Circle) Choose one

- Teacher reads a little from a book he's currently reading
- Teacher shows a couple of books from the school library that students may be interested in reading, in case someone hasn't chosen a book yet

Silent reading: Students may sit anywhere in the room

Reflection (2 - 3 minutes in circle, partners, or small groups; if there's time, a few share with whole group)

Students choose and answer a process or content question such as:

Describe some part of your book that interests you and tell why.

Do you enjoy silent reading? Why or why not?

What's difficult about reading for you? (partners only)

What percentage of the book have you read? Does it hold your interest?

Would you recommend this book to others in our advisory?

What have you learned from reading this book or article so far?

Plan for Success

Be sure to have interesting books and other reading material at various reading levels available so if students arrive with nothing to read, they can find something quickly. They will also get the message that you mean what you say about this time being used for silent reading for everyone, with no exceptions.

Establishing a silent reading time is like establishing other routines. You need to make clear from the start what the routine will be, model it, and reflect afterwards on how it went. Advisory usually allows for a fairly short amount of reading, so be rigorous. If anyone talks or does anything other than reading, redirect that person immediately. The plan is that *everyone* will read for 20 minutes. If need be, tell the straying person to take a break in another chair or in a designated break place to muster concentration before going back to her seat to resume reading.

Sometimes a story as enjoyable to middle schoolers as it is to elementary kids is told; audience participation happens regularly during these stories. When it does, middle schoolers can lose their coolness and really get as involved as a kindergartner. Of course, we'd never admit that!

—middle school advisory student, Minneapolis MN

READ ALOUD

Daily News

Greeting (1 - 2 minutes in circle)

Depending on the book to be read, choose a greeting that fits with its geography, characters, or culture. For example, for *Bud, Not Buddy*, the greeting could be "Hi, Lucille, I'm John, not Johnny." "Hi, John. I'm Lucille, not Lucy." The Basic Greeting is fine, too.

> Tuesday, February 10, 20__
>
> Salutations, Everyone!
>
> Today we'll read the next chapter in Gary Paulsen's <u>Hatchet</u>. Circle up for the greeting, and afterwards find a place in the room that will help you listen well. Today we're listening especially for small details that describe a person or scene or animal so you can picture it in your mind. When you hear one, snap your fingers so we'll all notice it.
>
> Reflection question I'll ask at the end: What is one detail you remember from today's reading?
>
> Here's to our reading enjoyment!
>
> Mrs. London

Activity (15 - 20 minutes)

Teacher reads a chapter or less from a novel

Spark: (Circle) Teacher reminds everyone of the story so far, or introduces the book if this is the first reading from it

Reading: Students listen, sitting anywhere in the room

Reflection (2 - 3 minutes in circle, partners, or small groups; if there's time, a few share with whole group)

Students choose and answer a process or content question such as:

Describe some part of the book that interests you and tell why.

What did you visualize as I was reading this chapter?

Summarize what has happened in the story so far.

How would you describe _____ (a main character) to someone?

Other questions having to do with motivation, intention, feelings, or predictions about what will happen.

Plan for Success

Read with gusto. Create drama in your reading so its characters come alive for the listeners. There is special intimacy in listening to a live read-aloud, but if you feel you are not skilled enough in oral reading, you might use a recorded reading. Another option is to have student readers, but only those fluent enough to read at an engaging pace and with some expression. The main purpose is to have students get caught up in a book together, not to give oral reading practice; if you can manage both, so much the better.

BOARD GAMES

One way to provide a relaxed setting for students to get acquainted is to set them together at a board game. They can quietly pay attention to each other while they play the game—fun and relationship-building at the same time!

Daily News

Monday, January 5, 20___

Greetings, Returning Students!

Happy first day back! To help you segue from vacation to school, we'll have a board game advisory today. Below is a list of games. Sign up for one you would like to play.

Cribbage Concentration   Checkers   African Stone Game   Other?

Remember our role plays on inviting people and asking to join. Game days are successful only when everyone has fun!

Playfully,

Ms. Brzynzski

Greeting (1-2 minutes in circle)

Name Card Greeting: *Pick a card from the pile and greet your partner with a high five.*

Activity (15 - 20 minutes)

Students set up and play quick board or card games of their choice. On a generic board game (see sample on page 278), players throw the dice and advance, pulling a card when they land on a "card space." The card tells you what to do. You can choose a focus for the game and create cards to match. For example, the focus could be "succeeding in school" and the cards could read: forgot my homework (move back two spaces); ate a good breakfast (move ahead two spaces); practiced asking probing questions (move ahead four spaces), etc.

Reflection (2 - 3 minutes in circle, partners, or small groups; if time, a few share with whole group)

Students answer a process or content question such as:

What was fun about the activity today?

What might you do differently next time?

Do you have any ideas for other games we can play in 15 minutes or so?

Plan for Success

To introduce board games, choose and demonstrate a game that everyone can play at the same time, such as cribbage, poker, gin rummy, or another card game. This gives you a chance to make sure that everyone learns the routine of board game days, that it's important to know the game rules and follow them, and that students need to exhibit good social skills during the time of play to have the privilege of more days with, eventually, a variety of games. Taking the time to establish the protocols of a new routine first pays off in fewer incidents of disruption and more enjoyment all around.

MAKING THE ADVISORY ROOM OUR OWN

Traditionally in many middle schools, advisories and homerooms do something to make their space their own. Posters, charts, names, photographs of the advisory students—all of these help create a sense of ownership and belonging.

Daily News

Wednesday, September 16, 20__

Felicitations, Eagle Advisory!

Today we get to create things that will give our advisory room a special look. Sign up for the project you want to work on. The limit is six people per project.

Eagle Door Poster   Our Class Agreements   Our Declarations   Greetings & Games Book

The materials for each project are located in the four corners of the room. Circle up and I'll give you your instructions there.

Go, Eagles!

Mr. Lopez

Greeting (1 - 2 minutes in circle)

Basic Greeting, Hand Jive Greeting, or any other quick greeting

Activity (15 - 20 minutes)

Making a door poster, a poster list of class or school rules, a poster list of advisory students and their goals for the year, a poster or ring book of CPR greetings and games

Spark: (Circle) Students sign up to work on one of the projects. Teacher provides a planning sheet to each group. They draw up a plan for what their poster will look like, what materials they will need, and who is working on the poster.

Work time: Students work in groups to fill out their plan sheets and bring them to the teacher for approval and/or recommendations. If there's time, students gather materials and sketch out the poster in pencil. Project is completed in 1 or 2 subsequent advisories.

Reflection (2 - 3 minutes in circle, partners, or small groups; if time, a few share with whole group)

Students choose and answer a process or content question such as:

What was fun about the activity today?

Do you think the poster you are working on will turn out well? What's your evidence?

What is one way that your group got along well to get the job done?

What is a problem your group had to solve?

Plan for Success

Establishing their own, special environment within which your advisory will meet each day will increase student enjoyment and sense of belonging. For the work quality to be good enough to display all semester or year, brainstorm standards for a good poster ahead of time.

PEER TEACHING

The strong desire for friendships makes peer teaching a natural for adolescents. When students pair up and teach each other something, both learn, and relationships are strengthened.

Daily News

Monday, March 20, 20__

Happy First Day of Spring!

Today we'll be sharing something we know with another person. Pick a number from the basket, find your partner with the same number, and sit next to each other anywhere you choose in the room. After a greeting, one of you will introduce the other to the game, tool, or recipe you brought and then, at a signal from me, you'll switch roles. You and your partner can decide what greeting you want to do. Each person will get 8 minutes to demonstrate. Be sure you leave time for your partner to give it a try, if that's appropriate in your situation.

I'll be sharing as well, so somebody get ready to knit!

Have fun,   Mrs. Thomlinson

Greeting (1 - 2 minutes in circle)

Name Card Greeting: *Pick a card from the pile and greet your partner with a high five.*

Activity (15 - 20 minutes)

Partners, formed by cards picked randomly in greeting, get together to show each other how to play a game, thread a needle, shuffle a deck of cards, do a trick, twirl a ball, knit—any skill or know-how that one has to show the other, then vice versa.

Planning: (Circle) Students sign up beforehand, in earlier advisories, to demonstrate or teach someone to do something. They can show at least several steps to the process in 6 or 7 minutes. Students may need help brainstorming skills they could teach. They must bring any necessary supplies.

Work time: Students in pairs teach each other how to do something. Work time ends by students thanking and/or acknowledging their partners.

Reflection (2 - 3 minutes in circle, partners, or small groups; if time, a few share with whole group) Students choose and answer a process or content question such as:

What was fun about the activity today?
What did you learn from your partner?
Each person describes what her/his partner taught.

Plan for Success

You can prepare students for random partners ahead of time. Explain that we will use random partners sometimes to help everyone get to know and work with everyone else. Sometimes it might be awkward or frustrating, but in the end, the community will benefit. It is a great preparation for adult life to learn to work with a wide variety of people, even though you may not want all of them as friends.

The important message to deliver is that we *all* can work with each other, and we will. The only option a student has who is not willing to live by that guideline is to sit out the activity.

HOMEWORK BUDDIES

As with peer teaching, the practice of homework buddies puts students together for positive purposes. A mutual support system, student-to-student, can make a big difference in homework success, and can help pull the advisory community together.

Daily News

Ciao, Mi Amici! ("Hi, My Friends" in Italian)

Today is Homework Buddies day. Find your buddy on the list* and decide what homework you will work on today. You have 20 minutes, so each person should get about ten. One option, if you both want to focus on the same thing, is to spend the whole 20 minutes on that. Be sure to raise a hand if you need my help. I'm the trouble-shooter during Homework Buddies.

Begin with a Fist-Tap Greeting.

Good luck!

Mr. DeAmato

*Note: Homework buddies are pre-assigned by the teacher. The homework buddies list roughly matches people strong in at least one academic subject with others who need support with homework in general or with a particular subject.

Greeting (a few seconds in work place)

Homework buddies greet with Fist-Tap Greeting

Activity (15 - 20 minutes)

Partners work together on any homework difficulties or confusions. Work time ends with students thanking and/or acknowledging their partners.

Reflection (2 - 3 minutes in partners)

Discuss a process or content question such as:
What new understandings did you have today?
What was something difficult about the homework?
How did the two of you get along?

If there's time, a couple of people share out with the whole group or you end with 1-5 fingers from everyone indicating what they accomplished today, how well the partners got along, or ask for someone to share one good idea for getting homework done right.

Plan for Success

To be successful, homework buddies require an advisory climate that feels safe and friendly. You may decide to defer this activity until such time as you have established a strong community. Even then, students may feel awkward when they see that you have paired weaker learners with stronger ones, at least in some subjects. Talk about differences ahead of time, and you may decide to make participation in the buddy work voluntary. Students who opt out may either work with the teacher or alone. During homework time, you would then circulate, helping students who you know need help.

TEAM-BUILDING AND TRUST-BUILDING ACTIVITIES

A session of team/trust-building activities can make a big difference in the health of the relationships within a community. When the activity calls for risk-taking and mutual support, students usually rise to the challenge, and breakthroughs occur.

Daily News

Thursday, October 24, 20__

Good Morning, Friends!

As promised, we'll be heading to the gym as soon as the bell rings. When we get there, circle up on one of the floor circles. After a greeting, I'll give you instructions for our team-building activity. (I hope we have time for two of them!) Be ready to share a quality you need to be a good team player.

Let's play!

Ms. Sanchez

Greeting (1 - 2 minutes in circle)

With Fist-Tap Greeting or Hand Jive Greeting, greet the person next to you in the circle. If you are doing team-building with another advisory or the whole grade level, you can do the Greeting in the gym or wherever you are meeting. If the group is large, skip the hand jive and have students greet as many people as they can in a One-Minute Mingle Greeting.

Activity (15 - 20 minutes)

Depending on the size of the group, the activity can take place in home room or in the gym. Students engage in one or two activities that build interdependence and cooperation (see Appendix A to find Team- and Trust-Building Activities)

Reflection (2 - 3 minutes, in circle if there's time)

Talk to your high-five partner about something that worked well in this activity today.
If time, follow Partner Shares with whole group questions (choose one):

What was fun about today?
How well did your group work together today? (Show with 1-5 fingers)
Share any ideas for doing even better next time solving problems as a group.

Plan for Success

Team-building activities are a powerful aid to building community at any time. At the beginning of the year, they can transform a group of virtual strangers into an interdependent group. Graduate them in order of the degree of risk, and build student capacity to work together. Save the riskier trust activities for later in the year when students are more willing to depend on each other in situations of vulnerability.

CROSS-ADVISORY GAMES

One way to build a grade-level or whole-school community is to invite another advisory to join yours to greet each other, have some fun, and reflect on it together afterwards. It's also gives you an excuse to talk about what it means to be a host or a guest, and allows students to practice the social skills they have been learning all year.

Daily News

Attention, Everyone!

Today is a B schedule day. Today is also the day we've been waiting for—we're launching the 7th grade cross-advisory games. We'll go to the gym as soon as the bell rings, and meet and greet the other 7th grade advisories. Every Tuesday this month we'll meet in the gym to play during advisory. Today's game is Continuous Kickball.

Let's have some fun!

Mr. Armado

Greeting (1 - 2 minutes in circle)

With Fist-Tap Greeting or Hand Jive Greeting, greet the person next to you in the circle. If you are doing games with another advisory or the whole grade level, you can do the greeting in the gym or wherever you are meeting. If the group is large, skip the hand jive and have students greet as many people as they can in a One-Minute Mingle Greeting.

Activity (15 - 20 minutes)

Depending upon the size of the group, the activity can take place in homeroom or in the gym. Students engage in a cooperative game suitable for large numbers. See Appendix A to find activities suitable to large groups such as multiple classrooms.

Reflection (2 - 3 minutes in circle, partners, or small groups; if time, a few share with whole group)

Talk to your partner about something that worked well in this activity today.
Whole group questions:
What was fun today?
How could we improve the game next time?
How well did people work together today? (Show with 1-5 fingers)

Plan for Success

If you are planning to play with another advisory group, make sure both teachers prepare students similarly for what is expected of them. Each room can make a Y-chart of how the games will look, sound, and feel if everyone is playing hard, safe, and fair. If you already work under the same rules, each teacher can ask her group how those rules will apply to the games. During the activity, responses to rule-breakers should be consistent, whichever room they are from and whichever teacher is handling the redirecting and consequences.

CONFLICT RESOLUTION

To know how to work through conflict with others is a premium life skill, and adolescents can learn it very well. Teach them a format, guide them while they are learning it, and do a follow-up whenever possible to provide some accountability, and you've got what it takes for a great conflict and stress manager—their conflicts, your stress!

Daily News

Monday, April 5, 20__

Good morning, Friends!

We'll be having an all-school assembly today at 10. I hear that a highlight will be the Talent Show Committee's announcement.

Advisory today will be about the skill of repairing relationships by settling quarrels in a nonviolent way. Describe your level of cool when you're in the middle of a conflict. Check the response that you most often use.

I lose it and fight   I fight with words only   I cool off on my own   I talk it out

Yours calmly,

Ms. Sampson

Greeting (1 - 2 minutes in circle)

Basic Greeting with or without a handshake, hand jive, or peace sign

Activity (15 - 20 minutes)

Demonstrate the Conflict Resolution process: HELPSOUT

Planning: Plan the demonstration ahead of time with selected students. Tell them or decide together on the conflict issue you will resolve. The teacher orchestrates the process by directing students through the steps (see page 272 for Steps of a Conflict Resolution).

Demo: The demonstration can be done in the circle, with the actors given extra space around them (they still remain in the circumference and do not go into the center of the circle, so they don't have their backs to some people).

Reflection (2 - 3 minutes in circle, partners, or small groups; if time, a few share with whole group)

Students choose and answer a process or content question such as:

What steps did we take in this conflict resolution process? Use the chart to help you remember.
How might this process help you resolve things when you have a quarrel with a friend?
What helps you calm down so you can resolve a quarrel peacefully?
What help would you need to go through this process?

Plan for Success

At first, the Conflict Resolution process requires the presence of a neutral adult to guide students through the steps and make sure they follow them appropriately. After students become familiar with the process, they can go through the steps themselves without an adult present, although the results of the process need to be recorded so the teacher can check in with both parties after time has passed to see if things have truly been resolved.

ROLE PLAY

Drama is a perfect device for teaching social skills. Students like the skits, and when they act out in a controlled setting the challenging social dilemmas that are a part of their everyday lives, they learn to stop, think, and make good decisions based not on impulse, but on what is reasonable and right.

Daily News

Tuesday, November 5, 20__

Good Morning, Thespians!

Student Council meets today at 3 p.m. in Mr. Lawton's room. Our advisory activity will be a role play on saying no. It's hard to do sometimes, and when we act out a situation where you need to say no, we'll come up with some words to use that may help. In a phrase below, describe a situation when you may have to say no to someone.

My daughter asks to use the car (Ms. R)_____

(students add situations, one each, & sign)_____

Thanks for your input!

Ms. Randall

Greeting (1 - 2 minutes in circle)

Basic Greeting with or without a handshake, hand jive, or peace sign

Activity (15 - 20 minutes)

Do a role play on a school social issue relevant to students such as:

- Saying no without hurting someone's feelings
- Asking someone to change his/her behavior
- Asking for a favor
- Asking permission to do something
- Apologizing
- Offering to help out
- Responding to gossip passed to you
- Responding to gossip about you, overheard or rumored
- Telling someone you've changed your mind
- Cleaning up after you've told a lie
- Admitting a mistake
- Comforting someone who is sad
- Calming someone who is mad
- How to reengage a group member
- How to decline an invitation
- How to invite someone over

- How to have a conversation
- How to give a compliment
- A student is left out of a game at recess
- Students repeatedly ask you to give them your homework answers
- Kids are pressuring you to join their gang
- A student consistently annoys you and your friends with his behavior
- How to tell someone you want to be his/her friend
- Telling a friend you are angry with him/her
- Showing others (students, your parents, a sibling) that you don't want to be disturbed
- Explaining to a teacher why you did something the teacher didn't like
- Telling a parent that you want to handle a difficult situation by yourself

Planning: Students can brainstorm a list of issues ahead of time. Add some of your own, write the issues on cards, and file them for future role play demonstrations. Plan the demo ahead of time with selected students. Tell them or decide together on the issue you will resolve. The teacher orchestrates the process by directing students through the scene and through the stop-and-think part (see page 271 for Steps of a Role Play). The teacher facilitates the discussion about possible ways to handle the situation constructively, chooses with the role play partners the option they will act out, "rewinds" to the beginning of the scene again, and takes it to a conclusion, using one of the group's suggestions. The teacher plays the key role in the play, the person who has a dilemma to resolve, unless he/she is confident that a student can handle it well.

Demo: The demonstration can be done in the circle, with the actors given extra space around them (they still remain in the circumference and do not go into the center of the circle, so they don't have their backs to anyone).

If there is time, students might act out, without the teacher, another one of the ideas suggested during the brainstorming. The teacher continues to be the director.

Reflection (2 - 3 minutes in circle, partners, or small groups; if time, a few share with whole group)

Students choose and answer a process or content question such as:
What were the steps we took in this role play process? Use the chart to help you remember.
How might this process help you resolve this issue in real life?
What helps you calm down so you can stop and think before you act?
Show with a thumb up (yes), sideways (maybe), or down (no) whether you think you might take this action if you find yourself in this situation.
Have students share out which other actions brainstormed they might rather choose.

Plan for Success

There is an urge in doing role plays to show people doing the wrong things—being rude, making mistakes, breaking rules. It can be entertaining , but that's the problem with it. What entertains us we remember, but what we want students to remember from these role plays is not the wrong things but the good solutions and choices they brainstorm together. Cut the action before it moves to the wrongdoing, and brainstorm solutions that would avoid mistakes yet also provide some emotional satisfaction to the people involved.

SOCIAL ACTION THEATER: ROLE PLAYS ON SOCIAL ISSUES

Theater makes things come alive, so when you dramatize distant and/or abstract events and issues, you get everyone's attention. That's what it takes to prompt both memory and thinking skills.

Daily News

Thursday, November 7, 20__

Good Morning, Sociologists!

Today we're going to look a social issue that is important to young people: underage drinking. We'll set up a role play which takes place in Minnesota, where it's against the law for adults to supply alcohol to teens. Two adults, a mother and her brother, are discussing a party that her son Johnny wants to have at their house. The mother says there can be no alcohol. Her brother is trying to get her to ease up about it.

Yours in solidarity,

Ms. Eisenbeis

Greeting (1 - 2 minutes in circle)

Basic Greeting with or without a handshake, hand jive, or peace sign

Activity (15 - 20 minutes)

Do a role play on a social issue relevant to students.

Ahead of time, compile a list by polling students about social issues and adding ones you think are important as well. Write the issues on cards and file them as a resource for future Social Action Theater demos such as:

- Eighteen-year-olds deciding whether to vote
- Getting into a car when you know the driver has had a drink
- Throw away or recycle?
- Buying by brand or value
- Saving money for the future
- Hanging out vs. loitering
- How loud is too loud?
- Fashion: who selects your clothes?
- Peaceful protest

Planning: Plan the demo ahead of time with selected students. Pick an issue to explore from among those compiled with students. The teacher orchestrates the process by directing students through a scene in which the issue is confronted or discussed, and then through the stop-and-think part (see page 271 for Steps of a Role Play). The teacher facilitates the discussion about possible ways to handle the situation constructively, chooses with the role play partners which acceptable option they will act out, "rewinds" to the beginning of the scene, and takes it to a conclusion, using one of the group's suggestions. The teacher plays the key role in the play, the person who has a dilemma to resolve, unless he/she is confident that a student can handle this role well.

Demo: The demonstration can be done in the circle, with the actors given extra space around them (they still remain in the circumference and do not go into the center of the circle, so they don't have their backs to some people).

If there is time, students (without the teacher) might act out another one of the ideas suggested earlier. The teacher continues to be the director.

Reflection (2 - 3 minutes in circle, partners, or small groups; if time, a few share with whole group)

Students choose and answer a process or content question such as:

Do you think the resolution of this social issue was a good one?

Responses can be oral, written, or a show with a thumb up (yes), sideways (maybe), or down (no). Students share out which other brainstormed actions they think would be better and why.

Partner Share on remaining thoughts about the issue:

What are your thoughts about this issue now that we've had this discussion? One or two share out.

Plan for Success

You can gather ideas for Social Action Theater from issues that are discussed during CPR's that focus on current events. Record events that are interesting to students and create Social Action Theater around the central issues of the events. For example, if an athlete is found to be using performance-enhancing drugs, the Social Action Theater can focus on the moment of choice when a friend tells him he is foolish to avoid the drugs, because many other athletes are getting away with it. Remember, focus on the moment of decision, not on the negatives.

PROBLEM-SOLVING MEETING

When the whole group (or many people) is involved in an issue, a Problem-solving Meeting is often the best structure to help everyone feel heard, to clarify what's at stake, to brainstorm some good solutions, and together make things better.

Daily News

Thursday, March 27, 20__

Good Morning, Problem-solvers!

Things have not been going well in PE for many of you. Mr. Constantine tells me that you spend more time standing around talking than exercising and playing, and that he keeps having to remind you of your tasks. Some of you tell me there's a lot of gossip going on. This meeting is to find out what we can do to get PE back on track. Get ready to share one idea about why students gossip and what we can do about it.

Peace,

Ms. Oliphant

Greeting (1 - 2 minutes in circle)

Basic Greeting with or without a handshake

Activity (15 - 20 minutes in circle)

Leader (the teacher or, if you have modeled and practiced the format sufficiently, a student) states the problem and the rules of Problem-solving Meetings, and asks for thumbs up regarding willingness to abide by the rules:

- Speak briefly and respectfully, without naming or blaming anyone.

- Listen carefully.

- Work to solve the problem.

- Abide by the solution, even if you don't participate in the meeting.

Leader gives each student a chance to comment on the causes and effects of the issue from his/her personal experience (e.g., "My feelings have been hurt by gossip" "I think people gossip because it makes them feel important."). Brainstorm solutions and select by consensus one solution to try. Establish a way to keep track of results and set a date to check in. See page 274 for Steps of a Problem-solving Meeting.

Reflection (2 - 3 minutes in circle)

Rate the quality of the meeting on a scale of 1-5 (thumbs process, page 26).

Plan for Success

If someone opts out of following the rules, he must sit out of the meeting, but he is still expected to abide by the group's decision. He is, in effect, giving up his own power, but he is not getting out of the obligation to follow whatever procedure the class decides upon.

COUNCIL

Sometimes adolescents simply need to express themselves and know they are heard. Council provides that chance, in a confidential setting, to speak from the heart and listen to others from the heart about issues that are important.

Daily News

Monday, December 9, 20__

Good Morning, Friends!

Today is an early release day. Dismissal will be at 1:00, so there will be no 5th and 6th hour classes. We'll use advisory, as we planned last week, for a Council meeting. Gather your thoughts about ambition: What is it? Whom do you know who is ambitious? How ambitious are you? Is ambition important?

Enjoy your day,

Mr. Slyzdyck

Greeting (1 - 2 minutes in circle)

Basic Greeting with or without a handshake, hand jive, or peace sign

Activity (15 - 20 minutes in circle)

A "talking stick" is held by the speaker (when someone else is to speak, the stick is handed to that person). The leader (teacher, or if modeled and practiced enough, a student) states the guidelines for Council:

- Speak only when you are holding the talking stick
- Speak from the heart and listen from the heart
- Don't speak across the fire (don't comment about or question what others have said)
- Double confidentiality: no one talks about what is said during Council to people not present or even to people who participated in the Council meeting

The leader begins the Council meeting by stating the topic or question and passing the talking stick to the person on his or her right for comment.

Our topic today is ambition—the urge to get ahead, to get things done, to accomplish, and to get the recognition that comes with accomplishment. Think about yourself. Are you an ambitious person, and if so, what are your ambitions in school or in life? Think about other people you know who are ambitious. What are their ambitions, and what chances do you think they have to achieve their ambitions? When the talking stick comes to you, you are invited to talk about what you see and think about ambition.

Each person has the opportunity to speak to the topic. If someone passes, the leader offers him/her another chance after the talking stick has made its way around the circle.

Martin, you passed. Do you have any thoughts now about ambition that you wish to share with us?

After everyone who wants to has spoken, the leader thanks the Council, reminds everyone of the confidentiality rule, and declares today's Council concluded.

Reflection (2 - 3 minutes in circle)

Oral or written. Choose one of the following questions:
Did Council help you to think in a new way? Explain.
Did we follow the rules and spirit of Council during this meeting?
Did you feel safe to speak from the heart in this Council meeting?

Plan for Success

Keep the topics for Council broad and safe at first such as:

- Heroes
- Siblings
- Helping your family
- People we admire
- Is it ever right to fight
- Caring for a pet
- Part-time jobs

Wait until you feel the group has become a caring community with everyone included before attempting to elicit thoughts on more difficult or emotional issues such as:

- Lying
- Stealing
- Reporting dangerous behavior to adults
- Dating
- A classmate's serious illness
- A student leaving school for the rest of the year

If and when you broach these sensitive subjects, keep the double confidentiality rule clear and strong for everyone by emphasizing it before and after the meeting. Council lends itself to intimacy, but let it come in its time.

SCHOOL SERVICE JOBS

Adolescent needs are well fed by service to their community. They learn skills and feel more competent; they often get to have some independence on the job; and they get to be with each other and have some fun. Taking the time to organize a way that your students can serve others will help them grow in cooperation, assertion, responsibility, empathy, and self-control—definitely worth it!

Daily News

Friday, January 15, 20__

Greetings, Service Providers!

This is our school service day, and we all have an assignment to accomplish. Sign up on the Choice Board for the project you want to work on. Then find a seat in the circle; after a quick greeting, we'll get started. Remember that everyone needs to be back here by no later than 8:30 so we can talk about what we've accomplished.

Thanks in advance for your willingness to serve your school.

Ms. Zander

Greeting (1 - 2 minutes in circle)

Basic Greeting, All Group Greeting, or any quick greeting

Activity (15 - 20 minutes)

Students work alone or in pairs on service jobs in the classroom and/or in the school. You can use one advisory activity time to generate the job list (brainstorm, or have students make suggestions in the interactive part of daily news).

Students can sign up for jobs on the daily news (use a separate sheet of paper so you have it for next time). Jobs can include classroom organization, recycling collection, memo delivery, etc. See page 281 for more school service job suggestions.

Reflection (2 - 3 minutes in circle, partners, or small groups; if time, a few share with whole group)

Students choose and answer a process or content question such as:

What was fun about your job today?

What is something you can improve for next time?

Do you think the job you did contributes to the school? What's your evidence?

What is one way that your group got along well to get the job done?

What is a problem your group had to solve?

Plan for Success

Not all service jobs will work in the short time period of advisory. It will take teamwork for your staff to divide up the available jobs among the different homerooms if you want all groups to engage in some kind of school service. Even if you have to go on a rotation system in which different advisories have jobs at different times, you will be demonstrating that we all share the work of supporting a clean, safe, attractive school environment.

CAREERS

Often by 5th or 6th grade, a student has reached conclusions about himself and his abilities, and may have already lowered expectations about what he might become in life. A focus on careers opens the doors and windows a bit, and may make a career seem possible that he had never before considered.

Daily News

Friday, April 12, 20__

Dear Advisory Students,

Mrs. Silva has agreed to talk with us today about her work as a lawyer. On a card below, write at least one question we could ask her to help us understand better the career choice of being a lawyer. Put your question in the basket before taking your seat in the circle. Rhonda will lead the greeting and will facilitate our conversation with Mrs. Silva.

Show your best stuff!

Ms. Montgomery

Greeting (1 - 2 minutes in circle)

Basic Greeting with a handshake. Student leader or teacher introduces guest and selects and leads the greeting.

Activity (15 - 20 minutes in circle)

Guest gives a 3 to 5 minute introductory talk about his/her career, followed by questions. Two possible question formats:

- Leader asks several questions chosen from the cards
- Leader invites students to ask their questions, written ahead of time or not

When there are about 5 minutes remaining in the advisory period, the leader makes a closing comment, thanking the guest for coming, and mentioning one or two things learned from his/her visit.

Reflection (2 - 3 minutes in circle)

Students answer a process or content question such as:

What is one thing you learned about the career we heard about today?

On a scale of 1-5, (5 being the most interested), how interested are you in a career in_____?

Plan for Success

Establishing protocols for guest speakers is worth the time. You may choose to spend an advisory preparing and practicing what will happen whenever you have a guest, such as:

- Wear nametags
- Greet the visitor as on arrival
- Prepare questions in advance
- Choose a person to lead the event
- Thank the guest
- Reflect on the experience

OPTION, OPTIONS, OPTIONS

The choice is yours. Use A+ types of activities as often as you wish to add variety to your advisory. You can also take a thematic approach, focused around a theme you want your students to explore. Chapter 5 offers 170 advisories, using both the CPR and A+ formats, organized by 28 thematic possibilities.

You might choose to mix and match, sometimes using a theme, at other times selecting from the A+ samples described above, or putting your own A+'s together using the extended activities and quick greetings found in Appendix A. Students can also use this approach when they start planning and leading A+'s and CPR's. See Chapter 4: Planning Advisories for a look at the range of ways to organize community-building in advisory or homeroom using the CPR and A+ formats.

CLASS HOURS FRAMED BY OPENINGS AND CLOSINGS

The Activity Plus format can be used successfully for any class hour. The need is the same and so is the effect: a routine that brings security, community, clarity, and closure to every class.

- **Daily news** welcomes students and tells them what's up for today.

- **Greeting** brings the community together and includes everyone

- **Activity** (extended) instuction and work time building academic and/or social skills

- **Reflection** creates closure through thinking about the quality of the activity

This framework also satisfies the need to make good use of the times when students are at their most attentive: at the beginning of the hour and at the end. David Sousa's Primacy-Recency theory shows that when we get everyone focused together for the assignment explanation and/or minilesson at the beginning of the class, we are capitalize on Prime 1 time, the period at the beginning of the hour where student attention is at its peak. Then we make use of Prime 2 time at the end of the hour by using it for reflection and planning for next time—high-level thinking that will improve performance (Sousa 2001).

The work time between the opening and the closing is energized when you allow students to actively practice their learning or produce a product rather than just fill out a worksheet or listen to the teacher talk about the subject. Adolescents lose focus and energy unless they can move, talk with others, explore on their own, manipulate materials, and sometimes choose what and how to practice and how to demonstrate what they have learned. Opportunities to use a variety of skills in a variety of ways give students the autonomy they crave and the differentiation they need for each to succeed (Rogoff 1990; Dewey 1938 & 1969).

Sample Class Hour Using A+ Framework

Here's what a class hour might look like using news and greeting as an opening and reflection as a close to frame the content.

Daily News

Upon entering the classroom, students see a chart or board with a message that greets them in a friendly manner and tells them what will be happening during the class period and what is the first thing they need to do to get started. (2 - 3 minutes)

Greeting

Students spend a minute or two face-to-face in a seated or standing circle acknowledging each other's presence with a quick greeting. (1 - 2 minutes)

Direct Instruction

Then, preferably with students in the circle so everyone can see and hear everyone and all behaviors are clearly under teacher scrutiny, the teacher uses this prime learning time to review relevant material and/or to present new material, to give specific instructions, to take questions, to invite students to talk with a partner about the topic and connect it to what they already know, and to make sure all are clear about what they are about to do during the next portion of the class. (5 - 20 minutes)

Work Period

Students work independent of the teacher's direct instruction, alone, in partners, or in small groups, depending on the teacher's plan. They practice skills, investigate and explore concepts, gather information, prepare a representation of their understanding in some form, and get help from the teacher when necessary to keep working productively. Most learning is practiced on a worksheet can be learned better if students show what they know visually, in a dramatic presentation, through a poem or song or letter, or in a 3-D project like a relief map or diorama. The projects can be quick ones that take no more than 20 minutes to complete or more elaborate ones that extend over several class periods. The teacher may be circulating, disciplining, meeting with a small group for some additional instruction, or working one-to-one with a student. (15 - 25 minutes)

Reflection

Several minutes before the end of the class period, the teacher asks for cleanup, then poses a reflective exercise, either questions to the whole group for written or oral response, or questions for partners or small groups to discuss about the learning during this class period. The teacher may use this time to check for understanding and remembering with content questions, or may ask about the process of working together and the quality of students' experience during this learning time. See Appendix E for a list of stimulating reflection questions. (5 - 10 minutes)

The reflection provides closure for everyone. It helps students think about the most important aspects of their previous hour of learning; it helps them grow in their ability to assess their own learning process and their skills in working together; it provides a satisfying and informative conclusion to each class period for the teacher; and it replaces rushing out to the next class with the feeling of an orderly, purposeful flow. Teaching energy is fed by this simple means of closing down the work with one group before beginning work with the next.

Whether it's the activity during advisory or the activities of a class hour, a familiar framework strengthens teaching and learning. Students and teachers begin to experience a feeling of community all day long.

An advisory class enjoys a student-led read aloud

CHAPTER FOUR

Planning Advisories

Historically, the bugaboo of advisories is the planning of them. Teams of teachers have spent long hours constructing curriculums for advisories, often around themes, trying to lift the burden of planning from their colleagues by making a basic curriculum that can be used each year. The approach we are suggesting substitutes a *repeatable format* for a specific curriculum, and a wide variety of content can be inserted into that format in order to ensure relevance, timeliness, and variety.

Payoffs in Planning a Format-based Approach

- The formats, once learned and practiced, become easy to both plan and implement

- The repetition of the format provides certainty and ease of routine

- Variety is assured by the availability of two different formats: the Circle of Power and Respect (CPR) and Activity Plus (A+).

- Freshness is assured by the variety of content that can be addressed within the same format

- Learning skills such as focus, memory, following instructions, teamwork, analysis, inquiry, logic, observation, and dialogue are built into the format and practiced daily, whatever the content, and without lengthy planning.

- Specific academic skill-practice can be inserted easily—reading, language arts, science, social studies, content recall, math, summarizing, problem-solving—using the same format with slight variations.

- Students can and should take over the leadership of parts of the format, and ultimately all of it, including some of the planning of content (always with teacher guidance)

COLLABORATIVE PLANNING CAN EASE THE BURDEN

Let's assume that each teacher on a team has introduced CPR to his or her students and they've used the format for a few weeks, so everyone is familiar with it. Next, the team tries some extended activities using the A+ format in a few advisories. How shall we continue to use these two formats? How shall we plan interesting, relevant, important advisory content for our students for the rest of the year?

Some teams have lightened the responsibility for planning the content of the advisories by sharing it or creating a regular pattern for it. This can be done in several different ways.

Team Approach

You can take a team approach to planning and assign different days, weeks, or months to different teachers. This way, one teacher or teacher partners plan the content of an advisory that everyone will implement for the designated time period. For example:

Mondays: Ms. Barker and Ms. Meow

Tuesdays: Mr. Wright and Ms. Lefft

Wednesdays: Ms. Smith and Mr. Jones

Thursdays: Mr. Robin and Mr. Cardinal

Fridays: Ms. Everest and Ms. Fujiyama

The day before the advisory, the planners responsible for that day distribute the plan, either for Circle of Power and Respect meeting or an Activity Plus, to everyone on the team. You could have planners take a week at a time, or even a month.

Some teachers plan their own advisories so they can match the mood, interests, and needs of their particular advisory students with the CPR or A+ advisory that suits them best. A good reason for team planning is that students will move into their day after advisory having all had roughly the same start-up experience during the advisory period. As students talk with each other about a fun game they all played or about what people said in their room during the discussion, the shared experience can boost feelings of connectedness throughout the school community.

Establishing a Rhythm

So you don't have to start at Square 1 each week deciding what needs to happen on each of the five days of advisory, set up a routine to follow that shapes what you do, but allows for variation. One possibility is that each day of the week would be designated for certain kinds of content.

Sample Advisory Schedule with Academic Focus

You'll notice in the samples below that even when there are lots of academics in advisory, there is still a personal connection. The Monday meeting is completely personal and social. We never want social-emotional elements absent from advisory, whatever the focus. See Appendix A to find the greetings, shares, and activities listed below.

<u>Monday: CPR, personal focus—what's going on in our individual lives</u>

Greeting: Is This Seat Taken? or any other playful activity to enliven spirits on the transition day into the school week

Sharing: Whip Shares or Individual Shares on weekend activities

Activity: Hmong Courtship Game OR Rare Birds OR any getting-to-know-you game

> Welcome Back!
>
> What was a highlight of the weekend for you?
>
> Or any question about the weekend, the weather, homework, future plans, etc. Discuss the personal responses to the question

Tuesday: A+, Silent Reading

Greeting: Share Greeting about books *(Good morning, _____. What book are you reading?)*

Activity: Silent Reading: designating every Tuesday as a day for 15 - 30 minutes of reading would strengthen reading habits and skills

Reflection: quick share: *What is one thing that interested you in your reading today?*

> Welcome All Readers,
>
> Today is a READING day! Choose a book from the table if you haven't brought one of your own to read.

Wednesday: CPR, academic focus—geography

Greeting: Formal Greeting *(Good morning, Mr. Landry; Good morning, Ms. Costello)*

Sharing: Whip Share or Individual Share: *Where have you lived or what places have you visited?* Places are located on a map of the United States and marked with pins or flags. May take more than one day to complete; at the end, group will be able to see where they collectively have been

Activity: Where Are You From? (chair-changing game) Students point to their markers on the map.

> Greetings, Geography Sleuths!
>
> Look up in an atlas the location of one of the following cities. Write your name next to the one you chose. (one location per person or per pair of students)

One week the academic focus might be geography (as above); the next week you might switch to math. Subject area teachers could designate a day to focus on their subjects, or all teachers could do language arts as their academic focus, so that you are teaching reading and writing across the curriculum. The choice is yours.

Thursday: A +, Cross-advisory Games in gym

Greeting: High Five or any Hand Jive Greeting

Activity: 7th grade advisories meet in the gym for a cooperative game of All Hit Moonball

Reflection: whole group questions: *What went well in this game? How could we make it more fun? More fair? More safe?*

> Hello, Friends!
>
> We'll go to the gym first thing for an all-7th Advisory Day! We'll circle up for a greeting and get instructions for All Hit Moonball. Think about last time we played, and how we can make the game even more fun this time.

Friday: CPR, current events

Greeting: Basic Greeting *(Good morning, ____.)* OR What's Happening? Greeting

Sharing: Whip Shares on a news item, moderated by a student; use a headlines approach, with each person announcing a headline for the story he/she read, followed by a one-sentence description

> Good Morning, Reporters!
>
> Choose an article to share from the newspapers articles available, and get ready to report on the gist of the story.

Activity: Around the World ("It" repeats as many headlines as he can before the ball returns to him) Discuss which news stories shared have the greatest relevance to students.

Sample Advisory Schedule with a Personal Focus

Advisories with a personal focus bring out experiences outside of school. They give students a chance to share what is most important to them, and they build understanding of each other.

Monday: CPR with personal focus

Tuesday: A+ using role play or scenarios on how to handle challenging social situations

Wednesday: CPR on current events (or other academic focus) and how these events connect to student lives

Thursday: CPR with personal focus

Friday: CPR with personal focus

Either of these schedules and any other regular schedule can be made more interesting by using a variety of greetings, games, sharing topics, and specific content.

Sharing builds connections to peers and to school work

PLANNING THE FORMAT AND LEVEL

Choosing between CPR and A+ Formats

The formats for advisory can remain basically the same, day after day. You can use a CPR meeting format every day, and the varied content will keep it interesting. Some teachers choose to use both the CPR format and the A+ (extended activity) format, alternating between them, with the CPR days more frequent than the A+ days. The A+ format lacks some of the most effective parts of CPR for building community (sharing, processing the news), so make sure you have at least three CPR's a week.

Either format, however, offers great variety. At the beginning of each year, start with the CPR format and use it heavily for several weeks so you and your students become familiar and comfortable with it. It takes a few weeks to build enough ease with the format to enjoy it and begin to move towards more challenging and varied greetings, shares, and activities. After CPR is firmly established, then you might add some A+ advisories so you can offer some extended activities that wouldn't fit into the 5 minutes or so allotted to activities in CPR. Eventually both formats will become so familiar that students can take the lead with them and thereby grow, especially in competence and their capacity for responsible autonomy.

Choosing the Challenge Level

The levels help you choose from all the greetings, shares, and activities the ones that will be best for your group. Think about the degree of safety or risk, familiarity or newness, that the various options present, and your group's level of self-control. Then select elements that will fit your students as well as stretch them a little.

All the greetings, shares, and activities are organized in the Resource section within three levels, according to the degree of self-control, risk, autonomy, and complexity they require. Because students need to be gradually introduced to activities that require high levels of self-control and a strong sense of safety within the group, you need to have an idea for each greeting, topic, or game of how much self-control and risk-taking are required in it.

> **Level 1:** elements are excellent to use early in the semester because they are the least risky and the least physically active.

> **Level 2:** items require a higher level of social skills and ask students to take some chances with each other. They sometimes require choices, which need to be made responsibly.

> **Level 3:** greetings, personal shares, and activities rely on a high level of self-control and other social skills, and a high comfort and trust level within the community.

Progress through the levels is not always continuous. Even after you have built your group to the point where you can regularly enjoy Level 3 activities, for example, there is no reason to avoid Levels 1 and 2 activities. Some of those may have become favorites. And when spring fever hits, or students are antsy just before a vacation, bring out the reliable Level 1 games. Everyone will enjoy them, and you won't be correcting so many misbehaviors. Nobody is at Level 3 in life all the time!

PLANNING WITH GENERAL CONTENT

You can plan the content of advisory according to the time of year, the perceived level of cohesiveness in the class, and the social and academic needs of the students at any particular time. At the same time, select greetings, share formats and topics, and activities with varied content: one day academic skills, another day laughter and fun for the twenty minutes you are together, and on some occasions, serious discussion of an issue.

Planning with general content means you think first about the level of challenge that suits your students at this time, then you select the news content, greeting, shares, and activity that suits that day, without reference necessarily to what you did yesterday or what you might do tomorrow.

You might also do it the other way around: think first about the content you want to include, and then aim that content at the level your students can handle. For example, if you want to have an academic focus in your CPR, decide which subject(s) you want to address, then look for the math, language arts, social studies, or science type activities or sharing topics at the social challenge level appropriate to your community.

Basically, either way what you are doing is picking and choosing from among the abundant possibilities for greetings, shares, and activities, the ones that seem best suited to your students at any particular time. There are enough examples in the Appendices to give you options for advisories all year for both CPR and A+ formats. The consistent use of those two formats provides your students with clear, familiar models that they will internalize. When they begin to lead advisory, the pick-and-choose approach works especially well to allow them to design CPR meetings or A+ advisories from scratch with a huge menu of possibilities.

Sample General Content Advisory Plans

See Appendix A to find the greetings, sharing ideas, and activities listed below.

Monday: CPR, Catching up with each other

Greeting: Double High Five or any Hand Jive Greeting
Sharing: Whip Share on weekend news; everyone gives a one-sentence report
Activity: When the Cold Wind Blows (chair changing game)

> Welcome, Everyone,
>
> How are you doing? Check the icon that best describes your mood today:
>
> Great   OK   Bummer

Tuesday: A+, Preparing for high school transition

Greeting: Basic Greeting (*Good morning, _____*)
Activity: Guest to talk about transition to high school; followed by student questions
Reflection: Acknowledgment of what was learned and thanking the guest

> Hi, Ready Learners,
>
> Today Carol DeSoto is coming from _____ High School to talk about transitioning into her school. She's the guidance counselor, a good person for you to get to know. Be sure to welcome her, and be ready with your questions.

Wednesday: CPR, Academics—math

Greeting: Skip Greeting (greet at intervals)
Sharing: Whip Share on confidence in math: *How confident do you feel about your math skills? Very confident   Pretty good   Not Very   Not confident at all* A student can tally the responses. The results can be translated into a graph of the group's math-confidence levels.
Activity: Eleven (groups tries to reach eleven by chance)

> Greetings, Mathematicians,
> Here's a math challenge for you. Put your initials next to a problem and be ready to solve it for us (we'll help too). You can use word problems, adding fractions, averaging, etc.

Thursday: A+, Preparing for adult life

Greeting: One-Minute Mingle Greeting (greet several people during one minute)
Activity: Silent Reading from career books
Reflection: *Share one fact from your book.*

> Good day, Future Workers,
> Today we'll teach each other a little about careers through books on the subject. Choose one of the books, and after our greeting, we'll all read a little about a career and have one fact to share about it.

Friday: CPR, Building community

Greeting: Introduce partner to group and tell one thing about him or her.
Sharing: Individual Share on community with closing comments
Activity: Rare Birds (students guess each other's identity based on clues)

> Good Morning, Friends,
> What do true communities look, sound, and feel like? Write your idea in the appropriate place on our Y-chart.

Each of these advisories has a general purpose, but the focus shifts from day to day according to what the teacher feels the group needs, or according to what resources are available (for example, the availability of a speaker). You could hold CPR meetings on Monday, Wednesday, and Friday, and A+ on Tuesday and Thursday. You don't have to use this pattern—a week of CPR meetings could still be varied and interesting, and a combination of four meetings and one A+ advisory in a week would also be fine. It's the presence of the familiar format that preserves the flow and modulates behavior.

PLANNING AROUND THEMES

Thematic clusters of advisories provide opportunities to work on one topic over a period of time using the two formats of CPR and A + advisories. Designing advisories around single ideas or topics of investigation allows you to focus in on those topics. Select the themes most beneficial to your students and then use the advisories to build understanding. Traditionally, teams of teachers select themes for the year together. From there, teachers can plan individually, or teams can use one of the collaborative approaches described above on pages XX.

Sequence of CPR and A+ Thematic Advisories

Working with a theme, decide whether to use the CPR or A+ format on a particular day. When you first introduce the CPR meeting, do at least four or five in a row so students will get the feel of the format, before introducing the alternate format of A+ advisory. A+ should not be used to the exclusion of CPR. The A+ format does not serve adolescent needs quite as thoroughly as CPR, so A+ needs to be mixed into weeks that also use CPR.

Criteria for sequence

After an introductory period, feel free to switch the order of CPR and A+ advisories around according to:

> **Variety:** Switching between formats provides variety for the early-morning experience, just as variety of content does.

> **Content:** Some topics call for a more extended activity, such as a role play or a more elaborate game. At such times, switch to the A+ format—it's designed to handle topics and activities that need more time.

> **Flow:** You may decide that to build a particular theme you want to use a certain sequence of meetings and/or extended activities. One sequence or another may serve you better.

> **Schedule:** On some days you may have a longer or shorter advisory, or there may be other priorities that have to be included, and one format or the other might work better under the circumstances.

> **Student request for format:** It helps build student autonomy for them to make choices in things that matter to them. Let them decide, for example, that on Thursday the class will do an A+ advisory in the gym with another group.

> **Teacher preference:** Some days you may simply prefer a quiet CPR in your room instead of a highly active game in the gym—your choice. You may find that the rhythm of doing a CPR every day is fun for your students, and gives you simplicity and consistency that make your teaching day more comfortable. Many middle level advisories thrive using only the CPR format.

Choosing Themes

The first step in creating themed advisories is deciding how many themes you want to explore and what the topics will be. A theme can be a quick, one-week look into a topic, or it can extend through weeks or even months, depending on the variety of ideas and the degree of student interest and need. For example, the theme Getting to Know Ourselves and Each Other builds relationship over the first four weeks of school; the theme Transition to High School could be a one-week look at 8th graders readiness for this transition towards the end of the school year.

Every theme listed in Chapter 5: 170 Thematic Advisories has the potential of meeting the basic adolescent needs of competence, autonomy, relationship, and fun. Every theme helps to build the skills in understanding and social interaction that make for a healthy adolescence.

Once you've chosen your themes, you'll find the CPR and A+ advisories you need for your theme planned and ready in Chapter 5. There are 5 to 16 advisories for each of the 28 themes listed above. Many include multiple possibilities for activities, greetings, and sharing ideas to allow for longer investigation of the theme. Teachers of advisories at different grade levels might select different themes, or the same themes with different variations.

PLANNING A MIXTURE OF THEMES AND GENERAL CONTENT

You may decide to follow a theme for a while with your advisory, and then do a couple of weeks of general content and personal advisories. Either way, you use the CPR format for meetings and the A+ format for extended activities, so the formats are consistent whatever the content. When students begin to lead CPR meetings, selecting from an assortment of greetings, shares, and activities (all at the appropriate level, of course) gives them freedom of choice. Perhaps students will suggest a theme they would like to explore in their CPR meeting.

The sample advisories in the following chapter are organized under themes. It's fine, however, to choose any CPR or A+ advisory that seems right for you. You may decide to follow one of the themes exactly as written for a week or two, and then shop through the lists of greetings, shares, and activities for a combination that appeals to you.

My Name

KELLI is my nickname
and also a rapper's nickname
that rapper's name is R. Kelly
my football team knows me this way
It sounds so handsome
my name rides smoother then a phantom (which is a car)
this name is sweeter than candy

Student exhibits
his work from an
extended activity

CHAPTER FIVE

170 Thematic Advisories

In this chapter there is more than a year's worth of sample advisories which support 28 themes organized into 6 units. Clustering advisory content around a series of themes relevant to middle level students has a strong presence in advisory planning. Circle of Power and Respect and Activity Plus advisory formats can easily be organized and flavored by such themes. In fact, CPR and A+ make a thematic approach even easier, since the structure of advisory remains the same even as the content varies.

There are many ideas about what topics are important for adolescents to address, but most of them involve addressing the major needs of young people—the need for a sense of autonomy and competence in life, the need to learn how to create and maintain relationships, and the need for fun. In addition, we want them to get some practical knowledge for getting along well in the world—eating right, exercising, and otherwise taking care of their health and wellbeing. We want them to know how to get along with a wide variety of people, and how to grow into their role as citizens of the world. Advisories can address all these issues. They can also serve the special function of facilitating students' entry into a new year and departing at the end of the year so that the beginnings and endings are effective transitions.

Notice that certain topics are not addressed in the advisory themes exampled here, such as drug and alcohol abuse, adolescent sexual activity, and gangs. These topics require an in-depth, comprehensive approach with lots of information communicated and safety structures built in that take too long for the typical advisory period. If and when your school addresses these complex and sensitive issues, you can still use the A+ format of beginning with a community-building activity like a greeting and ending with a personal reflection.

HOW TO USE THE THEMATIC SAMPLE ADVISORIES

Levels within Themes

The sample thematic CPR and A+ advisories described in this chapter that are designed to start off the year are designed for Level 1. After that, the advisories include greetings, shares and activities for all three levels. You can always substitute for the ones suggested if you feel that the level of challenge isn't right for your students at the time. You might use greetings, shares, or activities

- at the same level
- at a lower level to assure a sense of safety and high participation
- at a higher level when you want to challenge your group to grow towards a new level.

The first theme, Getting Acquainted, is presented at Level 1 because it is suggested for the beginning of the year. The Closing the Year theme is presented at Level 3, since it is used to wrap up the year, when the community is normally at its strongest and safest. If you're near the end of the year and your advisory students have slipped back, or a group never did quite come up to a level of community appropriate for Level 3 activities, use the level appropriate for them. The levels are guides, not formulas.

Organization of Themes

The thematic advisories are organized into six units. The themes are presented in an order that would work well over a year. However, many of the themes could be used in a different order. There are a few cases where it makes sense to do one theme before another, and those are noted. Otherwise, use the individual themes in whatever sequence seems right for your situation.

In some cases, specific CPR or A+ advisories require preliminary work with students—sessions to establish protocols or to prepare for susequent advisories. Watch for notes to that effect. All of these themes, to be explored enough to have an impact on students, need at least a few advisory days each.

Organization of CPR and A+ Samples within a Theme

For each theme you will find at least five advisory examples, usually at least three CPR's and two A+ advisory days. They are arranged with CPR's first followed by A+ advisories, but the order in which you use them is up to you. See Chapter 4: Planning Advisories for criteria for deciding the sequence of CPR's and A+'s.

Choosing Greetings, Share Formats/Topics, and Activities

In many cases more than one activity is suggested (and sometimes more than one Greeting or Share). This allows you choice and enough variety so that when you want to repeat an advisory, it still feels fresh. Don't be afraid to repeat! The familiarity of the greetings, games, and sharing structures, as well as the routine of the two basic advisory formats helps to increase student comfort and participation. Some elements may become favorites, and teachers may have to push students to try something new.

See the Appendices for complete descriptions of the greetings, shares, and activities listed in the themes.

Daily News: Expanding the Sample Messages

The daily news examples given with each CPR and A+ advisory are minimal. They present a direction necessary for the meeting, an interactive question or task relevant to the meeting, and potential vocabulary words are higlighted. To them you can add

- information about changes or highlights for the day
- comments about the previous day
- jokes, cartoons, quotations
- acknowledgments
- reminders appropriate for the day, your plans, and the time and space available.

4 CPR

Greeting: Basic Greeting
Sharing: Whip Share: *One thing I like to do with my family is....* Follow with a review from memory of what people shared. *Who remembers something someone shared that he or she likes to do with family?*
Activity: Toss a Name Game

> Buenos Dias, Advisory!
> Seating is something you have to **calculate** today. Put a check in the box next to the number of siblings you have, then sit by somebody with the same number of siblings.

5 CPR

Greeting: Name Card Greeting
Sharing: Whip Share: *One thing that went well for me the first week of school was....*
Follow with a review from memory of what people shared: *Who remembers something that went well for someone?*
Activity: Group Juggle

> Ciao, Students!
> Today we'll **evaluate** how things have gone so far. Write on the line with your number one thing that went well the first week of school.

6 CPR

Greeting: Language Greeting, using a language spoken by a student in your group
Sharing: Whip Share: *A fun thing I did this past weekend* [or yesterday] *was....*
The teacher should be the final sharer. After you share your experience, have students brainstorm and list questions they might ask to learn more. Students ask you questions chosen from the list.
Activity: Me Too OR Toss a Name Game OR Group Juggle

> Aloha, Friends!
> Today we're going to greet each other in a language other than English. Write on your number line a way to say hello in another language. Let's see how many different greetings we can **devise**.

7 CPR

Greeting: Whole Group Language Greeting OR Language Greeting
Sharing: Interview Share: *Three things about me are....* Interviews Shares can continue for several days if you wish to give each student a chance.
Activity: Heads or Tails OR Toss a Name Game OR Group Juggle

> Howdy, Learners!
> Write on your line below a question you would ask [fill in the name of a famous person] if he/she were here today. Try to make your question a **stimulating** one.

8 CPR

Greeting: Handshake Greeting (page 216, Basic Greeting variation)

Sharing: Snowball Share: *What is a quality you have or would like to develop?*

Activity: Rare Birds, using cards written by students and read at random. You can do several and save the others for another time.

> Good Morning, Friends!
>
> Today we'll spend a little **introspective** time thinking and talking about ourselves. Write on a card a little-known fact about yourself. Think about your preferences and write below on your number line where you would want to go for your dream vacation.

9 CPR

Greeting: Ball Toss Greeting

Sharing: Interview Share, using volunteers

Activity: Group Juggle

> Hola, Advisees!
>
> Let's evaluate how we've been doing in our advisory. Write down one thing you think we are doing well.
>
> OR: Check the **categories** below which you think we are handling well in our advisory:
>
> Getting to Know Each Other
> Treating Each Other Kindly
> Using Self-control

10 A+: Planning Meeting

Greeting: Question Greeting: *When is your birthday?*

Activity: Planning Meeting (page 273) *How should we celebrate our birthdays in advisory?*

Reflection: Whole group: *Why is it important to celebrate birthdays?*

> Happy Birthday!
>
> Even though today may not be your birthday, we're going to **anticipate** and plan for the day that really is your birthday. Think of some good ways we could celebrate people's birthdays here in our advisory, and be ready to share.

11   A+: Academic Assessment

Greeting: Handshake Greeting (page 216, Basic Greeting variation)

Activity: Journaling: list subjects on chart and ask students to assess their academic strengths and weaknesses.

- What subject do you find easiest?
- What is your hardest subject?
- What subject do you enjoy most?   Why?

Reflection: Students tally on chart using symbols for easiest (+), hardest (-), most enjoyable (☺)

> Good Morning, Advisory Students!
>
> Today is a day to think introspectively about yourself as a student. We'll be journaling on our academic strengths and weaknesses so that we can build **incrementally** on what's working and improve what is not.

12   A+: Personality Inventory

Greeting: High Five or any Hand Jive Greeting

Activity: Personality Inventory (page 268) fill out chart

Reflection: Whip Share: *Which type of personality do you perceive yourself to be?* Tally answers so you can see the whole advisory's personality make-up.

> Greetings to All!
>
> Have you ever thought about animals and their different personalities? Today we'll be thinking about our own personalities and linking them to various animals—a little strange, but you might learn something about yourself!

13   A+: Social Inventory

Greeting: Name Card Greeting

Activity: Journaling: self-assessment of CARES (Co-operation, Assertion, Responsibility, Empathy, Self-control) skills strengths and weaknesses (CARES, pages 19 and 163)

- What social skill do you find easiest?
- What social skill is most challenging for you?
- What is one thing you could do to help yourself develop in your most challenging area? (Write on Post-it)

Reflection: Volunteers share out their easiest and most challenging; tally the results. Everyone puts a Post-it on chart about an idea for developing a social skill.

> Guten Tag, Students!
>
> Find something else in common with someone who has a personality type the same as yours (Lion, Bear, Deer, Eagle). Sit in the circle next to your "something in common" partner.

14 A+: Goals and Declarations

Greeting: Handshake Greeting (page 216, Basic Greeting variation)

Activity: Spark thinking about what students want most from this school year. Choose one:

- Read a short book or story (see list of books that spark goal-setting, page 276)
- Tell a story of your own hopes and goals
- Invite a guest speaker—high school former student, elder, parent, etc. who is willing to share about her or his dreams in life
- Lead a guided visualization so that students can visualize themselves being successful at something they want to do

Think, Ink, Pair, Share: students write about something they want to accomplish or a hope for the year. Write that hope in the form of a goal, and make a declaration about accomplishing it: *This year I will ....*

Reflection: Partner Share: *Read your declaration to your partner.* If there is time, 1 or 2 volunteers may wish to share their declarations with the whole group. Collect the declarations.

Note: This activity may extend into two advisories.

> Good Morning, Friends!
> Here's a piece of poetry to think about:
> Hope is the thing
> with feathers
> that **perches**
> in the soul
> and sings the tune
> without words
> and never stops
> —at all.
>   Emily Dickenson
> Start thinking about what this school year could be if it were your best year ever.

15 A+: Creating Guidelines for Advisory

Greeting: Peace Greeting

Activity: Making Advisory Guidelines: use one of the methods described on page 24 to brainstorm rules with students and then combine and sort their ideas into a few broad rules that cover all situations and that everyone agrees to by consensus

Reflection: Whole group: student reads the final rules to the group and then volunteers try to name the rules without looking at them

Note: This process will probably take more than one advisory period. You can brainstorm and narrow down the rules in the first session, and in the second session, finalize them with a consensus decision, followed by a formal signing of the Advisory Guidelines. If your grade level team wants shared rules (a good idea), then representatives from your advisory meet with representatives from the other advisories to decide on a final list. Those rules are then presented in a clean, large format to each advisory to sign off on, and the whole team then supports the shared Advisory Guidelines.

> Dear Members of Advisory,
> Today we'll create our own **guidelines** agreement. We will think together about the agreement we can make to ensure that our community is a place where everyone feels safe and cared about. In any group of people, there are moments when people get upset with each other. Successful communities set up guidelines that describe the way the community wants people to act so that everyone can have the good year they hope for and meet their goals. Those guidelines act as a safe "fence" around the group at difficult times. Be thinking about the agreements our group needs to make.

16   A+: Acknowledgments

Greeting: One-Minute Mingle Greeting

Activity: Touch Someone Who

Note: Allow enough time for all to have a chance to be both the tapper and a receiver. Be sure to model an appropriate shoulder tap before beginning.

Reflection: Whole group:

What worked about that activity?

On a scale of 1-5 where 5 is completely comfortable, show with your fingers how you felt when you were a tapper.

Now do the same for when you were sitting in your chair while others tapped.

> Greetings, Awesome Ones!
>
> It's always nice to be appreciated. In fact, human beings thrive on sincere, specific compliments. So today we're going to practice giving **recognition** to one another in simple, direct, sincere ways. We're going to do an activity called "Touch Someone Who." Circle up, please.

THEME: GETTING TO KNOW FAMILY AND ADULT FRIENDS

Links between home and school are valuable. They help you fill out your understanding of your students. They give adolescents a look into each other's family customs, and help bridge differences. And perhaps best of all, they provide a reason for a family member to visit school and share in the fun of advisory.

---

1   CPR

Greeting: Formal Greeting (page 216, Basic Greeting variation)

Sharing: Individual Share: *Describe a cousin (or other family member) you know well.* Ask for questions and comments, including a closing comment for each share, from the group.

Activity: Configurations

> Top of the Mornin', Students!
>
> We'll be talking together this week about our families and adult friends. Below on your numbered line, write the number of people in your family whom you see regularly.

---

2   CPR

Greeting: Formal Greeting (page 216, Basic Greeting variation)

Sharing: Individual Share: *Describe a custom you share at home.* You can brainstorm before the sharing begins: *What are some questions we might ask after someone has shared about a family custom?*

Activity: Hands Up OR Concentration, with topic: Favorite food you eat at home

> Happy Tuesday, Everyone!
>
> Today we'll be sharing about family **customs** and food. Write on your number line a favorite food you eat at home.

---

3   CPR

Greeting: Ball Toss Greeting

Sharing: Individual Share: *What helps me trust an adult is....*

Activity: Passing the Hoop

> Welcome, Students!
>
> Today we'll continue talking about friends and family. Do you have an adult friend whom you trust and talk with?

---

4   A+: Guest Speaker

Greeting: Handshake Greeting (page 216, Basic Greeting variation)

Activity: A guest discusses family customs (can be a parent or other relative, friend, or the teacher). Students ask questions from brainstormed list.

Reflection: Partner and/or whole group: *What's the value of customs to a family?* Students acknowledge and thank speaker.

> Dear Students,
>
> Today we are lucky to have as our guest in CPR Ms. Jenkins, Phillip's mom. She'll share with us some of the ways her family celebrates holidays and other events. Please give her a warm welcome so she feels comfortable.

5   A+: Visual Image

Greeting: High Five/Low Five or any Hand Jive Greeting

Activity: *Make a collage that represents your family.* Have lots of magazines, scissors, glue, and colored paper available. (Model use of scissors and glue before providing these materials.) This may need to be a two-advisory activity; students may bring photos from home with permission to use them.

Reflection: Partner reflection: partners introduce their collages to each other.

Greetings, Family Members!

Today we'll have some fun making a **collage** of our lives outside of school. We have art materials and magazines for you to use, and if you've brought any photos from home, you can add them to your collage. We'll have a quick greeting and then get started.

UNIT TWO: HEALTH AND WELL-BEING

Goals

Our mission in this unit is to protect our young adolescent students from their own impulses towards behaviors that can cost them dearly. Because the portion of the brain (amygdala) that prompts the spirit of adventure and risk-taking is especially active at this time, students are prone to use bad judgment. We can balance that tendency with information and consciousness-raising activities that could literally save a life, or improve the quality of their lives, now and in the future. Additionally, better health allows better concentration and more learning.

THEME: SAFETY

So many car crashes involve adolescents that driver's insurance for them is extra expensive. Middle level students need to hear the facts before they take on driving and other activities that can be dangerous to their and others' well-being. These advisories are designed to help raise consciousness about danger, the price of bad choices, and the responsibility good friends have to help each other stay safe.

---

1   CPR

Greeting: Formal Greeting (page 216, Basic Greeting variation)
Sharing: Whip Share: *Name a safe driving rule.*
Follow-up: *What were the safe driving rules mentioned?* Group remembers as many as possible
Activity: When the Wild Wind Blows: *What do we need to do so no one gets hurt during this game?*

> Hi, Fellow Travelers!
> Today we'll discuss auto safety.
> What is something you've seen drivers do that is unsafe?

---

2   CPR

Greeting: Double High Five or any Hand Jive Greeting
Sharing: Individual Share: *Describe something you do to be safe.*
Activity: Arm Hockey OR Space Station

> Good Morning, Safe Students!
> Think about a time when you are/were careful to keep yourself safe in a **potentially** dangerous situation. There will be time for a couple of shares.

3　CPR

Greeting: One-Minute Mingle Greeting

Sharing: Partner share: *What are the biggest dangers for adolescents?* Ask for some people to share out.

Activity: Driven to Trust: *What do we need to do to ensure that the people blindfolded will be safe?*

> Hello, **Prudent** Pupils!
>
> Do you have your friends' backs? Put your initials below one of the phrases to indicate how willing you are to tell a friend that you think she or he is about to take a bad risk.
>
> It's not my problem
> Only for really good friends
> Once in a while
> Usually I will

4　A+: Read and Reflect

Greeting: Formal Greeting (page 216, Basic Greeting variation)

Activity: Reading on teenage driving and rate of crashes. See www.dosomething.org,

Reflection: Small groups discuss questions: *Was this information new to you? Surprising? What can/should be done about the high rate of crashes involving teenage drivers?*

> Good Morning, Good Drivers-to-be!
>
> One of the things you can do to prepare for being a really good driver is to learn and think about driving long before the day you actually get your permit. Today we'll talk about teenage driving, and note some of the things to watch out for.

5　A+: Guest Speaker

Greeting: Great Greeting

Activity: Visit from law-enforcement person, EMT, emergency-room staffer, or survivor of a crash who talks about teenage safety OR Film on teenage driving

Reflection: Write and share out: *Have you changed any of your ideas about safety?* Students acknowledge and thank speaker.

> Dear Advisory Students,
>
> We have a guest today. Her name is _____, and she is an EMT (Emergency Medical **Technician**) who has come to share some of her experiences with us. Please greet her and help her to feel comfortable.

THEME: FITNESS

American adolescents on average are becoming more overweight and less active decade by decade. The repercussions of youthful inactivity on our nation's health and well-being are beginning to look dangerous. For quality of life, our middle level students need to be physically active. In the following advisories they are given opportunities to see the value and fun of exercise. In the process, their brains will get that extra oxygen needed for good thinking throughout the day.

---

1 CPR

Greeting: Baseball Greeting or the Football Greeting variation
Sharing: Whip Share: *I exercise by ....*
Activity: Snake Toss

> Hola, **Compadres**,
>
> Feeling tired? Need some energy? The best way to get it is to give it—exercise! It builds the body and soothes the mind. Today we'll start investigating what regular exercise can do for you.

---

2 CPR

Greeting: Ball Toss Greeting
Sharing: Partner Share with topic: Adult fitness *Looking into the future, how will you get your exercise as an adult? How do you see adults getting exercise?* Volunteers share out.
Activity: Paper Toss

> Hello, Sports Fans!
>
> We all know that good athletes are usually in great physical shape. What sport to you think requires the greatest **aerobic** fitness? Write your answer on your number line.

---

3 A+: Aerobic Inventory

Greeting: High Five/Low Five or any Hand Jive Greeting
Activity: Students use *Exercise and Your Heart A Guide to Physical Activity*, a publication of the National Institute of Health to learn about their aerobic health; see http://www.pueblo.gsa.gov/cic_text/health/exercise-heart/index.htm. *Answer the questions on aerobic exercise in Keys to Success; establish your Target Heart Rate.*
Reflection: Partners share results

> **Heartfelt** Greetings to All!
>
> Today is an important day. We're going to gather information that will tell each of us what how well **conditioned** our bodies are. The heart is the engine of aerobic strength. Let's see how well we are doing in pumping oxygen when and where we need it.

4   A+: Jogging Program

Greeting: Greet Three Greeting

Activity: (in the gym) Jogging Program: begin with 5 minutes or less of jogging in between walking warm-ups and cool-downs. Measure and record heart rates.

Reflection:

What was your heart rate right after exercise?

How easy or difficult was this exercise for you?

Set a target of 10 minutes or less for your jogging for tomorrow.

> Hello, Friends!
>
> Now that we know our aerobic starting points, let's see if we can move towards our Target Heart Rates. We'll move to the gym immediately, begin with a greeting, then have some warm-up movement, 5 minutes of jogging, and then cool-down movement. Get ready to move!

5   A+: Jogging Program

Greeting: One-Minute Mingle Greeting

Activity: (in the gym) Jogging Program: each student sets a jogging time target (up to 10 minutes), and does walking warm-up and cool-down. Measure and record heart rate.

Reflection:

What was your heart rate right after exercise?

How much did you push yourself?

Are you willing to commit to an aerobic workout every day?

What will it be?

Keep a record of your heart rate each time, and we'll have a chance to share records in a future advisory.

> **Jambo**, *Joggers!*
>
> Now that we have the hang of it, set a time target for yourself (from 5 to 10 minutes of **continuous** jogging). Start with a walking warm-up, like last time, and end with a walking cool-down. Those with shorter targets will do more walking at the end. Take your pulse right after you finish the jogging to see how close you are to your target heart rate.

THEME: FOOD AND NUTRITION

One wonders how many lessons have been lost because students were focused on their hunger, or were sluggish or hyperactive from poor eating habits. These advisories help raise consciousness about personal eating habits and the lifelong value of learning to eat well.

---

1   CPR

Greeting: P & J Greeting
Sharing: Whip Share: *What eating adventures have you had with foods that were new to you?*
Activity: Macaroni and Cheese, limiting pairs to edibles (e.g., bread & butter, salt & pepper, hot dog & bun, peanut butter & jelly, etc.)

> Dear Daring Diners,
> Are you willing to try something new this week? Eat a food you haven't tried before, then tell us about it.

---

2   CPR

Greeting: Share Greeting (page 215, All Group Greeting variation) about favorite foods
Sharing: Whip Share: *What "power food" do you eat?*
Activity: Twenty Questions with topic: What food am I?
(See Power Foods on page 282.)

> Hello, **Discriminating** Diners!
> Today we're discussing the foods we eat, and the extent to which they provide power (energy, growth, health, brain power). Check out the list of power foods and be ready to share from the list one power food that you eat at least once a week.

---

3   CPR

NOTE: Prepare for this meeting by having students keep a food diary for at least one day.
Greeting: Slap Jack Greeting
Sharing: Whip Share: *What is something you learned from keeping your food diary?*
Activity: Sausages

> Dear **Diarists**,
> Today we'll share our experiences keeping track of what we eat. Indicate on your number line a fruit or vegetable you ate and recorded in your diary.

4 & 5 A+: Group Work

NOTE: Internet access is required for these meetings, preferably with a maximum ratio of four students to a computer.

Greeting: "Miss Mary Mack" or any Hand Jive Greeting

Activity: Power Meals: in small groups, students review the USDA food pyramid information found at www.mypyramid.gov, and explore MyPyramid Menu Planner, MyPyramid Tracker (diet and exercise assessment), and MyPyramid Plan (estimate what and how much to eat). Groups make a meal they would like to eat that is nutritionally balanced, a Power Meal. This process will likely require a second day.

Reflection: Groups share their Power Meals.

> Good Morning, Power Eaters! Today we'll get some information that could change your whole life. People who eat well live longer and have more fun! Circle up for a greeting, and then we'll get into small groups to design some menus for Power Eating.

THEME: EMOTIONAL WELL-BEING

One of the main impediments to success in school is what students often refer to as being "bummed," a state of feeling bad about yourself, your life, your looks, and/or your relationships. An adolescent who is depressed or angry or hopeless cannot learn very much. The following advisories are designed to open awareness about ways to cheer or calm yourself or a friend, to handle mistakes (your own or others'), and to find options to deal with anger or depression.

---

1   CPR

Greeting: Individual Greeting
Sharing: Partner Share: *What is something you do that makes you feel good?*
Activity: Something Bad About Something Good

> Greetings, Friends!
>
> We all have different ways to cheer ourselves up when we're feeling down. Think about something that helps you feel better, and be ready to share.

---

2   CPR

Greeting: Peace Greeting
Sharing: Individual Greeting: *Describe a time when you felt angry, but you didn't lose your temper with someone.*
Activity: Yes!

> **Ciao**, Calm Students!
>
> Think about a time when you were able to contain your anger toward someone and handle the situation without trying to get even or to hurt the person in any way. There will be time for a few shares.

---

3   CPR

Greeting: Sawa bona Greeting
Sharing: Partner Share: *Talk with your partner about the following advice:*

When you make a mistake, the most important thing to remember is to forgive yourself and try to fix it. Treat yourself like a good friend. Be gentle, and realize that you're a good person, even though you slip up sometimes.
Activity: Yes!

> Howdy, Partners!
>
> Today we'll work on recovering from instead of going down with our mistakes. What do you do when you mess up? Check your most likely reaction(s).
>
> I'm really hard on myself
>
> I get **defensive** and start making excuses
>
> I apologize a lot
>
> I start looking for ways to fix it

4   CPR

Greeting: Silent Greeting
Sharing: Individual Share: *What is a way you have reached out to someone who was feeling sad or scared or lonely? Did that help the person feel better?*
Activity: Honey, Do You Love Me?

> Greetings, **Generous** People!
>
> Put your initials below ways that help you cheer up when you feel bad.
>
> Listen to music
> Go to a special place
> Talk to a friend
> Other (please specify)

5   CPR

Greeting: Mimic Greeting
Sharing: Partner Share: triads talk about what the sayings on the chart mean
Activity: Partners look at a picture of someone and identify something attractive about the person. Clip pictures from magazines and try to get a great variety: young, old, big, small, dark, fair, various hairdos, different ethnicities, genders, facial features.
Reflection: Partners share something attractive about the person whose picture they have studied. They can also comment on why, in the American media, this person might not be considered attractive.

> Good Morning, Beautiful People!
>
> Beauty is relative. Beauty is in the eye of the **beholder**. Different strokes for different folks. Pretty is as pretty does. What do these sayings mean? Be prepared to share what you think.

6   CPR

Greeting: Handshake Greeting (page 216, Basic Greeting variation)
Sharing: Partner Share: *What makes a person popular?*
Activity: Change One Thing

> Hey, Stylish Students,
>
> "Clothes make the person." Or do they? Think about what makes a person popular. Is it: Clothes? Makeup? Grooming? **Hygiene**? Personality? Intelligence? Manners?
>
> Place a check under each one that matters, in your opinion.

7   CPR

Greeting: Gushy Greeting
Sharing: Whip Share OR Individual Share: *If you could eliminate one emotion from your life, which one would it be and why?*
Activity: Mrs. Mumble

> Welcome, Friends!
>
> What is a word that describes how you feel today? Write it below in one of the bubbles.

8   A+: Visual Image

Greeting: Handshake Greeting (page 216, Basic Greeting variation)

Activity: *Make a drawing or painting of a place you love.* These images can be made into a book that would be located at the Take a Break place. Colored pencils work well for this, as do watercolor. Demonstrate use of colored pencils and watercolors. Avoid markers—they don't allow for much subtlety or mood. Tip: Give each student a small piece of paper (e.g., half of an 8 xɪɪ sheet) and you'll probably get better work.

Reflection: Partner Share: *Why does your place make you feel good?*

> Good Morning, Friends!
>
> Today you'll get a chance to draw or paint an image of a place that makes you feel good. I'll give you instructions after our greeting. Keep in mind today our rule about caring for the **environment**. At the end of advisory, you'll need to put back in an orderly way any materials you use.

9   A+: Handwork

Greeting: Silent Greeting

Activity: Handwork for self-soothing (for example, finger weaving, origami, knitting, crocheting, needlepoint, paper airplanes, beading, or string games) Use your own expertise or draw upon skills and hobbies of colleagues or parents. Once introduced, a handwork activity can be practiced throughout the year for calming at stressful times. Quiet background music might add to the calm.

Reflection: *Does handwork help you feel calm? Do you do handwork outside of school? Is there a handwork skill you would like to learn?*

> Hello, Handy Folks!
>
> Today we'll chill out with some work with our hands. If you haven't done **handwork**, you may be surprise at how much it calms you. Choose three pieces of yarn before our greeting, and get ready to relax!

10   A+: Group Work

Greeting: Movie Star Greeting

Activity: Media Mania

Reflection: *What effect do style and advertising have on how people think about what is pretty or handsome?*

> Welcome, Media Watchers!
>
> How much effect do the media have on what we think and how we live our lives? Today we'll try our hand at **influencing** others to think the way we do (or pretend to) about beauty. I'll explain more after our greeting. Meet me in the circle.

UNIT THREE: ADOLESCENT NEEDS

Goals

The more we can address and somewhat satisfy the needs that drive young adolescents, the more likely it is that we will succeed in educating them. Besides the fundamental survival needs shared by all human beings, adolescents are driven to satisfy their strong needs for *relationship*, a sense of *competence and autonomy*, and the chance to have some *fun*. A day without these things is disappointing, and sometimes impossible for them to handle. One way or another, they will seek ways to satisfy their needs, so it behooves us, their teachers, to offer them ways to learn that involve social interaction, fun, structures to build competencies incrementally, and the safe scaffolding they require to achieve more and more responsible independence. The following advisories are designed to start the day with a boost towards satisfying those needs, as well as to raise students' awareness of their own needs.

THEME: LEARNING ABOUT OUR NEEDS

One cause of the angst of adolescents is their powerful needs for relationship, autonomy, competence, and fun. They often have little or no awareness that these developmental needs press upon all normal adolescents, nor do they have much of an idea of how to satisfy the needs in safe and responsible ways. It is very helpful to give them insights into who they are as developing human beings. They need to know that they sometimes feel bad because they lack certain skills that would boost their competence. They need to understand that the reason they are lonely sometimes is that they have not yet learned how to handle the challenges of relating to a whole range of other human beings. One reason that they are so angry at times is that they haven't achieved the level of autonomy they think they deserve, and they need to know that independence and responsibility are linked in the minds of adults. They also need to understand that their drive toward excitement and fun can be managed in such a way that they remain in balance and productive in school. It is important for us to take a little time to introduce them to themselves.

---

1   CPR: Relationship

Greeting: Introduction Greeting

Sharing: Whip Share: *Who is someone with whom you have a good relationship?*

Activity: Table Top:

What is one of your favorite ways to have fun with a friend?

What are some ideas for how siblings can get along better?

What is something you know about getting along with adults?

What is one thing you have learned about friendships?

> Greetings, Friends!
>
> We all need friends and relationships. Today we'll be talking about getting along with others, because the better we are at relating, the happier we'll be. How important are relationships to your happiness? Put your initials under your answer.
>
> Not important
> Somewhat important
> Very important

2   A+: Acknowledgments

Greeting: Handshake Greeting (page 216, Basic Greeting variation)
Activity: Acknowledgment Buffet
Reflection: Exit Card (page 103) *How did you feel about what was said about you on your plate? How did you feel about writing about other people in the group?*

> Good Morning, Good People!
> We're having an **acknowledgment** buffet today. Start thinking about the people in our advisory and the ways they behave that contribute to you or to the group in general.

3   CPR: Competence

Greeting: Language Greeting
Sharing: Whip Share: *What are some things you are good at in school?* Scribe writes down the list (with names).
Activity: When the Cold Wind Blows with topic: Things we are good at doing in school, e.g., *When the cold wind blows, it blows for anyone who thinks he or she is good at math.*

> Hidey Ho, **Competent** Students,
> Today we'll be talking about things we are good at doing in school. Think about your classes, sports, how you are with kids, how you are with adults, remembering stuff, appointments, etc., homework, staying awake all day—whatever you are good at doing, and be ready to share.

4   CPR: Competence

Greeting: Baseball Greeting
Sharing: Whip Share: *What are some things you are good at outside of school?* Scribe writes down the list (with names).
Activity: When the Cold Wind Blows with topic: Things we are good at doing outside of school, e.g., *When the cold wind blows, it blows for anyone who thinks he or she is good at taking care of little children.*

> Good Morning, Experts!
> Hobbies and other activities outside of school help us acquire skills. We can learn a lot outside of **formal** education. Think about things you know how to do at home, outside, on your job, etc., and be ready to share. Write on your number line an activity you do outside of school from which you've learned a lot.

5   A +: Giant Puzzle

Greeting: Peace Greeting
Activity: Competency Puzzle: cut heavy paper into puzzle pieces and hand out pieces to students. Each student writes on his/her puzzle piece something he/she does well. Reassemble puzzle to display the class' competencies as a whole. You can number the backs of the puzzle pieces to aid reassembly.
Reflection: Exit Card (page 103) *What is a way one or more of us shows competence?*

> Peace, Puzzlers,
> Today we'll put together a puzzle that will **illustrate** the many things the people in this advisory are good at doing—a "competency" puzzle. Pick up a piece of the puzzle and start thinking about the things you do well.

6   CPR: Autonomy

Greeting: Language Greeting
Sharing: Whip Share: *In what ways are you independent or partially independent?*
Activity: Eleven

> **Ciao**, Choosers!
>
> Today we'll have a choice of the language in which we will greet. Choices are great. They give us a voice in life. What is a choice you have in your life? Write your answer on your number line.

7   CPR: Autonomy

Greeting: Hand Jive Greeting, with each student choosing a hand jive to use
Sharing: Whip Share: *In your life, what ways do you want to have more autonomy, more independence?*
Activity: Configurations

> Greetings, **Autonomous** Ones!
>
> Today is a day for wishing. What ways do you want to be more independent in your life? Do you think you are ready for that autonomy? Write on your number line a characteristic or skill you have that will help you be responsibly independent.

8   A+: Game

Greeting: Greet Three Greeting
Activity: ESP
Reflection: Whole group:
Sometimes you get to do things your way, but in a group, sometimes you have to compromise and go along with the group.
What advice would you give to people about balancing between doing things your way and helping a group come to consensus?

> Good Morning, Advisory Members,
>
> Today we'll examine the ways that people in groups compromise in order to come to a decision on a course of action. Think about ways in your life that you **compromise**.

9   CPR: Fun

Greeting: Ball Toss Greeting with variations
Sharing: Individual Share: Tell about a time when you had a lot of fun.
Activity: Chase the Caboose, model and practice the chair changing

> **Felicitations**, Fun-makers!
>
> The best moments in life are when friends are together, having fun, and laughing **good-naturedly**, don't you think? At those moments, what preserves the good time for everyone is self-control, so nobody runs wild. What is one thing to remember when you're having fun? Write your answer on your number line.

THEME: LEARNING SKILLS

We operate from the premise that all students can learn. They need to understand themselves as learners, get acquainted with their brains, figure out how to get their homework done, and have positive experiences with the subjects they must study. In these advisories they experience themselves as learners having fun, a positive association that may move them along towards academic success. At the same time, students practice some academic skills, and recall some of what they have learned in a variety of subjects.

---

1 CPR

Greeting: Skip Greeting
Sharing: Whip Share: *What is your favorite subject? Why?*
Activity: Guess the Number

> Greetings, Smart Students!
>
> Check the subject you find the hardest **intellectually.**
>
> Math
> Science
> Language Arts
> Social Studies

---

2 CPR

Greeting: Choice Greeting
Sharing: Individual Share: *Tell about a time when you did something impulsive and either were glad or regretted it later on.* Bring in comments about brain development as students share (e.g., brain development and fun, page 15).
Activity: No, No, No

> Bonjour, Brainy Students!
>
> Here's a sketch of your brain showing the part that's very active at your age, the amygdala, and the part that is still developing, the **pre-frontal lobes.** It's the **amygdala** that gets you excited and urges you to look for adventures and take risks. The pre-frontal lobes help you stop and think and make good judgments.

---

3 CPR

Greeting: High Five/Low Five or any Hand Jive Greeting
Sharing: Whip Share: *What helps you get your homework done? What hinders you?*
Activity: Homework buddies (page 110) Students meet with homework buddies to exchange phone numbers, academic strengths, and schedules. Pre-arrange the buddies in groups of two or four, striving for a balance of strengths and weaknesses in each team. The first night, the assignment is to call each other to get the answer to a simple question, such as their buddies' favorite music or food. You can also build these

> Dear **Diligent** Students,
>
> Homework and school go together like peanut butter and jelly! On your number line, write a payoff and a problem related to homework.
>
> Payoffs
> Problems

partnerships by playing games in teams and/or creating a team logo or handshake. From time to time, tell students to learn something new about their buddies.

---

4   CPR: Reading

Greeting: Book Character Greeting
Sharing: Whip Share: *What is the book from which your character comes? Other reading meetings might ask: What is the title of a book you read recently? OR With what book character do you most identify?*
Activity: In the Manner of the Adverb

> **Bonjour,** Book People!
>
> What genre of books do you like best? Write your name in a category below:
>
> Fiction   **Historical Novel**
> Fantasy   Mystery
> Biography   Poetry
> Other (specify)
>
> Make a nametag with the name of a book character and pin or tape it on you (pins and tape below).

---

5   CPR: Social Studies

Greeting: Language Greeting
Sharing: Partner Share: each person shares a description of a typical school day while the partner draws a timeline illustrating the day he or she is hearing about
Activity: Around the World

> **Jambo,** Historians!
>
> Let's make a timeline of our birthdays. Write your name and birthday (month and day) on a Post-it and place it in the proper place in the timeline below.
>
> Sept._____Aug.

---

6   CPR: Math

Greeting: Skip Greeting
Sharing: Individual Share: *What tricks (memory aids, shortcuts, etc.) do you use to help in computation: adding, subtracting, multiplying, or dividing?* You can choose students ahead of time who can show the rest some shortcuts or ways to remember certain computations.
Activity: Count to Ten OR Guess the Number OR Pico Firme Bago OR One Frog

> **Guten Morgen,** Mathematicians!
>
> Show that you have detected the pattern by adding the next number.

7   CPR: Science

Greeting: Question Greeting: *What's your favorite kind of weather?*
Sharing: Individual Share: *Tell about an experience you had of wild weather.*
Activity: Observation Olympics OR Detective OR Someone's Missing OR Frogger with topic: A scientist needs to be an accurate observer

Salutations, Super Scientists!
Today we're going to learn about weather from each other, and we're going to practice careful **observation** while we play. How many letters of the alphabet are not present in this message? Write the number on your number line.

8   A+: Reading Across the Curriculum

Greeting: One-Minute Mingle Greeting
Activity: Silent Reading (page 104) of fiction or nonfiction in a subject area
Reflection: Exit Card (page 103) *From what you read today, write down a fact, an idea, a description of a character, or an incident.*

Good Morning, Ready Readers!
We'll spend advisory chilling out with a book. Use one you brought, or select one from the table. As you read, look for a **memorable** idea or description that you can share with us at the end of advisory.

9   A+: Role Play

Greeting: Telephone Greeting
Activity: Role play (pages 114 and 271) on a homework dilemma such as the distraction of TV or telephone
Reflection: Whole group: *On a scale of one to five (five being the most positive), use fingers to show whether you now feel better able to resist distractions and do your homework.*

Hello, Homeworkers!
You guessed it! Today we'll be dealing with a homework issue: the problem of **distractions**. Be ready to participate in a role play that will help us solve the problem. Meet me in the circle for the Telephone Greeting.

10   A+: Problem-solving Meeting

Greeting: High Five/Low Five or any Hand Jive Greeting
Activity: Problem-solving Meeting (pages 118 and 274) on the problem of late homework
Reflection:
How can we keep track of how we are doing in handing in homework?
When shall we check in again about this problem?

Howdy Again, Homeworkers!
Today's homework problem is the one where you don't do it on time. We'll **assemble** a problem-solving meeting on ways to get homework done and in when it's due. Circle up, and we'll begin with some hand jive.

THEME: SOCIAL SKILLS

Social and academic skills are interdependent. You can't have success in learning or in life without social skills. You can't concentrate, exchange ideas, listen, speak so others will listen, or work with others unless you have some basic social competencies. We use the list created by Elliott and Gresham to determine how social skills affect students' social and academic capacities (Gresham and Elliott 1990): Cooperation, Assertion, Responsibility, Empathy, and Self-control (CARES). We have devised advisories that help students explore each skill.

---

1   CPR: Cooperation

Greeting: Snake Greeting
Sharing: Partner Share: *Tell about a time in your life when teamwork was important, in or out of school.* A couple of volunteers share with whole group.
Activity: Helium Hoop OR Shrinking World

> **Ohieyo**, Students!
>
> Today we'll start talking about, practicing, and **implementing** social skills. Indicate how important you think social skills are to success in life by rating their importance below.
>
> Not important
> Sometimes important
> Very important

---

2   CPR: Assertion

Greeting: Choice of Voice Greeting (page 215, All Group Greeting variation)
Sharing: Individual Share: *Tell about a time when you stood up for yourself or for someone else.*
Activity: Honey, Do You Love Me? OR What Are You Doing?

> **Salutations**, Strong Ones!
>
> Here's the scene: You walk into a room with about forty people, all socializing in pairs and small groups. What do you do first? Answer on your number line.

---

3   CPR: Responsibility

Greeting: Partner Greeting
Sharing: Whip Share: *What was a time when you had to handle a lot of responsibility? You can follow up with questions for anyone. For example, what games did you play with the little kids at your sibling's birthday party?*
Activity: Obstacle Course

> Good Morning, Students!
>
> Today we're going to work with the "R" word, Responsibility. How often do you act responsibly? Write your initials under your answer.
>
> Never   Sometimes
>
> Usually   Always

4   CPR: Empathy

Greeting: Silent Greeting
Share: Individual Share: *Tell about an embarrasing moment you experienced.*
Activity: Talk Show OR One-Minute Talk

> Hello, Friends!
>
> Today's meeting gives us a chance to show support for one another. When is it hard for you to feel **empathy** or support for someone? Answer on your number line.

5   A+: Self-control

Greeting: Snake Greeting
Activity: Radio OR Tag Games OR Team Red Light OR Where Are You From?
Reflection: Whole group:

With fingers, show from 1to5 how well you think we did in self-control during the game.

Now with fingers, show how hard it was for you to use self-control.

Any ideas for how we could make the game more fun without losing our controls?

> Salutations!
>
> Today's social skill topic is the one John Dewey (an important influence in American education) said was key to success. Without self-control, not only do you get in trouble, but you can't succeed in school or in life. We have to teach ourselves to hold back on those **impulses** to break rules, and have fun anyway. Let's practice with a game!

6   A+: CARES Group Work

Greeting: Reach Out Greeting (page 217, Choice Greeting variation)
Activity: Divide students into five groups (one for each of the CARES skills). Give each group a list of games already familiar to the class. The group decides which one is best to practice their assigned skill and prepares to lead the group in that activity.
Reflection: Groups explain how their chosen activity teaches their assigned skill, and lead the whole advisory in playing it. After playing, whole group indicates with thumbs whether they agree that they practiced the designated skill while playing the game. You will need at least two advisory periods for all five groups to lead a game. Limit time of playing to a few minutes.

> Greetings, Everyone!
>
> We practiced self-control by playing a game. Other games can teach us other social skills, so today we'll divide into small groups, and each group will teach us a different social skill with a game. Get ready to think and play at the same time!

THEME: FRIENDSHIP

Since young adolescents are fixated upon their peers, it is important that they learn about the challenges of making and keeping friends.

---

1   CPR

Greeting: One-Minute Mingle Greeting
Sharing: Whip Share: *What is something you enjoy doing with friends?*
Activity: Copy Cat

> Welcome, Friends!
>
> One of the best things in life is good friends. Indicate below how important your friends are to you by putting an X on the **continuum.**
>
> _____
>
> Not   Crucially
> important   important

---

2   CPR

Greeting: Say Hi to _____ Greeting
Sharing: Partner Share: *Tell about a time when you participated in gossip.*
Activity: Telephone

> Howdy, Friends!
>
> Here are some questions about the practice of talking about people behind their backs. Put a **tally** mark next to "yes" or "no" for each question.
>
> Have you ever gossiped?
> YES   NO
>
> Have you ever listened to gossip? YES   NO
>
> Have you ever been gossiped about? YES   NO

---

3   CPR

Greeting: Gift Greeting
Sharing: Individual Share: *What was a meaningful gift you received?*
Activity: Magic Ball

> Greetings, Gift Givers!
>
> Gift-giving is a world-wide custom. Why do you think people like to give and receive gifts? Write your answer on a Post-it and put it on the daily news chart/board.

4 CPR

Greeting: Knock Knock Greeting

Sharing: Partner Share: *What characteristics do you appreciate in a good friend?* Partners write at least two qualities they admire in friends, each on a separate card or Post-it. Partners read their qualities to the whole group. Volunteers sort the qualities and make a list of what the advisory can call Five Star Friends on a poster.

Activity: Popcorn Acknowledgment OR I Sit in the Grass

> Top of the Mornin' to You, Friends!
>
> Today we'll be talking about the qualities of a good friend. Be thinking about what you look for and strive to be in your friendships, and be ready to share.

5 A+: Personal Reflection

Greeting: Silent Greeting

Activity: Individuals reflect on their own friendship qualities as identified by the group in the #4 CPR on friendship above. Teacher can write the qualities with continuum lines or with a scale (such as Never=1, Seldom=2, Frequently=3, Regularly=4, Always=5) to indicate how much you practice each quality. Students add up their numbers. The higher the number, the more you practice the qualities of what the group considers good friendship.

> Good Morning, Students!
>
> Today we'll think about how good a friend we know how to be. We've **compiled** a list of the qualities we think are important in a friend. Now you can decide how many of those qualities you demonstrate each day. After our greeting, I'll pass out our own Personal **Inventory** on Friendship Skills.

Reflection: *Does your number match the person you think yourself to be, or were you surprised? Circle qualities in which you are already strong. Put a triangle around qualities you would like to improve.*

6 A+: Role Play

Greeting: Inside-Outside Greeting

Activity: Role play (pages 114 and 271) Scenario: problems between friends. Both groups have written a scenario about a problem between friends. The inside group first role plays the scenario while the outside circle observes and responds, then the groups switch roles.

> Greetings, Advice-givers!
>
> Life is full of problems between people. You can't escape them, but you can learn how to deal well with them. Today we'll see how well we can solve a problem between Liz and Miranda. Meet me in the circle for our greeting, followed by a role play.

Sample scenario: Liz and Miranda are friends. Miranda has been invited to a party and Liz was not, even though the person giving the party is friends with both of them. Liz wants to go to the party. Miranda is hurt that Liz would even think of going since she (Miranda) was slighted by their mutual friend. *What could Liz do or say to work this out? What could Miranda do or say to make things better?*

Reflection: Written: *Have you been in a situation like this one? What are the words or actions that you would choose to handle this situation?*

7   A+: Small Group Discussions

Greeting: Basic Greeting in small group circles

Activity: Sticky Social Situations: each group writes a friendship problem scenario on a card. For example, Steven jokingly disses his friend Frederick when other people are around, and Frederick is sick of it. (For more examples, see Sticky Social Situations on page 269.) Groups exchange cards, and discuss what would be a good way to handle the scenario described on the card they receive.

Reflection: One person from each group reads his or her scenario to the whole group. Another person describes how the group recommends handling such a problem.

> **Buenos Dias,** Problem-solvers!
>
> Think about the things that can go wrong between friends, and get ready to share at least one idea with your group. Today we'll identify some problems and figure out good ways to handle them.

8   A+: Acknowledgments

Greeting: Name Card Greeting

Activity: Touch Someone Who

Reflection: Exit Card (page 103) *Write down an idea for a Touch Someone Who category to add to our list.*

> Welcome, Friends!
>
> One of the best things we can do for our friends is tell them something we enjoy and admire about them. Join me in the circle, where we'll play an **acknowledgment** game, Touch Someone Who.

THEME: COMMUNICATION

The following advisories give young adolescents some insight into the complex world of communication. It helps them see that developing the skills to use the appropriate and effective words and tone is worth working towards.

---

1   CPR

Greeting: Choice of Gesture Greeting (page 215, All Group Greeting variation)
Sharing: Whip Share: *Share your understanding of the communication word you chose.*
Activity: Charades

> Good Morning, Everyone!
>
> It's all in how you say it—that's a clue to good communication. Here are some words that will help us understand the mysteries of good give-and-take with others. Be prepared to share your understanding of one of the following words.
>
> | | |
> |---|---|
> | non-verbal | verbal |
> | tone of voice | body language |
> | sender/receiver | active listening |
> | feedback | encouragement |
> | slang | formal speech |

---

2   CPR

Greeting: Silent Greeting
Sharing: Partner Share: *What's the evidence that a person is really listening to you? What does it look, sound, and feel like?* Make a Y-chart of their ideas as students share out.
Activity: Non-Verbal Messages OR ESP

> Hello, Colorful Communicators!
>
> There are many ways that we communicate. Which do you think is the most potent way we send messages to each other when we are face-to-face? Vote below with a tally mark.
>
> The words we use
>
> Our tone of voice
>
> Volume of voice
>
> Facial **expression**
>
> Body language

---

3   CPR

Greeting: Elevator Greeting
Sharing: Partner share: *Describe a person with whom you have difficulty communicating and tell why you think communicating is hard with him or her.* One or two people share out to whole group.
Activity: No, No, No

> Good Morning, All!
>
> Sometimes it is really hard to get your message across to someone or to **comprehend** what you are being told. What's something that definitely doesn't work for you when you are talking with someone—your pet peeve in communication? Write below on your number line.

4   CPR

Greeting: Introduction Greeting

Sharing: Partner Share: *Do you have more than one communication style? Can you switch from informal to formal situations and make your communication style appropriate to each?*

Activity: Divide into two groups. Each group reads six words from the daily news message, and the other group has to come up with a more formal alternative.

> Dear Class,
>
> When one is speaking formally, instead of the following words, what more formal word might one use? Be ready to share a **synonym** or substitute.
>
> | | |
> |---|---|
> | Hi | S'up? |
> | How's it goin', man? | I ain't complainin' |
> | Whatcha doin'? | Gimme five! |
> | I'm doin' lousy. | I get the drift. |
> | Nah | Yeah |
> | See ya around. | Bye. |

5   A+: Role Play

Greeting: Guess My Greeting

Activity: Role play (pages 114 and 271) Scenario: two students meet at lockers. Tyrell is angry at Marcus because Marcus didn't wait for him after school yesterday as he said he would. (Of course, the role play could work with two female students, too.) Solve the problem by having both people use these four empathetic-language steps:

1. Describe what happened using descriptive, not judgmental, language.
2. Say how you feel or felt without blaming.
3. Say what you need or want.
4. Make a request for the future.

Reflection: Whole group: *How might these steps help us communicate with our friends?* Role plays can be done repeatedly. See page 114 for a list of scenarios.

> **Aloha,** Actors!
>
> Today is a role play day. The problem is posted below. We'll use some **empathetic** language to resolve the problem so that both parties are satisfied.

6   A+: Game

Greeting: Telephone Greeting

Activity: Rap a Rhythm

Reflection: Whole group, oral: *What did you enjoy about that activity? What ways might we make it more fun?*

> Hello, Students!
>
> Good communication depends upon how one person responds to another. Today we'll play with communication by responding to each other with **rhythms**. Circle up and we'll begin with a Telephone Greeting.

THEME: SERVICE

Young adolescents look both inward and outward. The larger world attracts them, and they are beginning to learn how to deal with it successfully. We want their growing awareness of life to include the idea that we are, at least in part, here to help one another. Discussing and experiencing service to others is a character-formation experience critical for middle level students. They seem to genuinely enjoy contributing to others, in part because it builds their sense of their own competence and independence.

---

1   CPR

Greeting: Handshake Greeting (page 216, Basic Greeting variation)
Sharing: Partner Share: *What does the quote from Kennedy mean? Do you agree?* One person from each partnership shares out to whole group.
Activity: Cumulative List: *I'm going to serve by ....*

> Welcome, Students!
>
> In his **inaugural** address, President John F. Kennedy said, "Ask not what your country can do for you. Ask instead what you can do for your country." Be ready to share what you think he meant and whether you agree.

---

2   CPR

Greeting: Formal Greeting (page 216, Basic Greeting variation)
Sharing: Whip Share: *How might a middle level student serve her or his community?* (or country? world?)
Activity: Configurations

> Good Morning, Friends!
>
> Adults have served the United States and others in the armed forces, the Peace Corps, the Job Corps, and Teach for America, to name just a few ways. What can students do to help **sustain** others? Be ready to share.

---

3   CPR

Greeting: One-Minute Mingle Greeting
Sharing: Think, Pair, Share: *How could students help their school?*
Activity: Count Up

> Welcome, Wise Ones!
>
> Today we're going to think about how we could make a contribution to our school. Here are a few ideas. Put a star next to the two ideas you like best. Be ready to add an idea or two during CPR meeting.
>
> Copy for office or teachers
> Set up recycling collection
> Recognize everyone on his/her birthday
> School Store
> Lunch time entertainment
> Talent show
> Organize **intramural** sports day

4   A+: Planning Meeting

Greeting: Basic Greeting

Activity: Planning Meeting (page 273) with topic: Choosing and organizing a school service project. See page 121 for more about school service jobs.

Reflection: Whole group:
Was our final choice of a project your favorite idea?
What do you think will be the outcome of our project?
Name one trouble spot you think we might have to deal with.

> Salutations, Servers!
>
> Get ready to make a decision today about the school service project our advisory will do. Look over the list we **generated** and be ready to choose your favorite.

5   A+: School Service

Greeting: Fist-Tap Greeting (page 216, Basic Greeting variation)

Activity: Work on school service project. Work on the project can occur on future days as well, until it is complete. See page 121 for more about school service jobs.

Reflection: Whole group:
What went (or is going) well?
What is something that needs improvement?
Do you have suggestions for improvement?

> Good Morning, Workers!
>
> Today is the day we begin our service project. Check the list below to see who your partner is and to which room(s) the two of you will go to **distribute** the survey. Pick up your surveys and stand by your partner. We'll greet each other in a standing circle, do our assigned tasks, and meet back here at 8:45 sharp.

THEME: PLAY AND FUN

The power of play to make the learning day a positive experience is a resource we are foolish to waste. If a quick game or joke or lively, interactive experience can focus and engage our young learners, let's begin every day with a taste of good fun!

---

1 CPR

Greeting: Tower Greeting
Sharing: Whip Share: *What is a favorite way you have fun?* (Be sure to indicate ahead of time that activities that include an element of violence or self-abuse are not included in this definition of fun.)
Activity: Chase the Caboose, with safety guidelines established before the game

> Welcome, Fun-loving Students!
>
> Although we enjoy having fun in any advisory, the next few will be specifically focused on fun, and how to have fun without hurting yourself or others. Have you ever **endangered** yourself while trying to have some fun? Indicate your answer with a tally mark.
>
> YES   NO

---

2 CPR

Greeting: High Five or any Hand Jive Greeting
Sharing: Partner Share followed by share out: *Tell about a time when you heard or were in any way a part of anti-fun. What did you do?*
Activity: Hoops

> Greetings, **Gregarious** Gigglers!
>
> Today we'll look at "anti-fun," trying to have a laugh at someone else's expense, such as sexist, racist, classist, anti-culture jokes, **sarcastic** humor, mocking imitations, or laughing at another's mistake. Every one of these anti-fun moves spoils the good time for everyone. You never know when you'll be the next victim of prejudice. The message is: this group is not safe. Think about what you do when you hear someone making such a joke, and be ready to share.

---

3 CPR

Greeting: Riddle Greeting
Sharing: Whip Share: *Who is the funniest person in your life?*
Activity: Mrs. Mumble

> Felicitations, Funsters!
>
> Check out the joke books on the table with a partner; each of you get ready to share one riddle and any other joke that's good, clean, silly fun.

4   CPR: Having fun with math

Greeting: Puzzle Greeting
Sharing: Snowball Share: *What's hard about math? What's fun about math?* Answer one question per side of the paper.
Activity: Count to Ten OR Pico Firme Bago OR Guess the Number

> Greetings, Magnificent Math-ematicians!
>
> We're investigating how to have fun while doing school work. To-day we'll look at math. Indicate with a tally mark below on the **continuum** how you feel about math.
>
> Not fun at all   Can be fun

5   CPR: Having fun with words

Greeting: Great Greeting (page 215, All Group Greeting variation)
Sharing: Whip Share: *What is a word you like? Why?*
Activity: Partners teach each other a new word by inviting them to take guesses first, looking at clues in the word itself (part of speech, parts of other words, association, etc.).

> Welcome, **Wordsmiths**!
>
> With a partner, find a word in the dictionary that you think will **stump** the class. Write the word (spelled correctly) on one side of the card, and its definition on the other.

6   CPR: Having fun with thinking

Greeting: Ball Toss Greeting, played forward and backward
Sharing: Cumulative Share (page 231, Whip Share variation)
Activity: Green Door OR Alibi OR Twenty Questions

> Greetings, Good Thinkers!
>
> Thinking can be fun. Here's a puzzler: connect these nine dots with one continuous line (you can never lift your pencil off the page to **relocate** it) that changes direction no more than three times. Copy the dot pattern and give it a try!
>
> •   •   •
> •   •   •
> •   •   •

7   A+: Active fun in the gym

Greeting: Slap Jack Greeting in pairs, simultaneously

Activity: All Hit Moonball OR Team Red Light Green Light OR Giants, Wizards, Elves OR any other active game that takes a big space; can play as cross-advisory games (page 112)

Reflection: Whole Group: *What was fun about this game? What might make it even better?*

Note: You may wish to invite other advisories to join you in this kind of active, big-space game. You can insert these games into your regular advisory schedule to offer a physically active change of pace.

> Hello, Playful People!
>
> It's a games day! Get ready to have some playful, **non-competitive** fun in the gym. We'll go to the gym together, do a quick greeting, and start All-Hit Moonball.

---

8   A+: Group project

Greeting: Basic Greeting

Activity: Partners make a Favorite Jokes book with illustrations to give to younger students, siblings, or to keep (e.g., 8½ x 11 paper folded in half and stapled down the center). Resources: books of riddles, puns, knock-knock, or other quick jokes. Or you can make your own fun with top ten lists:

- top ten excuses for not having your homework done
- top ten ways for greeting someone in the halls
- top ten phrases most often heard in middle schools.

> **Jambo**, Jokers!
>
> Do you know the difference between unlawful and illegal? (Unlawful is against the law and illegal is a sick bird.) Do you have a riddle, pun, knock-knock or other quick joke to share? If not, you'll be able to find one in the books on the table. Today we'll **compile** our own book of favorite jokes to share with our first grade buddies (or younger siblings or cousins). Remember, for the little kids, the sillier the better.

For "foldables," paper-folding patterns for mini-books, see Dinah Zike's book series.

Reflection: Whole Group: *Read us your favorite joke or riddle. What makes these jokes fun?*

THEME: HOBBIES

An arena of life that seems to motivate young adolescents intrinsically, without the urging of adults, is the special interests they develop on their own, usually outside of school. Giving students an opportunity to share hobbies and other interests can build community and spark interest in learning in general.

1 CPR

Greeting: Ball Toss Greeting
Sharing: Whip Share: *What is a hobby or interest you have, outside of school?* After the go-round, see what students can remember about what hobby/interest each has.
Activity: Alibi, using hobby as part of alibi

> Good Morning, Students!
> Today's CPR Meeting is about hobbies. The word "hobby" originally was used to signify a kind of horse with a slow, **ambling gait**, one that gentlemen or ladies rode in their **leisure.** What does the word mean today? Can you connect its current meaning and the original meaning? Get ready to share your theory.

2 CPR

Greeting: What Are You Doing? Greeting, connecting actions to hobbies
Sharing: Whip Share: *What is a hobby or interest you've never tried but are interested in?* Brainstorm a list of good hobby questions to ask when students begin to share about their hobbies. The brainstormed list will improve the quality of the questioning.
Activity: Fact or Fiction OR Cumulative List with topic: Hobbies or interests

> **Ciao,** Students!
> One thing that is said to help keep people happy in life is to have special interests or hobbies. Do you think hobbies are good for people? Why or why not? Sign in below your answer, and have your reasons ready.
> Yes   No

3 CPR

Greeting: Step In Greeting
Sharing: Individual Share with topic: Hobbies or interests
Activity: Pictionary OR Twenty Questions with topic: Hobbies or interests
Note: You may choose to have students share hobbies for several CPR meetings (or see A+ Advisory below).

> Hello, Happy **Hobbyists!**
> Think about your hobby or an interest outside of school. Is it a risk-taking kind of activity? Do you think this is something you'll do when you are an adult? All your life? Sign your name below under your answers.
> Risky?
> YES   SORT OF   NO
> Life-long?
> YES   MAYBE   NO

4   A+: Peer teaching

Greeting: Let Me See Your Walk Greeting, walks include a pantomime of doing hobbies

Activity: Partner Share: students demonstrate their hobbies to each other, teaching their partners a little about how to do that hobby or follow that interest. See page 109 for more about peer teaching.

Reflection: Partner Share: *What is something that interested you about your partner's hobby?*
Might it be something you would try doing?

> **Salutations,** Students!
> Be prepared today to talk with a partner about your hobby for three minutes each. We'll use the 3-1-3-1 approach, and each of you will talk for three minutes, and have one minute to tell back what you learned from your partner. See the posted list for partners.

5   A+: Collecting Information

Greeting: Roll Call Greeting, naming hobbies or things in the introduction

Activity: Hobby Survey: survey teachers in the school to find out their hobbies. To do this, divide the list of teachers among students. Students write the name of each teacher on an index card, and the hobby of that teacher if it is known. You can collect the data with a survey question circulated to every teacher, or by students asking each teacher in person. The in-person process will undoubtedly take more than one advisory.

Reflection: Whole group (If you haven't surveyed yet): *What are some hobbies you predict our teachers have?* Then you can compare your predictions with the actual data you gather.
(If you have teacher hobbies) *What is the most common hobby among the teachers? What teacher hobby surprised you?*

> Aloha, Advisees!
> Today we're going to investigate the hobbies of teachers in our school.

6   A+: Group project

Greeting: Cumulative List Greeting (page 218, Cumulative Greeting variation)

Activity: Begin an *All About Us* book which will describe not only the hobbies and special interests of each person in the advisory, but other pieces of information about the group—a kind of almanac of our advisory.

Reflection: Whole group: *What categories of information about us do we want to include in our Advisory Almanac?* (Give a few ideas to spark the process, such as birthdays, number of siblings, pets' names)

Note: This is an extended activity that could be worked on in several advisories.

> Good Morning, Fascinating Folks!
> An **almanac** is a reference book that is also a fun book to browse. Take a look at one of the almanacs on the front table. We'll start the greeting at 8:33.

THEME: MAKING CHOICES

Making good choices is a skill of crucial importance to middle level students. Sometimes their very lives depend on making the right choice. They are not yet equipped with a fully developed brain that would make the exercise of judgment easier, and they are programmed for risk-taking and the urge to say "yes" to excitement. They need our help to learn the elements of good judgment—how to stop and think before acting, how to line up the options and think about the outcomes for each of them, and how to make a choice that satisfies without selling out your best interests—one's health, safety, reputation, or success.

---

1   CPR

Greeting: Baseball Greeting
Sharing: Think, Pair, Share: *How do you make your choices? For example, what do you think about when choosing whether or not to go to a party?*
Activity: Continuous Tale

> *Good Morning, Advisory!*
>
> *Every day we make lots of choices. How many choices would you say you make in a day, from the time you awake until the time you fall asleep at the end of the day? Write your estimate on your number line.*

---

2   CPR

Greeting: Choice Greeting
Sharing: Post-it Share
Activity: Configurations: small groups choose from a list of subjects; at the end, they tell why they chose the one they did.
Note: Throughout the meeting, keep track of the kinds of reasons given for all choices made.

> *Ciao, Choosers!*
>
> *Here's a choice for you: Should we have pretzels as a snack at the end of CPR Meeting, or should we choose the mystery snack? Vote below by writing your name.*
>
> *Pretzels Snack   Mystery Snack*
>
> *Be ready to share about why you made the choice you did.*

---

3   CPR

Greeting: Greet Three Greeting
Sharing: Think, Pair, Share: *Which seems to you the best way for groups to make decisions: leader decides; majority rules; consensus?*
Activity: Create a consensus decision on the snack. Looking at the choices on the daily news, and come to agreement on either pretzels or the mystery snack.

> *Good Day, Deciders!*
>
> *Yesterday we voted for our choice of an after-CPR snack, so the majority ruled. Today we'll decide by* **consensus**, *which means that everyone has to be either for the choice or willing to go along with the choice, even if it's not his or her preference. Indicate with your name again:*
>
> *Pretzels Snack Mystery Snack*

4   A+: Group work

Greeting: Two students choose a greeting from the list, lead the greeting, and afterwards explain why they chose that greeting.

Activity: Small groups are each given choices to make. They list options for each side of the choice, and then make their choices.

Examples of choices:

- To go out for the basketball team or not
- Whether to have a friend over without telling my mother
- To watch TV or write a report that's due next week
- To save all my paycheck or spend some on a new pair of shoes
- Whether to stay home on a day when I have a slight cold and a science test
- Whether to cancel my babysitting job in order to go to a concert with a friend
- Whether or not to tell my mom that I broke a fancy vase
- To sleep later and skip breakfast or get up on time to eat

> *Good Day, Friends!*
>
> *Since making good decisions is one of the secrets to a great life, it's a good idea to practice decision-making. Today, in small groups, we'll study the options of a choice and come to a* **consensus** *on a good choice. Remember, life is a thinking person's game!*

5   A+: Group work

Greeting: Two students choose a greeting from the list, lead the greeting, and afterwards explain why they chose that greeting.

Activity: Students show that they know the elements of good choice-making by describing the options of a particular choice they have made or are going to make, and the arguments for and against each option. Students can choose one of several ways to do this:

- Make a *The Choice is Mine* mini-book
- Make a poster
- Write a narrative

Reflection: Exit Card (page 103) *Do you now know better how to make good choices? Do you think you will make good choices in the future?*

> *Welcome, Wise Ones!*
>
> *Decision-making practice continues! Today we'll look at real-life choices, and create a* **representation** *of your decision in the form of a mini-book, poster, or* **narrative.**

THEME: PLANNING AND ORGANIZING

Many students fail not for lack of ability but for lack of organizing skills. They never seem to get it together. Their lockers are a mess, they lose things constantly, they come to class unprepared, and homework is a hit-or-miss endeavor. Rather than assume our students already know how to get and stay organized, let's model organizational skills for them, and give them time to practice, step by step, what we demonstrate. For many, this may be the first time that anyone has carefully shown them the way.

---

1   CPR

Greeting: Huddle Up Greeting
Sharing: Whip Share: *Do you consider yourself an organized person? Why or why not?*
Activity: Configurations

> Good Morning, Students!
> It's time to get organized. What is something an organized person does? Write your idea on your number line.

---

2   CPR

Greeting: *Greet everyone whose name begins with the same letter as yours.*
Sharing: Individual Share: *Describe a time or place when/where you were/are either very organized or very disorganized.*
Activity: Sorting: groups are given a variety of materials and must sort them into groups and then explain the basis of their sorting. Materials to sort could include classroom supplies, magazines, books, recycling, papers, etc.

> Holá, Organizers!
> How important is being an organized person to your success in life? Write your name under your answer.
> Not important
> Somewhat important
> Quite important
> Very important

---

3   CPR

Greeting: Puzzle Greeting
Sharing: Partner Share: *Tell your partner about something in your life that needs organizing.* Partners give at least one suggestion for getting organized. A couple of people share out.
Activity: Key Punch

> Bienvenidos, Friends!
> Organized people get more done. Name a person you know who is well-organized. Write on your number line.

4   A+: Demo

Greeting: One-Minute Mingle Greeting
Activity: Demo on ideas for organizing homework assignments:

- Assignment books, calendars, organizers, trappers
- Getting the assignment right
- Gathering needed materials
- Preparing a location to work
- Working and handing in your work
- Handling breakdowns

Partners help each other organize for homework
Reflection: Plan to Keep Track: *We'll keep personal tallies of late or missing homework for the next five days on large index cards: write your name and classes, and leave a space across the card for five days of tallying.*

> Howdy, All!
>
> Today is your lucky day! We're getting organized, or at least learning how to get organized, about homework. You and your partner will help each other decide how to do so. First we'll have a short demo on what organized people do to get and stay in order.

5   A+: Demo

Greeting: One-Minute Mingle Greeting
Activity: Demo on organizing a locker: emptying the locker; organizing the contents; putting things back for future accessibility. Then, students organize their lockers
Reflection: Whole group: *What are the payoffs for being organized?*

> Hear ye, hear ye!
>
> Today we're applying our organizing skills to your home away from home—your locker. Out with mess! In with **ease**!

THEME: TRANSITION TO HIGH SCHOOL

Eighth grade students will soon be making the important transition to high school, and most middle level students are thinking about that transition. There will be adjustments to make, both academically and socially. It is important that students are prepared for those adjustments, and spend some time thinking ahead, planning, and perhaps making some changes now that will ready them for the next phase of their education. The following advisories will help raise their consciousness about that next big transition.

---

1   CPR

Greeting: Handshake Greeting (page 216, Basic Greeting variation)
Sharing: Whip Share: *What is one thing you are looking forward to in high school and one thing you are nervous about?*
Activity: Yes!

> Hello, Future Graduates!
> High school is just around the corner, so let's spend some time thinking about your **transition**. Think about something you are looking forward to and something you are nervous about, and be ready to share about both.

---

2   CPR

Greeting: Snake Greeting
Sharing: Partner Share: *What are some ways to make new friends in a new place?* Some share out to whole group.
Activity: Mix and Mingle

> **Buenos Dias**, Friends!
> What are some conversation openers? Write one on your number line.

---

3   CPR

Greeting: Choice of Voice Greeting (page 215, All Group Greeting variation)
Sharing: Individual Share: *Who knows someone in high school? Can you tell us anything you have learned about high school from him or her?*
Activity: Affinity Process

> **Salaam Aleichem**, Students!
> We'll be doing some high school site visits. What is something you want to see during your visit? Write your answer on your number line.

4   A+: Guest speaker

Greeting: Formal Greeting (page 216, Basic Greeting variation)

Activity: Guest from a high school—a student or educator. Students ask questions or make comments after a brief talk.

Reflection: Whole group: *What is one thing you learned from talking with our guest today?*

> Greetings, Advisory Students!
> Please greet and welcome
> _____, our guest
> from _____ High School.
> _____ is a senior this
> year, and has agreed to talk
> with us about how he made
> his **adjustments** from middle
> school to high school. Be ready
> to ask one of the questions we
> **generated** for him.

5   A+: Guest speaker

Greeting: Handshake Greeting (page 216, Basic Greeting variation)

Activity: Guest from a high school—a student or educator. Students ask questions or make comments after a brief talk.

Reflection: Whole group: *Who has a thank you acknowledgment about something you learned or enjoyed today?*

> Good Morning, Friends!
> Once again we have a guest who
> has generously agreed to talk
> with us about to expect when
> you move to high school. Ms.
> _____ is the **guidance**
> counselor at _____
> High School, and she is eager
> to meet us and share some in-
> formation. Please welcome her,
> and get your questions ready.

6   A+: Group work

Greeting: Greet and Meet Greeting, with discussion about success in high school

Activity: Partners write tips for success in high school. Collect all the tips, and make one list. Post in the room or give everyone a copy.

Reflection: Whole group: students read their tips aloud.

> Howdy, Future High-schoolers!
> Today we'll gather together all
> the ideas we've learned about
> making a good transition to
> high school and succeeding in
> our high school years. You and
> a partner will write down a good
> idea or two, and we'll **compile**
> them into a reminder list that
> will come in handy in the future.
> Start your thinking motors,
> and join me in the circle.

THEME: CAREERS

Even though middle schoolers' adult careers are years away, now is a good time to begin thinking about them. Students often have ideas about their interests and strengths, and even those who don't are at least curious about their futures. Hope for a good, productive life generated in early adolescence is good insurance against wrong turns that can tempt those with no belief in themselves. Alert students to their options. Encourage them to aspire to success in their work lives. Even if they don't believe they can do it, you can light the lamp and keep it burning, and maybe it will guide them to new possibilities.

---

1   CPR

Greeting: Formal Greeting (page 216, Basic Greeting variation)
Sharing: Whip Share: *Name a career that attracts you, say one reason why, and show your card.*
Activity: Shuffle 'em Up

> **Buenos Dias, Amigos!**
>
> Think about what you would like to do as your job in life, and write the career that attracts you on an index card. Hold onto your card, and be ready to play!

---

2   CPR

Greeting: Formal Greeting (page 216, Basic Greeting variation)
Sharing: Partner Share: *Do you have to be a certain type of person for certain kinds of careers? Explain your answer.* Partners share out. Tally yes and no responses and summarize explanations.
Activity: What's Your Job OR any chair changing game

> **Bonjour, Amis!**
>
> Careers sometimes seem to run in families. Why do you think that happens? Today we'll talk about whether only certain people are fit for certain jobs. For example, what are the qualities a person should have to be a doctor? Write one below on your number line.

---

3   CPR

Greeting: Formal Greeting with a handshake (page 216, Basic Greeting variation)
Sharing: Individual Share: *What career word did you choose, and do you think you would want to do this work.*
Activity: Hands Up, with each person saying the name of the career s/he has defined.
Note: See page 280 for a list of less-known careers.

> **Shalom, Chaverim!**
>
> The names of some careers may be unfamiliar to you. Look in the dictionary for an explanation of the kind of work that is done in one of the following careers, and write the career word and its meaning on **alternate** sides of an index card. Put your name on the list by the career name you have chosen. One apiece, no repeats.

4   A+: Guest speaker

Greeting: Formal Greeting (page 216, Basic Greeting variation)

Activity: Guest who shares about his/her career (page 122). Students have time to ask questions or make comments after a brief talk.

Reflection: Whole group: *What career would you like to learn more about?*

> Good Morning, Friends!
> Please welcome our visitor today. _____ is here to share with us about his career in _____. Check over our list of questions and be thinking about which ones will give us **enlightening** answers.

5   A+: Group work

Greeting: One-Minute Mingle Greeting

Activity: Books on careers are available. Partners select a book to browse and find at least one interesting fact about a career described in it.

Reflection: Whole group: *What is one thing you learned about the career you studied?*

> Welcome, Learners!
> One way to find out about career opportunities is to read about them in books and magazines. Today you and your partner will get a chance to investigate possibilities.
> We'll start with a One-minute Mingle Greeting and end with sharing with each other something we learned about a career.

THEME: MANAGING MONEY

Something wealthy people know that many others do not is that the way to grow your money is to manage it well. Young people who learn that lesson early in life are more likely to manage their finances well as adults. Middle school is a great time to begin exposing them to smart thinking and good habits about money.

---

1 CPR

Greeting: High Five/Low Five or any Hand Jive Greeting

Sharing: Whip Share: *If you were given $100, would you spend it or save it?* Follow with a discussion of the reasons for spending and saving.

Activity: Group Juggle, with a twist: Each item is worth money (say, $5.00); group sees how much money they can juggle at once. For example, if they can keep 10 balls or bean bags going at once they are juggling $50.00.

> Welcome, Advisory Students!
> Today we'll talk about money. What does the expression "The rich get richer" mean? What does it mean to be **financially** independent? Do you know of any examples of either expression?

---

2 CPR

Greeting: Cumulative High Five Greeting (page 217, Cumulative Greeting variation)

Sharing: Think, Pair, Share: *How much do the media affect how you spend your money?*

Activity: Count Up: small groups see how many coin combinations they can use to make a dollar. For example, ten dimes, or twenty nickels, or two quarters and five dimes

> Hi, Savers and Spenders!
> Fads come and go in the **marketplace**, but while they last, many people rush to buy what's considered new and cool. Do you? Tally your answer below.
> YES   SOMETIMES   NO

---

3 CPR

Greeting: Name Card Greeting

Sharing: Partner Share: *If you had more money than you needed to take care of your basic needs, would you give some to charity?* Volunteers share out.

Activity: Heads or Tails: if your community is strong, you might give a little prize to whoever is left standing at the end, thereby demonstrating that getting money by luck is not only chancy and inequitable, but also often creates jealousy and resentment. Most lottery winners do not consider their lives happier after winning, and most are in financial ruin a few years after they "win."

> Good Morning, Money Managers!
> People do many things with money—spend it, save it, give it away, gamble it, lose it, bury it, find it. The trick to successful money management is to be **intentional** and smart about what you do with it, not to leave your money to whim or luck. Then you're on your way to being able to take care of yourself money-wise.

4   A+: Board game

Greeting: Formal Greeting with a handshake (page 216, Basic Greeting variation)

Activity: "Save or Spend" board game on a generic game board (see sample on page 278): players pick "save" and "spend" cards that determine how much money each player has at the end.

Instructions: Throw the dice and advance, pulling a card when you land on a "card" space. The card tells you how much money to save or spend, and what you'll get for what you spend. By luck, you end up with a certain amount of money and/ or goods and services. Teacher or students can make the Save and Spend cards indicating amount of money and what is purchased (see page 279 for examples).

Reflection: Whole group: each person writes the amount of money she/he has at the end of the game on a chart (or the board). For the biggest saver, compute the amount of money he or she would have in ten years if the amount were invested at 5%. In 15 years, $10,000 would more than double. Student can use a calculator with a compound interest function or the formula:

$$M = P(1 + i)n$$

M is the final amount including the principal.
P is the principal amount.
i is the rate of interest per year.
n is the number of years invested.

What does the game demonstrate about saving and spending money?
What are the rewards of spending?
What are the penalties?
What does it take to be a saver?
What is the payoff?

> Greetings!
> Today we're going to see how much money we can save and/ or spend in a board game called "Save or Spend." Circle up for the greeting, and we'll discuss the instructions.

5   A+: Guest Speaker

Greeting: Formal Greeting with a handshake (page 216, Basic Greeting variation)

Activity: Banker or accountant visitor. The guest could focus on investments, interests, and/or credit. Students have time to ask questions or make comments after a brief talk.

Reflection: Whole group: *What is one thing you learned today about money management?*
Students acknowledge and thank speaker.

> Good Morning, Friends!
> Please welcome our guest to-day, Ms. _____, from _____ Bank, who is here to give us the inside story on banking, saving, and **investing**. This may be your lucky day!

UNIT FOUR: MULTICULTURAL UNDERSTANDING

Goals

In our fractured, factionalized world, hope is renewed when young people show acceptance of people who are different from them. Young adolescence can be a time when a young person decides, perhaps without even realizing it, that he or she accepts, likes, or will hang out with only people who seem a lot like him or her. We can intervene with advisory experiences that open eyes and hearts to the importance of learning about cultural variations, the cost of refusing to mingle or tolerate, and the possibilities for those who understand the rich lives available to people who have the courage to take a stand for inclusion and tolerance.

THEME: CUT FROM COMMON CLOTH

A good way to begin to break down the barriers among people is to encourage them to know one another. It soon becomes apparent that we are all cut from basically the same human cloth, and that although the cloth may vary somewhat from group to group, we have a great deal in common. Our differences can be the spice of our lives together, so the challenge is to recognize our similarities and enjoy our differences. Middle level students do this well if we set up the right structures and make attractive invitations.

---

1   CPR

Greeting: Sawa Bona Greeting
Sharing: Think, Ink, Pair, Share: *Write on a Post-it as many cultures or countries as you know from which you are descended. Share with your partner, and put your Post-it on the chart or board.* Read all the cultures of the advisory, including your own.
Activity: Where Are You From?

> Jambo, Advisory Students!
> America is sometimes called a "melting pot," a "gorgeous **tapestry**," or a "tossed salad." Today we'll get some insight into why. Which phrase do you think better represents the mixture of cultures in the United States? Write your name under your answer.
> MELTING POT
> GORGEOUS TAPESTRY
> TOSSED SALAD

2   CPR

Greeting: Language Greeting

Sharing: Individual Share, with teacher sharing about one culture in his or her heritage. Whole group brainstorms questions to learn more about a person's culture or background. A few of these questions can be asked of the teacher if there is time.

Note: In sharing on days to follow, students highlight a custom or tradition, and may bring in an artifact or picture related to the custom. You can create a sign-up list for volunteers to share about their heritage. You can focus on these for several weeks, or you can intersperse heritage shares during the semester.

Activity: Hands Up, with students naming their own culture or any culture, one apiece, no repeats

Note: For a sample list of ways to say "hello" in different languages, see page 220. You can also make a list available to students. See www.elite.net/~runner/jennifers/gmorning.htm for more examples.

> **Dzien Dobre**, Friends!
>
> That's a Polish greeting. Do you know how to say "good morning" or "hello" in a language besides English? Do some research at home or online to find out how your ancestors may have greeted each other. Check out our list for ways to say "hello" in different languages. If possible, learn a game popular with your cultural group that we could play in advisory.

3   CPR

Greeting: Language Greeting: match the choice of language to the heritage of the student sharing that day

Sharing: Partner Share: *How did you get your name? What is its significance?* A few volunteer may share out. Take a hand count of how many students know where their names come from. Suggest that those who do not know find out, so that all can share the origins of their names when they do their heritage shares.

Activity: Me Too OR I Never OR When the Cold Wind Blows

Note: Students can share the possible origins of their customs with a partner after you read the daily news together.

> Buenos Dias, Amigos! (You can match the greeting to the heritage share for the day.)
>
> One fine thing about the variety of cultures in the world is that they have invented many interesting and enjoyable customs. Write below on your number line a family custom you enjoy. Be ready to share about how you think that custom came to be.

4 A+: Game-playing (classroom or gym)

Greeting: Language Greeting

Activity: Students try out games from different cultures; may do it as cross-advisory games (page 112). Examples: Hmong Courtship Game; Cup and Stick Game; Inuit High Kick; Tug of War

Reflection: Whole group: *What is one thing you now know about _____ culture?*

Note: As illustrated, heritage shares can take place in either CPR or in an A+ advisory—your choice.

> **Boozhoo** (pronounced boo-ZHOO), Friends! (Ojibwe greeting)
>
> People all over the world like to have fun, and they have invented thousands of ways to play. Today we'll try out some games that are very old, but perhaps new to us: the Cup and Stick Game and String Games. Start **flexing** your fingers— these are games of dexterity!

5 A+: Drawing

Greeting: Shape Greeting

Activity: Inside-Outside Shape *Draw an outline around yourself (someone else can trace around you) and fill the figure in with words or small images of the people, places, customs, and family, friends, neighborhood, school influences that have shaped you and continue to shape you.*

Reflection: Written: *Name the three biggest influences upon you. What percentage of who you are would you say was shaped by those influences?* (The percentages should add up to close to 100%.) Possible influences:

- Family
- Friends
- Neighborhood
- School
- Religion
- Sports or other interests
- Media (TV, Internet, advertising, etc.)

> Welcome, People!
>
> We'll be making full-length **portraits** of ourselves today, visual and verbal. After we draw an outline figure, we'll fill it in with words that describe us, our family, customs, friends, favorite things to do, see, eat, and listen to. These are the things that help shape us into the people that we are.

THEME: THE COST OF US VS. THEM

The world has paid a big price for prejudice and exclusion in the past and we continue to pay the price today. It is crucial to our thriving—maybe even our survival—that we find ways to include each other, with all our differences. Biodiversity makes nature thrive; cultural diversity brings similar benefits for people.

1   CPR

Greeting: Huddle Up Greeting, with categories of differences between people, for example:

- gender
- age (e.g., 12 or younger; 13 or older)
- family size (big families—3 or more siblings
- smaller families—2 or fewer siblings)
- birth order (1st, 2nd, 3rd, etc.)
- jobs (student and teacher)
- height (5' 2" and under; 5' 3" and over)
- place of birth (city, state)

Sharing: Partner Share: *What sort of person do you like to spend time with?*

Activity: Me Too OR When the Cold Wind Blows

> Good Morning, Group!
> How much do we have in common as a group? Before CPR begins, find someone with whom you share some **characteristic**, and sit by that person.

2   CPR

Greeting: Huddle Up Greeting, using new categories

Sharing: Think, Pair, Share: *Tell about a time when you felt you were the only one in a group that was different in some way (e.g., you were new, or you were older or younger, or you were the "new kid," or you were the only person of your gender, race, culture, etc., in the group).* Volunteers share out.

Activity: Passing Game

> Greetings, Friends!
> Most of us have had moments when we felt like the odd person, the one who was different in some way. People seem to want to hang out with others who are like them in some way. But **diversity** is everywhere, so the ability to socialize and work with people who are different from us is an important personal strength. How good are you at hanging out with people who are different from you? Indicate which category fits you best.
> I avoid mixed groups
> I get along with most people
> I enjoy variety in the people I **associate** with

3   CPR (with a guest)

Greeting: Color Coded Greeting

Sharing: Individual Share (guest only shares) The guest is a person with a trait (class, color, culture, age, or an invisible trait such as sexual orientation) often in the minority in US culture. Whoever the guest is, he or she must be willing to share about his/her difference(s), apparent or not.

Activity: Rare Birds: *Write about a way that you are different from most of the people you know* (e.g., I like to eat eggplant; I speak two languages).

> Greetings, Rare Birds!
>
> Today we're going to look at differences among us. Be thinking about a way (big or small) that you are different from lots of other people you know. We have a guest, so be sure to greet and welcome him if you have a chance before CPR begins.
>
> Sharing: What are some qualities, interests, or **preferences** you share with the people with whom you enjoy hanging out? (e.g., We all like basketball; we all like to read; we all like to listen to the same kind of music, etc.)

4   CPR

Greeting: Name Card Greeting

Sharing: Whip Share: *Are you a stay-at-home or an explorer? In other words, are you a person who prefers to hang out with kids who are very similar to you in looks and lifestyle, or are you an explorer, who likes to mingle with a variety of folks, many of whom seem to be different from you?*

Activity: Affinity Process

Note: When processing the news, ask for a show of hands on the question: *Are your groups mostly homogeneous, heterogeneous, or some of each?* (Make sure students understand the definitions of those words.)

> Hello to All!
>
> Our advisory, of course, is a group that has members. Think about other groups you spend time with, in or out of school. To how many different groups (formal or informal) do you belong? Write the number on your number line.

5   A+: Read Aloud

Greeting: Good Morning, Friend Greeting

Activity: Read Aloud: *Star-Bellied Sneetches* by Dr. Seuss. Divide into 4 groups each with a copy of the book and do round-robin reading and showing pictures. See page 106 for more about Read Alouds.

Reflection: Whole group: *Name some qualities that can distinguish ourselves as different from others* (brainstorm a list).

> *Buon Giorno*, Friends!
>
> "The world is so full of number of things. It's a wonder we all aren't happy as kings!" One of the reasons people are unhappy is the trouble we have getting along with people who are different from us. That's the problem in the book we're going to read aloud this morning, The Star-Bellied Sneetches, by Dr. Seuss.

6   A+: Council

Greeting: All Group Greeting
Activity: Council meeting (page 119) with topic: Exclusion *Tell briefly about a time when you felt excluded, or when you excluded someone else, or when you saw someone being excluded.*
Reflection: Written: *Describe something you learned from listening to stories of exclusion.*

> *Greetings, Good Students!*
> *Today is a Council Meeting day. Circle up, and we'll listen and talk about the topic of* **exclusion**.

7   A+: Simulation

Greeting: Language Greeting
Activity: Competing for Resources Around the World
Reflection: Whole group: Each small group answers questions in turn.

> *Hello, Advisory Students!*
> *Many people frequently go to bed hungry. Our exercise will give us some* **insights** *into why.*

What did you notice about the way the world's population is divided?
What did you notice about the way the world's resources are distributed?
Is the present arrangement fair?
Is the arrangement practical? What does it cost the world?
What price might we (U.S.) or you personally pay for the present disparity?

THEME: EACH DEPENDS UPON THE OTHER

In spite of the differences among people in the world, we are all much more connected than we seem to be. In a sense, the entire population of the planet feeds from the same source, breathes the same air, uses the same limited supply of resources. Today it is more apparent than ever that as humans we depend upon each other for our well-being.

---

1 CPR

Greeting: Cumulative Greeting
Sharing: Whip Share *Who is someone you depend upon? Why?*
Activity: Key Punch: in the last round, everyone plays against the clock for best time

> Dear Earthlings,
> Experts tell us that we are all **dependent** upon each other in small and big ways. Think about someone you depend on, and think about someone who depends on you. Be ready to share.

---

2 CPR

Greeting: Silent Greeting
Sharing: Whip Share: *How are you connected to the governor of our state?* (Or select another public figure.) *How does he/she affect you directly or indirectly?*
Activity: Continuous Tale
Note: Process a few ideas for each question after you read the chart.

> Good Morning, Fellow Humans!
> Scientists tell us that everyone and everything is connected. How can it be that the **flutter** of a butterfly wing in Brazil is connected to a tornado in the midwestern U.S.? How do professional sports affect you, even if you don't watch any teams play? Think about it and be ready to share an idea.

---

3 CPR

Greeting: Whole Group Language Greeting (page 221, Language Greeting variation)
Sharing: Partner Share: *What would be fun and what would be hard for you living on a commune?*
Each partnership shares out to whole group.
Activity: Five People Standing

> Howdy, Partners!
> In the course of American history, there have been many groups who have attempted **communal** living. What is a skill it would take to live closely within a group? Write an idea on your number line.

4   A+: Visual Image

Greeting: Puzzle Greeting

Activity: Puzzle Picture: Make a numbered grid on top of a large, colorful poster that is not too detailed. (e.g., American flag, famous sculpture or monument, abstract painting, or a map of the world) Students are each assigned a numbered square to reproduce with colored pencils or markers, crayons, Craypas, or collage (everyone must use the similar materials). Then the advisory group tries to assemble all the parts they have made to recreate the whole image. This activity will probably take more than one advisory. Students can also work on their square at home. The exciting moment is when the image is reassembled. The process teaches close observation, accurate work, and collaboration.

Reflection: Whole group: *What was a highlight of this project for you? What might you do better next time in such a project? How would the skills we used to complete this project be useful in the world of work?*

> Hello, Puzzlers!
>
> Today both our greeting and our activity will involve puzzles. Puzzles are a good **metaphor** for separate things (or people) coming together to make a whole. When everything fits, it's very satisfying.

5   A+: Visual image

Greeting: Climbing a Tree Greeting (page 226, Tower Greeting variation)

Activity: Tree of Life: students make a collage tree from colored paper and place in its branches the names the members of their family, friends, neighbors, pets, and others important in their lives. In this exercise, "family" is taken to mean all those whose lives touch and influence yours.

Reflection: Partner Share: *Name two strong points about your partner's work. Ask a question about the members of your partner's Family Tree.*

> Good Morning, Sunshine!
>
> Here are the lyrics from an old song:
>
> "It's a Tree of Life to those who hold fast to it, and all of its supporters are happy."
>
> What do people mean when they talk about the "Tree of Life"? We'll talk about the great Tree today.

6   A+: Game

Greeting: Silent Greeting

Activity: ESP

Reflection: Whole group processes the activity:

What made your group decide to change?

What made your group decide to stay with what you had?

Why do you think some people were reluctant to take on a different sound or gesture?

What helped you compromise?

What dangers to a group do you see in individuality?

What dangers to a group do you see in compromise?

> Good Morning to All!
>
> We'll play a magical game today called ESP, **Extra-sensory Perception**. Somehow or other, we human beings find ways to communicate with each other, even when we are not talking. This will be a fun way to see how good we are at coming to agreement without a specific plan to do so.

THEME: A WORLD IN FLUX

Things are moving and changing constantly. What looks like a stable environment is really altering in big ways and small every moment. This is good news when you think of some of the problems we have around the globe. As long as things are changing, there is hope that we can guide that change towards a better world, one in which people finally figure out how to get along.

---

1   CPR

Greeting: Wild Card Greeting
Sharing: Whip Share: *What is one thing you have gotten better at doing?*
Activity: Something's Changed OR What Are You Doing?

> **Ciao,** Changers!
>
> Between the time you came into this room and the time you leave, you will have changed in many ways. It's a fact! Put your initials under each of the ways below that you think we will all have changed (no matter how small the change) before advisory is over.
>
> Physically
> Feelings
> Ideas & information
> Relationships

---

2   CPR

Greeting: Choice of Voice Greeting (page 215, see All Group Greeting variation)
Sharing: Whip Share: *How flexible are you? Is change easy or hard for you? Give one example for your answer.*
Activity: Zumi Zumi OR Copy Cat

> **Felicitations,** Flexible People!
>
> Scientists tell us that big changes (and sometimes small ones) are challenging for people, and if a lot of things change all at once in your life, you may experience that as stressful and upsetting. Show with your initials under one of the numbers below how many big changes are going on in your life these days.
>
> None   1   2   3   More than 3

---

3   CPR

Greeting: Movie Star Greeting
Sharing: Individual Share: *Tell about a time when you had to adapt to a change.* You may want to share first to model.
Activity: Chase the Caboose OR Is This Seat Taken

> Greetings, Friends!
>
> One comfort we have when things aren't going well is that things never stay the same. The change and **flux** of life may be an advantage. Write on your number line one good thing about change.

4 A+: Game

Greeting: One-Minute Mingle Greeting
Activity: Four Corner Thinking: students group and regroup within the room to reflect their opinions on a series of subjects.
Reflection: Whole group: take a few responses for each question.
What did you notice about this activity?
How many of you took the opportunity to change your position?
How many were tempted, but didn't? (Show of hands for these questions)
How did you feel about publicly taking a stand on a topic?
Why is it important to make your opinion public sometimes?
What are the benefits of changing your point of view? What are the costs?

> Hello, Advisory Students!
> Scientists tell us that the ability to change and adapt to new **circumstances** is one of the most important survival qualities that animals have. Today we'll see how flexible we are in our opinions.

5 A+: Drawing

Greeting: Fist-Tap Greeting (page 216, Basic Greeting variation)
Activity: Exquisite Corpse, with small groups (about 6-8 people per group). Each group circulates one paper and gives their completed drawing a title. The person who started the drawing shares her group's drawing and title, and explains the image she originally had in mind.
Reflection: Partner Share followed by volunteers sharing out (1 or 2)
This activity forced things to change. How open are you to changing when you are in the midst of a project or a game or a conversation?

> Good Morning, Students!
> Today we'll be creating an image on paper together. It will be a mystery to all of us until it is revealed at the end. Welcome to the **Exquisite Corpse!**

6 A+: Inside-Outside Circle

Greeting: Inside-Outside Greeting: use the variation that has students trying new gestures each time
Activity: Inside-Outside Circle with topic: Ways that I have changed/am changing.
Since you started 5th grade, in what ways have you changed the following:

Clothing size	*Sleeping habits*
Exercise	*Eating habits*
Friends	*Music*
Homework	*Having fun*
Relationships with family members	
Reading, math, writing, science, history	

> Boker Tov, Transformers!
> It's one thing to be changing all the time (whether we want to or not!) and another to be aware of your changes. Today we'll try to become more aware. Think about at least one important way in which you have changed in the last couple of years, or are currently changing.

Reflection: Exit Card, signed (page 103) *What is one way you would like to change? What is one way you think you ought to change?*

THEME: PERSONAL POWER: THE COURAGE TO TAKE A STAND

The power that lies within humans seems to be much stronger than the power people have over each other. Part of that personal power is the ability and willingness to take a stand and declare yourself in support of what is good for all of us.

---

1 CPR

Greeting: Name Card Greeting

Sharing: Partner Share: *Describe someone you know who is brave enough to stand up for something or someone.*

Activity: Me Too, saying *I admire people who....* Each student adds a quality or behavior they admire. Example: *I admire people who tell the truth.* First, discuss with students the kinds of community-building qualities we are looking for, and what sorts of qualities would be inappropriate to refer to in this game.

> Good Morning, Friends!
> Today we'll be discussing people who are brave enough to take a stand for something important. Be ready to share about someone in your life who seems brave enough to do that and what that person would, or does, stand up for.

---

2 CPR

Greeting: Reach Out Greeting (page 217, Choice Greeting variation) Students make an effort to greet someone they haven't talked to yet today.

Sharing: Partner Share: *What is one thing you would be willing to do to make school a safer, more inclusive place?*

Activity: Twenty Questions: person in the middle is a well-known hero (or group) who took a stand for something important.

> Good Day, Fellow **Agents,**
> Some people step up to a situation and do something about changing it. They are sometimes called "Change Agents." Think about a way that you could be a Change Agent in our school and make it a safer, happier place to be. Be ready to share.

---

3 A+: Read Aloud

Greeting: Sawa Bona Greeting

Activity: Read a "Giraffe" story, a story about someone who has taken a stand and made a difference. See page 106 for more about Read Alouds.

Reflection: Think, Pair, Share: *What would it be like if we had a world in which no one stood up and called for change?*

> Good Morning, **Allies!**
> Today we'll read a story about someone who had the personal power to take a strong stand for something he believed in. That is how most of the major changes in history have happened: one person took a stand and held fast. Maybe you are or will be such a person!

4   A+: Scenarios

Greeting: Good Morning, Friend Greeting (page 221, Language Greeting variation)

Activity: What Would You Do? As a second step, partners make up a What would you do? scenario about a social issue (e.g., A friend tells you that a girl/boy likes you. What do you say or do?) and exchange questions with another pair. Give partners about 2 minutes to write their question on a card, and 3 to 5 minutes to pose the questions to partners.

Reflection: Acknowledge your partner for the work done.

> **Aloha, Activists!**
>
> Today we're going to spring into action—at least in our minds! Get ready to think quickly and make a courageous decision on the spot. That's the stuff that heroes (and giraffes) are made of!

---

5   A+: Reflection

Greeting: Reach Out Greeting (page 217, Choice Greeting variation) *Greet someone you don't see much outside of school.*

Activity: Taking a Stand: each person folds a paper into four quarters and writes the following four headings in the four quarters:

1) I excluded

2) I was excluded

3) I saw someone excluded and didn't do anything

4) I saw someone excluded and spoke up

Write an example from your life of each one of these situations.

Reflection: Exit Card (page 103) *I am willing to take a stand and speak up in the future when and if I or someone else is excluded or otherwise pre-judged. Indicate Yes or No on your card.* Report the results at the next advisory.

> **Buenos Dias,** Brave People!
>
> Today is a day you can stand up and be counted. We'll look at opportunities to take a stand, and you will be invited to make a commitment. It might be the most important invitation you ever received!

UNIT: SOCIETAL ISSUES

Goals

Our students will soon step into a larger world. The following advisories help them prepare to live in the world successfully, by sparking their interest in current events, citizenship, and the crucially important arena of education.

THEME: CURRENT EVENTS

One way to participate effectively in your society is to keep yourself aware of what's going on and why. This means that we not only need access to the news, we also need tools to understand it. Practice in reporting and discussing current events helps students develop habits of mind that are inquiring, accurate, interpretive, and tolerant of diverse points of view.

---

1 CPR

Greeting: Greet Three Greeting

Sharing: Individual Share: student shares by telling the topic of a news story. You can go first to model the format. From a list of posted questions, students ask questions and share answers.

- Who was involved?
- What happened?
- When did it happen?
- Where did it happen?
- Why did it happen?
- What does this have to do with us?

Activity: Quiz Show, with a news story topic

> *Good Morning, Readers!*
>
> *Today is [date], and we'll be looking at some of the news of the world. Clip out of a newspaper an article that is interesting and appropriate for our advisory to hear about, and be ready to report.*

---

2 CPR

Note: Create in advance a "News Fact Form" containing the following questions and space for answers: *Who is the story about? What happened? When did it happen? Where did it happen? Why did it happen?*

Greeting: What's Happening? Greeting

Sharing: Individual Share: student shares a news item, and individuals from the advisory ask the fact-finding questions: *Who? What? When? Where? Why?* while a scribe records. For the closing to each share, ask for someone to re-tell the story, based on the facts described in the scribe's list. Then ask the group: *Why does this matter to us?* Have a couple of shares if time.

Activity: Park Bench: students who have not yet shared their article talk about all the facts except *What* facts. Class tries to guess what happened.

> *Good Morning, Reporters!*
>
> *You and a partner choose a clipping from yesterday or cut one from today's paper and be ready to **analyze** it for its basic facts: Who, What, When, Where, Why. Use the News Fact Form provided to record your answers for your news story.*

3   CPR

Greeting: Formal Greeting (page 216, Basic Greeting variation)

Sharing: Individual Share: *Share about your own life in a way that tells listeners the answers to the fact questions: Who, What, When, Where, and Why.*

Activity: Connections

> *Good Morning, News* **Analysts!**
> Write each type of fact about a news story on a separate card, i.e., one card each for the answers to Who, What, When, Where, and How. We'll be playing a game with the cards this morning in CPR.

4   A+: Game

Greeting: Introduction Greeting

Activity: Four Corner Thinking, focused on a news story. Teacher reads a brief news story, reads a series of statements about the story, and students group and regroup within the room to reflect their opinions about the statements. Teacher calls on one or two students in each corner to give their opinions and at least one fact to support or illustrate them. Example statement: *Mr. Smith was to blame.* Strongly agree fact: *I agree because he was aware of the problem first.* Strongly disagree fact: *I disagree because the boys were responsible for their own actions.*

Reflection: Whole group: *With fingers 0 to 5 representing easy to difficult, how hard is it to base your opinions on facts? With fingers 0 to 5 representing easy to difficult, how important is it to base your opinions on facts?*

> *Good Morning, Newscasters!*
> Newspapers and news broadcasts contain both facts and opinions. Opinions are only as good as the facts they are based upon. Today we'll hear your opinions on what's happening in the news. Be ready to **cite** facts to support your opinion.

5   A+

Greeting: One-Minute Mingle Greeting

Activity: Students write on a Post-it an opinion with facts to support it. Example topics:

- Pop machines on school premises
- School uniforms
- Graduation requirements
- Lock-in parties at school

You can assign one topic to everyone, or allow choice.

Reflection: Place all the Post-its on chart or board (under the topic if you've given a choice).   Read opinions with their supporting facts to determine collective class opinion. *Have we been persuasive with our opinions? Thumbs up, down, or sideways.*

> *Hello, Opinion-makers!*
> Today you'll write a short opinion piece on the following topic:_____. Make sure you support your opinion with at least one fact; unsupported opinions aren't very **convincing!**

THEME: CITIZENSHIP: RIGHTS AND RESPONSIBILITIES

Being a citizen is a mixed bag. In a democracy it gives you certain rights, and it also requires that you exercise responsibility, so that your exercising rights does not infringe on those of others. In a society—or in any group—you give and take. The challenge is to keep the balance fair and just.

---

1   CPR

Greeting: Basic Greeting, repeating *Shalom,* _____
Sharing: Partner Share, followed by partners sharing one idea with the whole group
What is social responsibility, and what does it have to do with being a good citizen?
Activity: Shrinking World

> Dear Advisory Students,
> You are a **citizen** of our school community. As a citizen, you have rights and responsibilities. Name one of each at your number line.
>
> \#   Rights   Responsibilities

---

2   CPR

Greeting: Basic Greeting, repeating *Namaste,* _____
Sharing: Whip Share: *Whom do you consider a leader in your community? Why?*
Activity: Knots

> Good Morning, Leaders!
> People have a wide variety of ideas about what makes a good leader. Write on your number line one **characteristic** you think a leader should have.

---

3   CPR

Greeting: Greet and Meet
Sharing: Partner Share: *Discuss the list of characteristics of a good leader from yesterday and put a tally mark next to the one you and your partner think is most important.*
Activity: Knots with a designated leader for each group OR Line Ups with a designated leader

> Greetings, **Fellow** Citizens!
> Here is the list we made yesterday of characteristics of a good leader. Today we'll decide which are the most important ones. Think about which ones stand out for you, and be ready to vote.

---

4   A+: Team-building Game

Greeting: Shape Greeting
Activity: Shape Up, with and without a designated leader
Reflection: Whole group: *How did the leader help the group? Was it easier to make the shape when you had a leader? Was it as enjoyable?*

> Good Morning, Today's Leaders!
> A good leader can make a task easier and more enjoyable. Today we'll work as teams with and without leaders to see what difference leadership makes.

5 A+: Opinion Game

Greeting: Handshake Greeting (page 216, Basic Greeting variation)

Activity: Four Corner Thinking or Line Ups

Use corners or a lineup as a way to sort out opinions, with one end or certain corners representing "strongly in favor" and the other "strongly against." Read statements about leadership, and have students decide where they stand. Use the samples below or make your own. You may decide to read only a couple, and give groups more time to talk about their points of view, and individuals time to change their positions if they wish to.

Statement examples: *A good leader...*

Gets all citizens to vote.

Redistributes money so that everyone has enough.

Bans hugging in schools.

Makes sure that everyone has health care.

Requires everyone between ages 13 and 18 to do community service.

Sets high standards for graduation from high school.

Sets high standards for who may drive.

Keeps religion out of public education.

Cuts taxes and governmental spending.

Raises taxes to pay for better schools, roads, and health care.

Reflection: Exit Card (page 103)
Respond on a scale of 1 to 5, with 5 being the strongest "yes."
Did this exercise make you think hard?
Did this exercise help you understand some of the issues a citizen must consider?

> Dear Citizens,
> Today you are called upon to express your opinions about matters important to our state and country. Get ready to think carefully. Have facts and examples to support what you believe.

---

6 A+: Carousel

Greeting: One-Minute Mingle Greeting

Activity: Carousel: *List ideas you have about ways a citizen could contribute to his or her school; neighborhood; city; state; country; world.* Groups of 4 or 5 visit each of the charts with a few minutes to write ideas under each topic. End with a Gallery Walk

Reflection: Exit Card (page 103) *What was one good idea you contributed or read about during the carousel?*

> Welcome, Good Citizens!
> Today we'll brainstorm ways that good citizens can contribute to their schools, neighborhoods, cities, states, countries, and world. Get ready to think hard!

THEME: EDUCATION

Although our students are currently immersed in education, it is a topic they may not think about very often. They can deepen their commitment to learning and broaden their understanding of what learning entails by looking together at the purposes and purviews of education in general, and their own education in particular.

---

1   CPR

Greeting: Handshake Greeting (page 216, Basic Greeting variation)
Sharing: Partner Share, followed by partners sharing one idea with the whole group:
What is (are) the purpose(s) of education?
Activity: Hands Up OR Concentration with education topics

> Greetings, Good Students!
> This week we're setting out to prove that school can be both meaningful and fun. Be thinking about what is the purpose and **purview** of education. Why is it a law in our country that all children must be educated in either a public, private, or home school?

---

2   CPR

Greeting: Snake Greeting
Sharing: Whip Share: *What should students at the middle level be taught that they are not taught today?*
Activity: Green Door

> Dear Thinkers,
> What if you were in charge of the subjects and topics students must learn in middle school? Think about the **curriculum** you would establish—what's important to know at this stage of your learning?

---

3   CPR

Greeting: Ball Toss Greeting
Sharing: Affinity Share: *What are the most important things you have learned in school so far?*
Activity: Simultaneous Clap

> Good Morning, Lucky Learners!
> Look back and **contemplate** your education so far. What grade was the hardest for you? What grade have you enjoyed most so far?
>
> Name   Hardest/Most Enjoyable

4   CPR

Greeting: Name Card Greeting
Sharing: Whip Share: *What are some qualities of a successful learner?*
Activity: What's in a Name? *Our topic is you as a successful learner. What are some things you have done or attitudes you have that have helped you learn?*

> G'day, Mates!
>
> Here's a **survey** to complete. Think about teachers you have had, and indicate with a check beneath the two qualities you think were most important in the teachers with whom you learned the most.
>
> SENSE OF HUMOR
> FAIR
> STRICT
> KIND
> KNOWLEDGABLE

5   A+

Greeting: Cumulative Greeting
Activity: Associations, with topic of education
Reflection: Whole group:
What was fun about this game?
What might make the game better?
What can you learn from this game?

> Howdy, Partners!
>
> Today is a day when work will be play! Get ready for a game that **revs** up your mind.

6   A+

Greeting: Greet Three Greeting
Activity: Charades OR Pictionary in partners or small groups
Reflection:

In today's game, how were CARES skills demonstrated?
How were academic skills demonstrated?
Can we think of other games we played this year that required similar CARES or academic skills?

> Greetings, Gamers!
>
> Today is another day of learning fun. We'll play a theater game about education. Pick a subject card from the box and think about something you have learned in that subject. Soon you'll get to share with all of us.

UNIT: DOWN MEMORY LANE—CLOSING THE YEAR

Goals

The learning year must not be allowed to trickle away. Students need help thinking about what kind of learner they have been during the year, and what's possible for next year, so they are prepared to stretch and grow. In a healthy school there is some sadness in the last weeks of school, whether students admit it or not. For some students, school is the safest, most positive place in their lives, and they are unhappy that the doors will close until the next school year. Relationships have been built, and the last weeks of advisory are a perfect place to reflect on what we have come to mean to each other, acknowledge our community, and celebrate our accomplishments. Accomplished people reflect on what they have done. Good advisories at the end of the year offer closure and help prepare students for their next steps.

1   CPR

Greeting: Snowball Greeting
Sharing: Whip Share: *What is something you'll remember from this year?*
Activity: CARES Acknowledgment

> Dear Advisory Students,
>
> As we come to the end of the school year, we'll take time to reflect on the year. We will especially notice the **highlights** of learning and friendship. Be ready to share about something you'll remember from this year.

2   CPR

Greeting: Great Greeting (page 215, All Group Greeting variation)
Sharing: Think, Pair, Share: *As you think about what you have done this past school year, what is something you are proud of?*
Activity: Twenty Questions, with names of classmates

> Aloha, Accomplished Ones!
>
> Looking back on this year in school, think about ways you have worked hard in your subject classes and in friendships. Maybe your major **accomplishment** this year has been in the area of social skills. For example, perhaps you are getting a handle on your self-control. Be ready to write and share about something you have accomplished.

3   CPR

Greeting: One-Minute Mingle Greeting
Sharing: Snowball Share: *What is something someone has done to help you in this advisory?*
Activity: Fan Mail

> **Holá,** Helpful People!
> We've spent the school year together learning, playing, talking, and helping each other. Think about the people in this advisory and the helpful things you have seen people do during the year. Can you think of a time when you were helpful to others in our group? Be ready to share.

4   CPR

Greeting: Ball Toss Greeting
Sharing: Whip Share: *What qualities or characteristics make for a good game?* Have a couple of students scribe the answers, putting tally marks to signify repeats. Read the list at the end, and ask for comments or questions directed to the whole group.
Activity: Around the World with topic: Games we have played during the year

> Greetings, Game-players!
> We have had fun together this year playing a lot of games. Write the name of a game we've played in one of the bubbles. Let's see how many we can remember. One **apiece**—no repeats!

5   CPR

Greeting: Silent Greeting
Sharing: Individual Share: *Tell about a memorable moment from this year.* Have a brief conversation with students first about what is appropriate to share.
Activity: Freeze Frame with topic: Memorable moments depicted by small groups; class gets three guesses, and then the group tells the story.

> Dear Students,
> When you look back on this year, some things will remain in your memory—maybe for your whole life! Think about something **memorable** from the year that stands out for you.

6   A+

Greeting: Syllables Greeting
Activity: What's in a Name? *Write a list of your strengths, accomplishments, and high points this year.*
Reflection: Gallery Walk: each student has one Post-it note to write specific, descriptive, positive comment(s) about one person's work.

> Good Morning to All!
> What's in a name? Our names are important to us for many reasons. Today we'll use our names to make a list of positive qualities about ourselves. Think about your good points, and (in all **humility**!) the ways that you shine. We'll be writing today.

7   A+

Greeting: Name Everyone Greeting
Activity: Reflection Book: assemble a simple book (e.g., 8 ½ x 11 paper folded in half and stapled down the center) to collect student reflections. *Write about highlights, accomplishments, or events in this past year.*
Reflection: Whole group: *What was one thing you mentioned as a memory from this year?*

Welcome, Advisory Students!

Today we'll start recording our memories from this year in a hand-made reflection book entitled Memories of [year]. Pick up your materials and read the instructions for making the book.

8   A+

Greeting: Crystal Ball Greeting
Activity: Reflection Book: *Write about your hopes and plans for next year in your book.*
Reflection: Whip Share: *What is one goal you have for next year?*

Greetings, Good People!

Today we'll continue writing in our **reflection** books, thinking about what we want to happen next year. Planners are more likely to get what they want than those who just wait to see what happens!

9   A+

Greeting: High Five or any Hand Jive Greeting
Activity: Reflection Book Autographs: students exchange notes and signatures on the autograph pages of their memory books.
Reflection: Whole group: *What is something you will remember from our advisory?*

Buenos Dias, Amigos!

Today is the day you've been looking forward to—we'll be signing each other's reflection books. Remember to keep it short and positive, so there will be lots of room for everyone to show her or his support for each person.

10   A+

Greeting: Choice Greeting
Activity: Touch Someone Who
Reflection: Cheers, individuals name something to cheer about and the kind of cheer the group will do

Au Revoir, Mes Amis!

This is our last advisory of the year, and I am sad to say goodbye to you. I will remember all the good times and interesting conversations we've had together. Today we'll spend our time acknowledging each other for the ways we have been friends. Have a great summer, and thanks for being who you are!

Greeting, Share, & Activity Index

GREETING	Level	Quick	Page#
	Social Challenge: Level 1: Acquainted Level 2: Familiar Level 3: Comfortable	Good for A+ advisories	
All Group Greeting	1 Acquainted		215
Ball Toss Greeting	2 Familiar		215
Baseball Greeting	1 Acquainted		216
Basic Greeting	1 Acquainted	Quick	216
Book Character Greeting	2 Familiar		217
Choice Greeting	2 Familiar		217
Choice of Voice Greeting	2 Familiar		215
Choice of Gesture Greeting	2 Familiar		215
Climbing a Tree Greeting	1 Acquainted		226
Color-Coded Greeting	1 Acquainted		217
Crystal Ball Greeting	3 Comfortable		217
Cumulative Greeting	2 Familiar		217
Cumulative High Five Greeting	2 Familiar		217
Cumulative List Greeting	2 Familiar		218
Double High Five Greeting	1 Acquainted	Quick	219
Elevator Greeting	1 Acquainted	Quick	218
Fist-tap Greeting	1 Acquainted	Quick	216
Football Greeting	1 Acquainted		216
Formal Greeting	1 Acquainted		216
Gift Greeting	3 Comfortable		218
Good Morning, Friend Greeting	1 Acquainted		221
Great Greeting	2 Familiar		215
Greet and Meet	3 Comfortable		218
Greet Three Greeting	1 Acquainted	Quick	218
Guess My Greeting	3 Comfortable		219
Gushy Greeting	3 Comfortable		219
Hand Jive Greeting	2 Familiar	Quick	219
Handshake Greeting	1 Acquainted		216
High Five Greeting	1 Acquainted	Quick	219
High Five/Low Five Greeting	1 Acquainted	Quick	219
Huddle Up Greeting	1 Acquainted	Quick	219
Inside-Outside Greeting	1 Acquainted		219
Introduction Greeting	1 Acquainted		220
Knock Knock Greeting	3 Comfortable		220
Language Greeting	2 Familiar		220
Let Me See Your Walk Greeting	3 Comfortable		221
Mimic Greeting	3 Comfortable		221
Miss Mary Mack Greeting	2 Familiar		219
Movie Star Greeting	3 Comfortable		221
Name Card Greeting	1 Acquainted		221

ACTIVITY	Level	Specific Types	Content	Large Group	Page#
	Social Challenge: Level 1: Acquainted Level 2: Familiar Level 3: Comfortable	Getting-to-know-you Chair-changing Acknowledgment Team-building Trust-building Extended time Quick	Can be used for academic content	Suitable to more than one classroom	
Acknowledgment Buffet	2 Familiar	Acknowledgment; Extended			233
Affinity Process	2 Familiar	Getting-to-know-you		X	233
Alibi	1 Acquainted				233
All About Us Book	1 Acquainted	Extended time			176
All Hit Moonball	1 Acquainted	Team-building; Extended	X		233
Arm Hockey	2 Familiar				234
Around the World	2 Familiar		X		234
Board Games	1 Acquainted	Extended	X	X	107, 278
Careers	1 Acquainted	Extended	X		122
CARES Acknowledgment	3 Comfortable	Acknowledgment			234
Carousel	1 Acquainted	Extended	X	X	235
Charades	3 Comfortable		X		235
Chase the Caboose	3 Comfortable	Chair-changing			235
Cheers	1 Acquainted	Acknowledgment		X	264
Competency Puzzle	2 Familiar	Extended			158
Competing for Resources Around the World	1 Acquainted	Extended	X	X	235
Concentration	2 Familiar		X		236
Configurations	1 Acquainted	Team-building		X	237
Conflict Resolution	1 Acquainted	Extended			113, 272
Connections	2 Familiar		X		237
Continuous Tale	2 Familiar		X		237
Copy Cat	2 Familiar				237
Council	2 Familiar	Extended			119
Count to Ten	2 Familiar		X		237
Count Up	1 Acquainted				238
Cross-advisory Games	2 Familiar	Extended		X	112
Cumulative List	1 Acquainted		X		238
Cup and Stick Game	1 Acquainted	Extended	X	X	238
Driven to Trust	3 Comfortable	Trust-building; Extended		X	238
Eleven	1 Acquainted		X		238
ESP	2 Familiar	Team-building; Extended	X		238
Exquisite Corpse	2 Familiar	Extended			239
Fact or Fiction	1 Acquainted		X		239
Fan Mail	2 Familiar	Acknowledgment			239
Five People Standing	1 Acquainted				239
Four Corner Thinking	2 Familiar	Extended	X	X	240
Freeze Frame	3 Comfortable	Extended	X		240
Frogger	2 Familiar				241
Gallery Walk	1 Acquainted	Extended	X	X	241
Giants, Wizards, Elves	2 Familiar		X		242
Gone Missing	2 Familiar				242
Green Door	2 Familiar		X		242
Group Juggle	1 Acquainted	Team-building			242
Guess the Number	1 Acquainted		X		243

ACTIVITY	Level	Specific Types	Content	Large Group	Page#
Hands Up	2 Familiar		X		243
Heads or Tails	1 Acquainted		X		244
Helium Hoop	1 Acquainted	Team-building	X		244
Hmong Courtship Game	1 Acquainted	Getting-to-know-you	X		244
Hobby Survey	1 Acquainted	Extended			176
Homework Buddies	2 Familiar	Extended	X		110
Honey, Do You Love Me?	3 Comfortable				244
I Never	1 Acquainted				244
I Sit in the Grass	1 Acquainted				245
In the Manner of the Adverb	2 Familiar		X		245
Inside-Outside Circle	1 Acquainted	Quick or extended	X	X	245
Inside-Outside Shape	1 Acquainted	Extended			189
Inuit High Kick	2 Familiar	Team-building	X		246
Is This Seat Taken?	2 Familiar	Chair-changing			246
Joke Book	2 Familiar	Extended			174
Journaling	1 Acquainted	Quick or extended	X		143
Key Punch	2 Familiar	Team-building; Extended	X		246
Knots	3 Comfortable	Team-building; Extended	X		247
Line Ups	1 Acquainted	Team-building		X	247
Macaroni and Cheese	3 Comfortable	Trust-building; Extended			247
Magic Ball	2 Familiar				247
Making the Advisory Room Your Own	1 Acquainted	Extended			108
Me Too	1 Acquainted		X		248
Media Mania	3 Comfortable	Extended			248
Mix and Mingle	2 Familiar	Getting-to-know-you	X		248
Mrs. Mumble	2 Familiar				248
Name Game: Name Us All	2 Familiar				248
Name Game: Name with Gesture	1 Acquainted				249
Name Game: Toss a Name Game	1 Acquainted				249
No, No, No...	2 Familiar				249
Non-Verbal Messages	2 Familiar				249
Observation Olympics	1 Acquainted		X		250
Obstacle Course	3 Comfortable	Trust-building; Extended	X		250
One Frog	2 Familiar		X		250
One-Minute Talk	3 Comfortable	Getting-to-know-you		X	251
Paper Toss	2 Familiar		X		251
Park Bench	3 Comfortable	Extended	X		251
Passing Game	2 Familiar				252
Passing the Hoop	2 Familiar	Team-building		X	252
Peer Teaching	2 Familiar	Extended	X		109
Personality Inventory	1 Acquainted	Extended			268
Pico Firme Bago	1 Acquainted		X		252
Pictionary	2 Familiar		X		253
Planning Meeting	1 Acquainted	Extended			273
Popcorn Acknowledgment	2 Familiar	Acknowledgment			253
Power Foods	1 Acquainted	Extended	X		152, 282
Power Meals	1 Acquainted	Extended	X		153

ACTIVITY	Level	Specific Types	Content	Large Group	Page#
Problem-solving Meeting	1 Acquainted	Extended			118, 274
Puzzle Picture	1 Acquainted	Extended			194
Quiz Show	3 Comfortable	Extended	X		253
Ra-di-o	3 Comfortable				253
Rap a Rhythm	2 Familiar				254
Rare Birds	1 Acquainted				254
Read Aloud	1 Acquainted	Extended	X		106
Reflection Book	3 Comfortable	Extended	X		207
Role Play	1 Acquainted	Extended			114, 271
Sausages	2 Familiar				254
Save & Spend Board Game	1 Acquainted	Extended			186, 279
School Service Jobs	1 Acquainted	Extended			121, 281
Shape Up	1 Acquainted	Team-building; Extended	X		255
Shrinking World	3 Comfortable	Team-building; Extended	X		255
Shuffle 'em Up	2 Familiar				255
Silent Reading	1 Acquainted	Extended	X		104
Simultaneous Clap	1 Acquainted	Team-building		X	255
Snake Toss	1 Acquainted	Team-building		X	256
Social Action Theater	2 Familiar	Extended	X		116
Something Bad about Something Good	2 Familiar				256
Something's Changed	2 Familiar				256
Space Station	3 Comfortable				256
Stay and Stray	2-3	Extended	X		241
Table Top	2 Familiar	Extended	X	X	257
Tag Game: Elbow Tag	2 Familiar	Extended		X	257
Tag Game: Freeze Tag	1 Acquainted	Extended		X	257
Tag Game: Partner Tag	2 Familiar	Extended		X	257
Tag Game: Toilet Tag	2 Familiar	Extended		X	257
Talk Show	2 Familiar	Extended			258
Team- & Trust-building Activities	1-3	Extended		X	111
Team Red Light Green Light	2 Familiar	Team-building; Extended	X		258
Telephone	2 Familiar				258
Touch Someone Who	2-3	Acknowledgment			259
Tree of Life	1 Acquainted	Extended			194
Tug of War	3 Comfortable	Extended		X	260
Twenty Questions	2 Familiar		X		260
What Are You Doing?	3 Comfortable				260
What Would You Do?	2 Familiar	Extended	X		260
What's in a Name?	2 Familiar				261
What's Your Job?	2 Familiar	Chair-changing			261
When the Cold Wind Blows	2 Familiar	Chair-changing			261
Where Are You From?	2 Familiar	Chair-changing		X	261
Yes!	2 Familiar	Chair-changing			262
Zoom	1 Acquainted		X		262
Zumi Zumi	3 Comfortable				262

GREETINGS

• All Group Greeting

A student is selected to begin. She greets everyone: *Good morning, everyone!* She is greeted back by everyone in unison: *Good morning, Antonia!*

Variations:

1. **Choice of Voice Greeting**: students greet the group and then ask to be greeted back in a special voice. *Good morning, everybody. I would like to be greeted in a deep* (or sad, or gleeful, or British accent, etc.) *voice.* Group responds: *Good morning, Gerome!* (in the voice of choice)

2. **Choice of Gesture Greeting:** students greet the group, adding gestures to their names. *Good morning, everyone. I'm Josie* (with a waving gesture). Group responds: *Good morning, Josie* (imitating the waving gesture).

3. **Great Greeting:** each student greets with a different word that means "great." *Good morning, everybody, I feel fabulous* (or terrific, fantastic, etc.). Group responds: *Good morning, Tyril, you are fabulous.*

4. **Share Greeting:** use this in Activity Plus to create a quick share. Each student greets everyone and then gives a one-sentence share on a topic. When everyone has had a chance to share, you may wish to invite students to ask clarifying questions of one or more students. For example, on the topic of news from yesterday: *Good morning, everybody. Yesterday I sprained my ankle playing soccer.* Group responds: *Good morning, Jimmy.* At the end, someone may ask Jimmy how long it will take for his ankle to heal.

• Ball Toss Greeting

Materials: a soft, indoor ball or equivalent (bean bag, stuffed animal, etc.)
A student is selected to begin and is given a ball. She greets another student and then tosses that student the ball (model a safe, on-target, underhanded toss first). The recipient of the ball returns the greeting, greets someone else, and then tosses him the ball. This continues until all students have been greeted and have received the tossed ball. The last student greeted closes the loop by greeting and tossing the ball to the student who went first.

Variation: Add more balls during the greeting to increase the challenge, do a second round by reversing the order of ball toss and the greeting, starting with the last person and ending with the first.

• Baseball Greeting

Four kinds of baseball hits are singles, doubles, triples, and homeruns. Students use one of these four types of hits to greet someone else. Stand in a circle and select a student to begin. If he chooses a single, he greets the student next to him; those who choose a double will greet the student two chairs away, and so on. Students who choose double, triple, and homerun greetings may "high-five" students yet to be greeted as they pass by. Except for the first greeter, once a student has been greeted, she sits down and will no longer exchange high fives or be greeted again. The greeting continues until everyone has been greeted, with the last greeter greeting the first, to close the loop.

Variations: Other sports metaphors can be used for this greeting. Apply the appropriate scoring for different sports. **Football greetings** use a touchdown, field goal, safety, or extra-point format. Basketball greetings use free throw, two-point, and three-point baskets.

• Basic Greeting

A student is selected to begin. She greets the student next to her in the circle, *Good morning, _____;* he responds, *Good morning, _____,* turns to the person next to him and greets him, and the process is repeated around the circle. The audience's job is to watch each greeting carefully and quietly.

Variations:

1. **Handshake Greeting:** students greet with a handshake. Model and discuss how you want handshakes to look and feel. Components of a good handshake include body position (standing 12 to 18 inches apart), eye contact, grip, squeeze, flow, duration, release, etc. Handshaking is an important social skill. It's often assumed that students know how to execute a handshake properly, although they may not. *Good morning, _____* with a handshake.

2 **Formal Greeting:** students use only last names (*Good morning, Ms. Roberts. Good morning, Mr. Garcia.*), with or without a handshake.

3. Greet using different beginnings, such as *Ahoy, mate; Top o' the morning;* or *G'day (Ahoy, mate, Jessica.* Response: *Ahoy, mate, Tyrone).*

4. Rather than greeting one at a time, while others watch, students greet those to their left and right, all at the same time, waiting if the person is busy greeting another.

5. **Fist-Tap Greeting (Pound It!):** students greet using Basic Greeting format, adding a gentle bumping of fists with each of their partners. Leader may choose to make this a silent greeting, or use the Fist Tap Greeting as a quick simultaneous greeting when time is short. Model and practice fist-tapping technique before beginning: make a tight fist, then gently tap partner's fist as *Good Morning, _____* is exchanged.

• Book Character Greeting

Materials: nametags, markers

Each student makes a nametag naming their favorite book character and wears it as they greet others. Afterwards, students share what book their character is from and why they like him/her.

• Choice Greeting

Students choose whom and/or how they greet. Choices can be made intentionally or randomly. The key thing to guard against is "shopping," where students size up each other before deciding whom to greet.

Variation: Reach Out Greeting: students simultaneously greet one another, using this greeting as an opportunity to expand their social world a bit. Leader chooses the degree to which the greeter "reaches out," for example:

Greet someone you haven't talked to yet today.
Greet someone you know a little but would like to know better.
Greet someone you haven't greeted in several days.
Greet someone of the opposite gender.

• Color-Coded Greeting

Materials: red and blue pieces of cloth or paper

Each student receives either a blue or red paper or strip of cloth; students don't get to choose the color. They make their color visible by either holding it or wearing it in plain sight. The Basic Greeting (*Good morning, _____*) goes around the circle, but Reds may greet only Reds and Blues may greet only Blues, so students must bypass people who are of the other color. Review the greeting by asking students how it felt.

• Crystal Ball Greeting

Students include a positive prediction for the future for the person they are greeting. *Good morning, _____. In my crystal ball I see that next year you will be playing on a hockey team.* The response is simply, *Good morning, _____, and thank you.* The greeting can go around the circle, one greeting at a time, or can happen among many pairs simultaneously.

• Cumulative Greeting

Each person greets everyone who has preceded him in the greeting. The first student greets the student next to her; that student greets her back, and greets whoever is next to her in the circle. This student greets her back, and also greets the first person. This cumulative process continues until the last greeter must respond to being greeted by greeting everyone in the circle.

Variations:

1. **Cumulative High Five Greeting:** students add high fives, either with each new greeting or during the cumulative greetings. Model and practice how to give gentle high fives prior to beginning.

2. **Cumulative List Greeting:** students add sharing. Leader selects a topic for the share part of the greeting and goes first, for example: *What are you doing this weekend?* OR *What's one of your favorite types of music?* As the greeting accumulates, each new greeter repeats what those before her have answered. Leader asks first but answers last, after greeting has made its way around the circle.

Cumulative List example:

Bob: *Good morning, Ray; what are you doing this weekend?*

Ray: *Good morning, Bob. I'm heading for the beach.* (Turns to Doris) *Good morning, Doris; what are you doing this weekend?*

Doris: *I'm working on a retaining wall in the backyard with my mom, Ray, and you're heading to the beach.* (Turns to Rebecca) *Good morning, Rebecca, what are you doing this weekend?*

Rebecca: *I'm dropping a new transmission into my brother's '69 Camaro, Doris, and you are working on a retaining wall in your backyard with your mom, and Ray's heading to the beach.* This greeting takes time and concentration, and actually functions as greeting, sharing, and activity rolled into one.

• Elevator Greeting

Students stand close together facing the same direction as if pressed together in a crowded elevator. Each person greets and is greeted by two or three of the people closest to him/her (*Good Morning, ____*), while everyone keeps their eyes fixed on an imaginary space above the elevator door. Challenge students to make the greeting friendly even though they are not looking at one another.

• Gift Greeting

Students greet each other and extend an imaginary gift to the person they greet. The gift should demonstrate a level of relationship between the greeter and the student being greeted by being related to an interest the student being greeted has.

Good morning, _____, this is a _____ for you because you are interested in _____. Reply: *Thank you, _____!*

Good morning, Chuck, this canteen is for you. I'm giving it to you because I know you like rock climbing. Reply: *Thanks, Isabel!*

• Greet and Meet Greeting

Students stand, form groups of three, greet each other, and then talk about the sharing topic provided by the leader. To foster inclusion, groups are encouraged to invite into their cluster those who are having difficulty finding a group of three, even if it means creating a group of four. Have topics ready before you begin.

• Greet Three Greeting

Students make eye contact from across the circle, move and greet each other using a greeting of their choice, and repeat this process two more times. All students are greeting simultaneously. Model and practice how to do this gracefully among several students while greeting.

• Guess My Greeting

Materials: index cards

Leader writes names of emotions on index cards, one per card, and gives one to each student. Students greet each other one at a time around the circle, in voices that reflect the emotions indicated on the cards. Students are challenged to show the emotions of fear, pain, delight, etc. while saying *Good morning, _____*. After a greeting, students may guess which emotion a greeter was trying to represent.

Variation: Once the group is familiar with the greeting, students greet each according to *both* the emotion and the action indicated on their cards. *Good morning, Jake* (e.g., showing the emotion of boredom while brushing your teeth). *Good morning, Tamara* (e.g., showing the emotion of fearful excitement while riding a bucking bronco).

• Gushy Greeting

One at a time around the circle, students greet each other using an over-the-top, "gushy" voice. This greeting must be theatric and extreme to work well, so model and practice first. *Hey, Shawna, how is it gooooooing?* Response: *Oooooooh, it is just grrrrrrand, Roxy).*

• Hand Jive Greeting

Moving in sequence around the circle, students greet each other with a rhythmic hand-clapping or body gesture pattern. Start with a basic, easy-to-do clapping pattern such as:

> **High Five:** students exchange a high five. *Hi, Arie.* Reply: *Hi, Roxanne*
>
> **Double High Five:** students greet with two high fives.
>
> **High Five/ Low Five:** a student greets and high fives his neighbor. The neighbor greets and low fives him back. *Hi, Roberta* (high five). *Hi, Jake* (low five).
>
> **"Miss Mary Mack":** students adapt this traditional hand jive to suit a quick greeting.

Use more complex rhythms as needed to keep things interesting and fresh. Model and practice each pattern as it is introduced. Many middle school students will enjoy an opportunity to create patterns of their own to use for this greeting.

• Huddle-Up Greeting

Students come to the middle of the circle when a statement is made that applies to them. Leader makes a statement and students come to the middle of the circle and greet the others in the middle. Those for whom the statement doesn't apply stay where they are, quietly waiting for the next statement.

Example: *Huddle up if you enjoy watching football.* Everyone who likes to watch football comes to the middle of the circle and greets everyone else who shares this trait, while those who don't enjoy watching football remain where they are.

• Inside-Outside Greeting

Form a double circle (one inside the other), and as the inside circle rotates, members of the inside circle greet people in the outside circle with a handshake and *Good morning*. Many variations are possible. For example, high fives or low fives can replace handshakes.

• Introduction Greeting

A "host" is chosen, and everyone stands. The host introduces each student to the rest of the group. The group greets the student being introduced by name, and the student being introduced responds.

Host: *Good morning, everybody. I'd like you to meet Janice Morgan.*
Class: *Good morning, Janice.*
Janice: *Good morning, everyone.*

• Knock Knock Greeting

Students brainstorm knock-knock jokes (use joke books as resources). Leader makes it clear that students need not worry about the quality of each joke, only that it be school-appropriate. A student is selected to begin. She turns to her neighbor, greets him, and tells him a knock-knock joke. He participates politely in her joke-telling and thanks her when she's finished. Then he turns to his other neighbor and tells him *his* joke, and the greeting continues around the circle.

Variation: Students pair up, greet each other, and tell each other their jokes.

• Language Greeting: Variations on "Good morning" and "Hello"

Leader chooses a language for the greeting, preferably one spoken by a student in the class. All students greet in this language, either around the circle or in the All Group Greeting format. (All Group format: *Buenos dias, everyone.* Group responds: *Buenos dias, Carla.*) Leader can list and model and practice the greeting possibilities ahead of time to facilitate pronunciation.

Good morning /Hello variations:
Japanese: *Ohayou gozaimasu* (Good morning)
Spanish: *Buenos dias* (Good morning)
Swahili: *Jambo* (Hello)
German: *Guten Morgen* (Good morning)
Fijian: *Bula* (Hello) *Yadra* or *Ni sa yadra* (Good morning)
Hebrew: *Shalom* (Peace) or *Boker tov* (Good morning)
Polish: *Dzien dobre* (Good morning)
French: *Bonjour* (Hello)
Arabic: *Sabaah el kheer* (Good morning)
Hindi: *Namaste* (Hello)

Variations:
1. Each student chooses to greet in a language of his/her choice, either one at a time around the circle or in the All Group Greeting format, with neighbors or the whole group responding in the greeter's chosen language. For example, one at a time around the circle:
    Carlos: *Bonjour, Samatha.*
    Samantha: *Bonjour, Carlos.*
    Samantha: *Namaste, Phyllis.*
    Phyllis: *Namaste, Samatha.*

2. **Whole Group Language Greeting:** A student announces to the whole group the language in which he would like to be greeted. The group fills the request by greeting him in unison in that language. *Good morning, everyone. I'd like to be greeted in Greek this morning!* Group responds: *Kalimera, Chad!*

3. **Good Morning, Friend Greeting:** as they greet one another, students add the word "friend" in a language other than English.
   Good Morning, Friend examples:
   Spanish: *Buenos dias, amigo/amiga*
   French: *Bonjour, mon ami/amie*
   Swahili: *Jambo rafiki*
   Mandarin: *Ni zao pinyin*
   Hindi: *Shubha prabhaat dost*

• Let Me See Your Walk Greeting

A student is selected to begin. He pantomimes his favorite hobby as he walks across the circle to another student. He greets her and asks to see her "walk." She returns his greeting, they exchange places, and she proceeds to pantomime a favorite pastime as she crosses the circle towards another student. This is repeated until all students have been greeted.

Example: Ted's hobby is golf, so he mimes swinging a golf club as he walks across the circle to Shalana. He says, *Good morning, Shalana, let me see your walk.* Shalana says, *Good morning, Ted, watch this!* and crosses the circle pretending to paint a canvas.

• Mimic Greeting

One at a time around the circle, students greet their neighbors in a manner of their choice, and neighbors mimic the greetings in return. Leaders can limit the words of the greeting (e.g., *Good morning,* _____), or give students choice of both the words and manner in which they greet.

• Movie Star Greeting

Introduce yourself to everyone using your middle name as your first name and your pet's name or the name of the street you live on as your last name. For example, Harold James Starling of Bushberry Lane with dog, Lucky, becomes James Bushberry or James Lucky. The audience listens, and then frames the student in question by pretending to look through a viewfinder in the manner of a movie director or cinematographer, and says, *Ohhhhh, yeeeeaaahhhhh!* in an exaggerated way.
Harold Starling: *Good morning everyone, I'm James Bushberry.*
Group responds: ("framing" Harold, like a movie director) *Ohhhhhh, yeeeaaahhhhh!*

• Name Card Greeting

Materials: notecards
Students' names are written on notecards and placed, randomly arranged, face down in a pile in the middle of the circle. One at a time, each student selects a card, reads it, and greets the student indicated.

Variation: Place nametags in a pile in the middle. Students greet and exchange seats with the person indicated on the cards they draw.

• Name Everyone Greeting

A student greets everyone in the room individually by name and with eye contact. When she has greeted everyone, everyone greets her back in unison. The greeter may remain where she is as she greets, or she may walk around the circle, greeting each student from a closer perspective. This is a good challenge greeting/activity after a couple of weeks of learning names (see Name Games in Appendix D).

• One-Minute Mingle Greeting

Each person greets as many students by name as possible in one minute. Model how to efficiently complete a greeting before starting. Give examples of how to be greeted and return a greeting, maintaining eye contact, before moving on to the next person.

• P & J Greeting

Materials: index cards

Leader creates pairs of index cards, each of which has a word which complements a word on another card. Each student receives one card. Students mill about, looking for the student who holds the index card that complements theirs. Students may say their word aloud, hold their card aloft for all to see, or mime an action that goes with their word to assist partners in locating each other. When partners find each other, they greet.

Pairs examples:

> Salt, Pepper
> Ketchup, Mustard
> Wind, Sailboat
> Bicycle, Handlebar
> Dance, Music
> Paintbrush, Van Gogh
> Astronomy, Telescope
> Winter, Ice
> Forest, Trees

• Partner Greeting

Any greeting done in pairs, simultaneously, rather than around the circle in the usual style—great when time is short or risk level needs to be lowered.

• Peace Greeting

Students form pairs, greet each other verbally, *Peace, _____*, and make a peace sign to each other. This may also be done using the Basic Greeting format, one at a time around the circle.

• Puzzle Greeting

Materials: notecards or colored card stock

Cut notecards or any piece of heavy, colored paper into two or three pieces each (no two cards the same color), hand out pieces to students, and have students find the rest of their group by matching pieces till they make a complete card. All in the newly formed group greet each other.

• Question Greeting

Students pair up; one student in each pair is chosen to greet the other first. She says, *Good morning,*_____, and follows her greeting with a question. Leaders may brainstorm and post a variety of getting-to-know-you questions prior to beginning.

Question examples:

What's your favorite food?
Do you have siblings?
What is a book you've read and enjoyed?
Whom do you admire, and why?
How often do you offer to help with chores around your home?
Where would you like to go to college? Why?

• Riddle Greeting

Materials: a supply of riddles in books or on cards

Leader makes sure everyone in the circle has a riddle to tell and supplies one to those who can't come up with their own. Students can greet and share their riddles in pairs, in small groups, or one at a time, as in the Basic Greeting.

Jeanna: *Hi, Terrell. Do you know what goes around the school and in the school but never touches the school?*

Terrell: *Hi, Jeanna. I don't know; what goes around the school and in the school but never touches the school?*

Jeanna: *The sun!*

• Roll Call Greeting

A rhythmic chant from Barbara McCutcheon in Baltimore, MD

Leader starts a steady rhythmic clap that all students join. Along with the clap, students chant the following:

Roll call, check the beat,
Check, check, check the beat
Roll call, check the beat,
Check, check, checka begin!

As the rhythmic clap continues, individual greetings begin.

A student is selected to greet first, and says: *My name is* _____*!*

Group response: *Check!*

Next, the student says: *They call me* (nickname)*!*

Group response: *Check!*

The student says: *I am a student!* (or something else, as long as it's positive)

Group response: *Check!*

The student says: *That's what I am!*

Group response: *That's what s/he is!*

The roll call chant is taken up again by the entire class: *Roll call, check the beat....*

When the chant ends (*Check, check, checka begin*), the student to the right of the first student says, *My name is_____!* the group responds with *Check!* and the greeting continues until all have had a chance to introduce themselves.

• Sawa bona Greeting

This African greeting uses two phrases: "Sawa bona," which means "I see you," and "Sikhona," which means "I am here." Except for the person who starts the greeting, students' eyes are closed until they are greeted. A student is chosen to begin; she opens her eyes, turns to the person to her right or left, and greets that person by name, saying, *Sawa bona, _____.* That student opens his eyes and responds, *Sikhona, _____,* turns to the student on his other side and greets him by name: *Sawa bona,_____.* The greeting continues around the circle in this fashion until all have been greeted.

• Say Hi to _____ Greeting

Each greeter greets his neighbor to the right on behalf of himself and for the student on his left, who asked him to say hi. Each greeter also asks the student he is greeting to greet the following student for him. The responders can greet *only* the person who directly greeted them or they can respond to the greeter and the one who sent the greeting through the greeter. When there's time, you can make the entire greeting cumulative!

Example: Dennis is selected to begin. He says *Good morning, Damon* (the person on his right), and adds, *Say 'hi' to Linda for me* (Linda is one person beyond Damon). Damon returns Dennis's greeting, turns to Linda, and says, *Good morning, Linda; Dennis says 'hi' and so do I. And would you pass along my regards when you greet Samantha?* Linda answers, *Good morning, Damon* (or *Good morning, Damon and Dennis*). *I sure will...* and so on.

• Shape Greeting

While greeting in pairs, one student makes half a shape with her hands; her partner completes the shape by mirroring the other side.

Example: *Good morning, Al* [makes a v-shape with fingers]. *Good morning, Nicole* [makes a v-shape of his own with his fingers and connects his fingertips to hers, completing a diamond shape].

• Silent Greeting

Students brainstorm types of silent greetings. Model and practice some of them, such as nod heads, smile, eye contact with raised eyebrows, handshake, wink, etc.

One at a time around the circle, students greet each other silently using one of the modeled silent greetings, or have students look across the circle and connect with at least three of their classmates. When everyone has been greeted, you may discuss what it felt like to be greeted silently and the power of non-verbal communication. Also, you may brainstorm times when your class might want to use a silent greeting such as:

1. We are in the middle of a lesson and a student returns from an activity outside the classroom.

2. We see a friend at lunch talking with someone else and we don't want to interrupt.

• Skip Greeting

Stand in a circle; select a student to begin. Agree on a designated number of spaces to skip along the circle and send the greeting around. After greeting, students sit and watch carefully and quietly until everyone has been greeted.

• Slap Jack Greeting

Students stand in a circle. A student (Student #1) is selected to begin. She faces her neighbor (Student #2) and places her hands out in front of her, palms up. Student #2 places her hands palms down, above but not touching Student #1's; they freeze for an instant, making eye contact. Student #1 then tries to gently slap the backs of Student #2's hands, while Student #2 attempts to avoid being slapped by pulling her hands away the moment Student #1's hands move (but not before). Whether a gentle slap is achieved or not, as soon as they finish, they greet each other. Student #2 then turns to her other neighbor (Student #3) and the greeting continues around the circle.

Variation: Students pair up and greet simultaneously to save time and lower the level of risk, since there is no longer an audience.

• Snake Greeting

A student stands up, greets a neighbor, gets greeted in return, moves on to greet the next person, and so on. As the leader moves on, the student she greeted stands and follows her, greeting the same people she greeted, in the same order. A constantly growing "snake" of students forms behind her. Once the leader has greeted everyone, she sits—she's the first to return to her seat—and others follow in order, shrinking the size of the snake, until everyone has sat back down.

• Snowball Greeting

Materials: paper, pencils

Students write their names on paper, then crumple paper into a ball and toss it on the floor. Each student picks up a paper ball, opens it up, reads the name on it, and greets the student indicated. Can be done simultaneously or one at a time.

• Step In Greeting

Students stand in a circle. One by one, students step into the circle and greet everyone: *Good morning, everyone.* Class responds in kind, adding the student's name: *Good morning, Jasmine.*

• Syllables Greeting

A rhythmic greeting. One at a time, the whole class greets each student in unison, making a crisp clap with each syllable of the student's name.

Whole group: *Good morning, An* [clap] *toine* [clap]

Antoine: *Good morning, everyone!*

Whole group: *Good morning, E* [clap] *liz* [clap] *a* [clap] *beth* [clap]

Elizabeth: *Good morning, everyone!*

Variation: Reverse the order of the greeting. Each student greets the class and the whole group returns the greeting, clapping the syllables of her name.

• Telephone Greeting

Students silently maintain eye contact with someone across the circle. They work together to determine who greets first, and to try to mimic picking up a phone at the same time. The greeter greets the person she has chosen, holding a pinky near her mouth and a thumb near her ear. The person being greeted does likewise, responding in kind. This can be done simultaneously or using the circle format.

• Theatrical Greeting

Each student selects a role to play that reflects a mood or dramatic situation, for example, a person feeling excitement, arrogance, worry, or love. Students may need to brainstorm a list of possibilities first. As they greet, each student assumes the voice and mannerisms of a character of her choice and greets the group. Everyone responds to that student in the same voice and manner. Greet around the circle or use the All Group Greeting format.

Example: (someone late for an event) *Oh, hi, everyone, hi. I'm late! I'm really late!* Group responds: *Hi, Georgie!*

• Tower Greeting

This is modeled on the old-fashioned method of selecting which baseball team bats first by having captains alternate grabbing a bat, starting at the bottom of its barrel and continuing to exchange grips until one captain grips the knob end, thereby winning first at-bats for her team. Here, starting at waist level, partners alternate placing a hand on top of the other's, moving them higher and higher until their arms form an arch between them. They look at each other under the arch and greet each other. Greeting continues around the circle.

Variation: Climbing a Tree Greeting: students stand. Partners mime climbing a tree together. When their arms are well above their heads, they stop climbing and greet each other.

• What Are You Doing? Greeting

One student begins the greeting by miming an activity. The next student watches the student miming, and says, *Hello, _____, what are you doing?* The first student replies by naming an activity *other than* the one she is miming. The student who asked then mimes the activity named, and a third student, watching the second person mime the activity the first student named, says, *Hello _____, what are you doing?* This continues around the circle until all have had a chance to be greeted, to mime some-thing, and to decide what is to be mimed next.

Example:
Tom mimes knitting a sweater.
Shawn, watching Tom: *Hey, Tom, what are you doing?*
Tom: *I'm milking a cow!*
Tom stops and Shawn begins to mime milking a cow.
Ana, watching Shawn: *Hey, Shawn, what are you doing?*
Shawn: *I'm practicing the tuba!* Ana starts to mime practicing the tuba.
A brainstormed list of activities may help students come up with new ones when they're on the spot; also, a discussion of school-appropriate content for this greeting may be necessary.

• What's Happening? Greeting

One at a time around the circle, students ask how their neighbors are doing in one of several ways: What's happening? What's up? How's it going? Or you could use Span-ish slang: Que mas? Que hubo? Que dices? Que honda? Or French: Salut! Ca va toi? Any of these can be combined with a standard or casual handshake.

• Wild Card Greeting

Materials: list of greetings used to date (optional)
A student is selected to begin. She greets the student to her right or left, using any greeting from a menu of those already implemented in advisory. The student she greets responds in kind, but then chooses a different greeting from the menu to use when she greets the next student.

Shares

• Affinity Share

Materials: notecards

In pairs, students come up with ideas related to a topic provided by the leader, and write these on notecards. Pairs double up (forming groups of four) and combine their comments, eliminating duplicates; next is a meeting of 8, then 16 (the number of ideas will grow at each meeting), until the whole group is working on one list; duplicates are eliminated at each meeting. One person reads the final list.

• Brown Bag Share

Materials: a brown paper bag for each student

Leader gives each student a brown bag; students may decorate them. Students place into their bag three to five objects that are of significance to them (help to symbolize who they are). Students will need a few days to select and gather their objects. Brown bags are then shared on a predetermined date. Sharing of bag contents can be done using format of the Inside-Outside Share, Partner Share, Individual Share, etc. If leader chooses to use Individual Share, allow for enough days for everyone to share, assigning two or three students to share per day.

Variation: The student sharing removes her items from her bag, places them in front of her without speaking, and invites her audience to make comments, including inferences. She may respond by indicating whether the comments or inferences are accurate.

• Heritage Share

A student highlights a custom or tradition related to her heritage, and may bring in an artifact or picture related to the custom. The student sharing may wish to entertain questions or ask for comments after sharing.

• Individual Share—the basic personal share

A student chooses a topic to share. He frames an interactive conversation by making a brief statement or two about the topic. Classmates then ask questions or comment about the topic; each question or comment is directed to the sharer. The quality of the share hinges on the audience's ability to participate fully and ask interesting, open-ended questions. The sharer fleshes out her story by answering questions and responding to comments to the best of her ability. To increase the challenge, the leader can set a time frame (1 to 3 minutes) for the sharer or for the questions and comments that follow.

Example: *I'm going to spend next weekend at my cousin's house. It's his birthday on Saturday. I'm open for questions or related comments.*

Leader is responsible for determining the format in which questions or comments are to be stated. The format should vary: at times questions can be mandatory going around the circle. At times raising hands and volunteering can be invited. Whichever format is used, leaders encourage full participation.

• Inside-Outside Share

Students form two groups and stand in concentric circles. Inside circle faces out, outside circle faces in. Students form pairs with whoever faces them from the other circle. Leader provides a question or topic for discussion and a time limit. Each pair greets each other and discusses the item. When time expires, pairs thank each other. Leader invites members of one of the circles to move one or more spots to the left or right and greet their new partner, and then sharing continues. Leader may choose to move through several rounds of sharing or limit sharing to one or two rounds. Leader also determines whether to have each new pair discuss the same or a new prompt.

• Interview Share

Topic: Three things about me are....

A student or teacher shares three pieces of information about him or herself. A student scribe is selected. Brainstorm and scribe a list of questions that might be asked of the sharer. Students then interview the sharer by taking turns asking those questions.

• Partner Share

Leader provides a topic and specifies a length of time to share. In pairs, partners share their ideas about the topic. Leader may choose to model listening and asking socially inclusive questions, like *Emmitt, what's your opinion?* Leader may also issue a time warning halfway through the share to ensure balanced sharing/listening in each pair.

Variations:
> 1. **High Five Partner Share:** students turn to their right- or left-hand neighbors and form the partnership with a "high five," and proceed to discuss the topic.
>
> 2. **Partner Plus Share:** Partner Share is followed by reporting to the whole group highlights of what was discussed during the share.

• Popcorn Share

This format moves students toward unregulated conversation skills. Students form a circle and stand. A topic for sharing is introduced. Students respond by spontaneously stepping ("popping") into the circle and speaking up, without raising hands. When finished, they step back into their spot and another student from anywhere in the circle steps in to share. Each student's response is brief. A key to success is merging gracefully into and out of the conversation: waiting until the prior student is finished before "popping" in, trying to avoid having multiple people speaking at the same time, etc. Leader may choose to limit each student to one comment. Participation is optional, but strongly encouraged.

• Post-it Share

Leader provides a topic. Students write responses on Post-its and place them on a board or chart. Responses are read by the group.

This form of sharing can take many forms. Responses may be individual, silent, and anonymous, or students may partner up (or form small groups) and discuss a prompt before composing a collective response on their group's Post-it. Alternatively, leader may issue multiple Post-its and have students respond to a single topic in more than one way.

Example using "Pros and Cons":

Partners discuss, write, and post their answers on a chart or board titled: *I'm unexpectedly invited out with my friends on a school night. I have homework. Should I go?* Blank space is provided underneath for "Pros" and "Cons" Post-it responses. A benefit of this sharing approach is that information shared can be kept for future reference.

• Snowball Share

Students write a question on a piece of paper, crumple it up like a snowball, and throw it into the middle of the circle. Each student picks up a "snowball." Students form pairs and ask and answer questions found inside their snowballs.

Variation: Teacher announces a discussion topic on which students focus their snowball questions or teacher asks questions and students answer in their snowballs.

• Think, Ink, Pair, Share

Materials: pencil and paper

Leader provides a sharing question or topic. Students quietly think about a response for 1 or 2 minutes. Next, they write their thoughts on paper. Then students form groups of two or three and share what they've written. Leader functions as timekeeper, assuring balanced participation within each group. For a final step, volunteers can share the questions and comments they wrote with the entire group

Variation: Think, Pair, Share: remove the writing step. Students receive a prompt from leader, reflect on prompt for a short period of time, and share their thoughts with a partner (or small group), and volunteers share out to whole group.

• Whip Share

A topic is introduced by the leader. Each student offers a brief response to the topic; responses quickly "whip" around the circle. *One of my goals this year is...; Our family likes to...; My favorite type of music is... If I could change one thing about the world....*

Variation: Cumulative Share: each student responds to the topic and also repeats the ideas shared by those who preceded her.

Activities

• Acknowledgment Buffet

Materials: paper plates

Leader gives each student a paper plate. Students write their names in the middle of the plates. Plates are collected, shuffled, and redistributed. Students read the name on the plate they receive and write an acknowledgment for that student. Plates are exchanged as often as time permits. The final writer returns the plate to the student whose name is on it. If possible, give students time to read and reflect on what has been written. Review essentials of appropriate acknowledgment before plates are exchanged.

• Affinity Process

A student finds someone with whom she has something in common. Then she and her partner find another twosome and discover a characteristic they all share. Next, foursomes create groups of eight and come up with a shared characteristic and so on until all are in one large group. The common characteristic discovered is likely to be different each time a new group is formed.

• Alibi

One student is chosen the Detective and leaves the room. Leader decides on a mishap or crime and chooses a student to be the Perpetrator of the mishap. Everyone thinks of a personal alibi. Detective returns. Leader announces details of the crime or mishap. Detective asks each student where he or she was during the crime or mishap. Each student gives an alibi; the Detective listens carefully. After the Detective has gone around the circle once, she asks around the circle a second time. Each student must give exactly the same alibi except for the Perpetrator, who changes her alibi slightly. The Detective gets three chances to identify the Perpetrator.

Variation: For a memory challenge, all students close their eyes and the leader taps the perpetrator silently. Then only the leader and the perpetrator know and everyone else must listen closely to catch the changed alibi.

• All Hit Moonball

Materials: beach ball

One-Team Version: Students scatter on a basketball court, open field, or any open space. A beach ball is hit aloft, and each student must hit the ball at least once before it falls. The ball may not be grabbed or held. Students may hit the ball more than once as long as they're helping keep it in play; play continues until all have hit it.

Variations:

1. Keep the ball aloft for as many hits as possible before it falls. Set a goal (30, 50, 75 or 100 hits) to add incentive.

2. **Two-Team Version**: Students form two teams. Teams stand on either side of a line or series of cones. Keeping the ball aloft at all times, teams must hit the ball at least twice on their side before sending the ball to the other team. Possible goals: keeping the ball in play among the whole group for as many hits as possible; passing the ball from one team to another as many times as possible while keeping to the two-hits-per-side minimum; hitting the ball among teammates 5 times (or some other number) before returning it to the other team.

• Arm Hockey

Students stand in a circle, each student's legs a little wider than shoulder width apart. Neighbors' feet touch. Students use their opposite arm—the one they don't normally use—to try to hit the ball between another student's legs. The ball must be hit with an open hand and may not be hit into the air.

Variations: Teams may be formed and a game played up to a predetermined score. Or students may be declared out if they allow a goal to be scored through their legs. In this case, they are allowed back into the game when another student is scored upon.

• Around the World

Materials: an object to pass around the circle

Students pass an object around the circle quickly while the person who is "It" tries to name examples in a content category selected by the leader. Model and practice passing the object around the circle before playing. Leader gives It an object to pass and starts the game with a command. Players begin to pass the object while It tries to name as many items in the category as possible before the object has passed all around the circle and returns to It.

Variation: The group can set a goal for the number of examples to state before the object completes its travel around the circle (a smaller circle has less passing time and therefore calls for fewer items to list).

Topic examples:

Name fractions equal to one-fourth

Name adjectives

Name bones in the human body

• CARES Acknowledgment

Students acknowledge one another using CARES (Cooperation; Assertion; Responsibility; Empathy; Self-control) social skills as a guide: *I noticed Roberto was responsible and got his homework in on time. I want to acknowledge Ingrid for using cooperation and inviting me into her group.* After each acknowledgment, students may choose to clap, bow, snap fingers, cheer in unison, etc. See Cheers on page 264.

• Carousel

Materials: chart paper, markers

Leader writes a different topic or question at the top of each of four or five large pieces of chart paper and places them around the room. Students form as many groups as there are questions or topics, i.e., one group per chart. Leader assigns a group to each chart and gives them a time frame (usually 2-4 minutes) to write their responses to the posted questions or topics. Leader may choose to assign a different-colored marker to students within each group to insure equal participation. When time expires, leader moves groups to a new chart along the carousel. This process is repeated until all groups have visited and responded to each chart. When finished, leader may choose to post the charts, have groups report on the results of their charts, and refer to them later as needed. Also, students may go around a second time and use Post-its to add to the previously-written comments.

• Charades

Leader prepares a list of vocabulary words. Before playing, decide on an appropriate form of guessing (raising hands, blurting, ringing bells, etc). Also, while planning, players should agree on whether using hand gestures to signal the number of syllables in a word is allowable. To play, a student (or pair of students) is selected. Leader assigns that student or pair a vocabulary word without disclosing it to the whole group. The word is mimed while the rest of the class tries to guess it. New students are selected to mime each new word.

• Chase the Caboose

Students sit in chairs in a circle. A student is selected to be "It" and stands in the middle, creating an open chair. Play begins when the player to the left of the vacant chair moves into it; her vacated chair is then slid into by her neighbor, and so on. The process of moving quickly and efficiently from chair to chair should be modeled and practiced before playing. The student in the middle attempts to sit in an open chair; to do so requires forethought, grace, and assertiveness, for she must beat someone else to it without engaging in any reckless physical contact. When she succeeds, the player left standing is It and the game continues.

Variation: After playing safely and well for a time, students may choose to slap the open chair with their hands occasionally to reverse the direction in which the circle is moving.

• Competing for Resources Around the World

Materials: one chair per student

Create eight areas of the room to represent eight regions. Distribute students with their chairs into these areas in apportioned groups based on regional population. (See chart below for percentages and examples. Leader or students can calculate the correct number of students in each group. For "partial" students, round up or down.) Discuss what students notice about global population distribution. Leader then introduces the wealth-distribution statistics, explains that the chairs now represent percentages of wealth, and moves chairs to match the wealth on each continent.

(For "partial" chairs, you can bring in a few extra, and round up or down or mark portions.) Leader asks everyone to sit down. There will be too few chairs for some groups and a surplus for others. Students discuss what they notice about wealth inequities and how it feels to have enough or not. Good for multiple advisories.

Leader may choose to distribute fake money instead of using chairs to illustrate wealth inequities.

Percentage of world population and wealth: example with 25 students

Region	Population	Wealth	25 Students	Chairs
North America	6.1%	34.4%	1.5	8.6
L.America & Caribbean	8.2%	4.3%	2	1.07
Europe	14.9%	29.6%	3.7	7.4
Africa	10.2%	1.0%	2.5	.25
China	22.8%	2.6%	5.7	.65
India	15.4%	.9%	3.8	2.25
Wealthy Asia-Pacific	5.0%	24.1%	1.2	6.02
Other Asia-Pacific	17.5%	3.0%	4.3	.75

• Concentration

A hand-clapping, rhythmic workout for the mind. Students form a circle. A basic, four-beat rhythmic pattern is established by leader, using thigh-tapping, clapping, and/or finger snapping. Leader also creates and teaches an introductory theme (statement) that will be chanted in unison before playing. Leader (or selected student) offers a topic to be used during the first round of play. One at a time, students respond to the topic, keeping to the tempo and rhythm selected. Start with basic rhythmic patterns, then try adding more complex ones as students get the hang of things.

Example of four-beat rhythmic pattern:

> Beat 1: left hand pats left thigh
>
> Beat 2: right hand pats right thigh
>
> Beat 3: snap fingers, left hand
>
> Beat 4: snap fingers, right hand

Introductory chant example:

Here come da judge! Here come da judge! (Begin rhythmic pattern after this statement)
Con-cen-tra-tion
Now in ses-sion
Can you keep the
Groove pro-gres-sion?

A category is then introduced:

To-day's top-ic
Tel-e-scop-ic
And we'll call it ___[states]_____ (OR opposites, prime numbers, elements, etc)
A-ri-zon-a; Kan-sas (The new state starts on the rhythm downbeat, so continue the pattern until you get there.)

• Configurations

Students form teams of three to eight players. Leader assigns each group an object to "build," using only the parts of their bodies such as a bus, helicopter, merry-go-round, washing machine, waterfall, etc. Create rules about proper touch before starting. Other groups guess what object/machine is being depicted.

• Connections

Leader creates card sets that correspond to about 5 news stories. The total number of cards should equal the number of students playing the game. Four or five cards should be created for each set. Each card within a set is labeled and provides an answer to who? what? where? when? or why? Card sets must not contain more than one card from each category. Leader shuffles cards and gives one card to each student. Students mix and mingle, try forming clusters with others who have the same event on their card. After the clusters are formed, the group tells the story represented by their cards. See how close they come to the actual news story.

Variation: Students receive a card. When mixing and mingling, they cluster with students who have cards from a different category, regardless of whether the information on the cards relates to the same story. Students form groups that include a who, what, where, when, and how question. "Stories" are read. Nonsense abounds!

• Continuous Tale

Students form a circle. A student is selected to start a story by contributing its first phrase or sentence. Each subsequent student adds a sentence or two to the story; the last few students must bring the story to a conclusion. Model or discuss good listening before beginning.

Variation: Before the first person begins, everyone selects a prop they must work into the story.

• Copy Cat

Form a circle. Leader instructs students to watch one other player in the circle without revealing whom they choose to watch. Each student imitates the actions of the student he is watching. Debrief after approximately thirty seconds.

• Count to Ten

Form a circle. Play moves around the circle, sequentially. The whole group counts to ten, one student at a time; each student may add one or two numbers to the number they receive. A student is selected to start. She begins by counting aloud, starting with One: She may say, *One*, or, *One, two*. The next player may say one or two numbers as well, so if the first student ends on one, the next student may say, *Two*, or, *Two, three*. Counting continues around the circle until the number reaches 10. The player who has to say 10 is out and must sit down. Play resumes immediately—the next student begins by saying, *One* or, *One, two*, and continues until only one is left standing. Model and discuss how to lose gracefully before beginning.

Variation: Students may count up three numbers and must sit down on 11, 13, etc.

• Count Up

Students count to ten as a group. Only one person may speak at a time, and students must blurt out numbers from random positions in the circle, without following a pattern or sequence to help them take turns. If multiple students say a number at the same time, the group starts from one again.

• Cumulative List

This is a game of concentration. The goal is to generate a list of some kind—hobbies or special interests are good. Students form a circle and one student is selected to start. She says, *I have some spare time, and I'm going to____,* naming an activity. The students who follow repeat the activities previously mentioned before they add their own. The game gets more difficult each time a new student adds to the list, so the leader may decide to allow students to choose where to sit according to how much challenge they're looking for. You can easily use academic content in Concentration.

• Cup and Stick Game

Materials: pencils, string, durable paper cups, tape (optional)

Persistence required! Students construct their own devices for play by attaching one end of a piece of string to the lip of a paper cup and the other end of the string to a pencil. When attached, one or two feet of string should separate pencil from cup.

To play, students grab the tip-end of their pencil and use an upward, swooping/flicking motion to elevate the cup, trying to get it to land atop the pencil's eraser end. Leader encourages students to keep trying. It's not easy, but with practice, it's possible!!

• Driven to Trust

Students form pairs. One student is the car, the other the driver. The car has its eyes closed or blindfolded. The driver stands behind the car and directs it through touch. Forward: driver's hand is between car's shoulder blades. Reverse: hand is on car's lower back. Right: hand is on right shoulder. Left: hand is on left shoulder. Stop: hands off. Emergency stop: both hands on shoulders. A high level of trust is necessary for this activity.

• Eleven

Students form clusters of four, their hands concealed behind their backs. A leader is chosen to give the signal to start each round of play. On leader's signal, group members flash fingers simultaneously. Their goal each time is to flash a total of eleven fingers. Collaborative strategizing is prohibited. Rule: players must flash a different number each time.

• ESP (Extra-sensory Perception)

This is a game with a connection to consensus-building. Students form at least three or four groups. Each group huddles up for a moment and comes up with a dramatic movement and sound they'll act out together for the rest of the group. Each group demonstrates its movement and sound, after which the leader shouts, 1,2,3, ESP! and all groups perform their action and sound at the same time. Leader instructs groups to continue "looping" through their performance for approximately 10 seconds, and to look around and try to notice what other groups are doing. After 10 seconds, leader tells groups to huddle up and decide whether to keep doing what they did last time or switch to another group's idea for round two. The goal is to come to consensus—to end up with all groups doing the same action and sound. It may take several rounds as groups learn to compromise. Leader should discuss how empathy and "giving to get" are important parts of coming to consensus. The game may be played with large groups.

• Exquisite Corpse

Materials: paper, pencils or colored pencils

This game originated with the Surrealists in the 1920's as an effort to draw from the irrational as the source of art and insight. In this version, the first person folds a piece of paper accordion-style twice, then draws on one third of the paper, extending the lines slightly into the space of the second third. After drawing, she folds the paper so the next person can see only the few lines extending into the second third. The next person then draws in the second third, integrating the lines from the first drawing, extending into the last third, and folding over to hide his drawing in the same manner as before. He then passes it to the next person who draws in the last third, integrating lines from the previous drawing. When the last third is complete, students find the drawings they initiated and open up the completed drawings.

• Fact or Fiction

In a circle, a student is selected to begin. She tells three things about herself: two facts and one piece of fiction. Others try to guess which item is fiction. The student who guesses correctly, volunteers, or the next student in the circle may go next.

Variation: Can be used to review academic content. Students tell two things that are correct and one that is not in any subject area. For example, three kinds of rock are: Volcanic, Deciduous, and Metamorphic.

• Fan Mail

Materials: paper, pencils

A student puts his name on top of an 8½ x 11 piece of paper, folds back the name part, and passes it to the student to his right, who reads the name and writes an acknowledgment underneath the fold line. This student then folds the paper again the opposite way (over her acknowledgment) so the name is the only thing visible. It is then passed to another student and the process continues for several rounds with the paper folded back and forth in paper fan style. The final student hands the paper to its owner and each player may share her acknowledgment "fan" with a partner.

• Five People Standing

A game of intuition. Students sit in a circle. Goal of activity is to have five people stand simultaneously—no more, no less. Leader signals for play to begin. No talking or non-verbal communicating is allowed; students must try to sense the proper instant to rise, with four others, to win the game. Each time one or more student(s) rise(s), play is temporarily suspended to count them. Play can continue for a specific amount of time or until group has been successful a predetermined number of times.

• Four Corner Thinking

Students stand in a line. Leader designates the four corners of the room as strongly agree, somewhat agree, somewhat disagree, strongly disagree. Students are to move to the corner that represents their position on the statements leader will read. After moving, leader gives each group a moment to discuss why they have chosen their corner. Leader then repeats the statement, giving students a chance to change their position after hearing others' reasoning. Depending on the nature of the statement, the leader may choose to call on one or two students in each corner to give their opinions and at least one fact to support or illustrate them.

Statement examples:

I enjoy eating French fries.

I enjoy eating green vegetables.

I enjoy participating in sports.

I enjoy watching sports.

I enjoy making things with my hands.

I enjoy listening to music.

I enjoy making music.

School is a fun place to be.

Girls and boys are treated equally in our school.

Women and men are paid equally for the same jobs in our country.

A curfew is needed for young adults in our town/city.

Talking can solve many problems.

Fighting can solve many of the world's problems.

Many people are prejudiced in our country.

Some kids get excluded at our school.

Children should have more rights.

Middle level students watch too much media.

Students should be able to use the Internet without restriction.

Some censorship is good for society.

Students should be allowed to quit school whenever they want.

Being open-minded pays off.

• Freeze Frame

Students form small groups. Leader gives students a few moments to plan out a frozen scene or "freeze frame" that relates to a topic. After displaying each group's freeze frame, audience guesses the subject of the freeze frame. Audience may not ask questions before guessing. Leader may wish to play a team- or trust-building game prior to introducing this activity to acclimate players to working together in close proximity.

Example with social topic—Memorable events from the school year:

> Freeze frame a funny (or exciting, surprising, difficult, fun, etc.) moment from this past school year (best done towards the end of the year).

Example with academic topic—Presidential election:

> Freeze frame a debate (or voting, stump speech, swearing in, etc.) scene from the presidential election

• Frogger

Students form a circle, lower their heads, and close their eyes. Leader chooses a student "Frog" by touching someone. Students raise their heads and open their eyes. To play, Frog secretively makes eye contact with and sticks his tongue out at other students, trying to avoid being seen by anyone but the target. When the Frog does this to a player, that player is "put to sleep" and slumps in his chair for the rest of the round. The rest of the players are also trying to determine who the Frog is. When a player thinks he knows, he tells the leader. If he is wrong, he goes to sleep. If he is right, the round is over and a new round starts.

Variation: When a player thinks he knows the identity of the Frog, he whispers it to the leader. If the guess is wrong, the guesser must go to sleep. If the guesser is right, he stays in the game. A new round starts when three have correctly guessed who is the Frog.

• Gallery Walk

Materials: wall and/or table space, Post-its, notecards, sheet paper for comments

Students create products and exhibit them around the room, on tables or walls. Students then "walk the gallery" to see each other's work. This can be used for art work, writing, projects, mind maps, etc.

Variations:

1. **Stay and Stray:** students create products in groups of three or more and exhibit their work. One student from the group "stays" with the work to explain it to viewers while others select another product and "stray" to it, where they learn about it from other student "stayers." Teacher signals a switch every minute or so, whereupon a different student from each group returns to his group's product to explain it with the display, while others stray to another product.

2. As they proceed along the Gallery Walk, students write questions for the author of each piece of work they see. Later, they ask their questions. Or students may write questions on Post-its attached to the exhibit piece.

3. Each product has a student-generated assessment question accompanying it; viewers write answers on Post-its as they have a look.

4. Partners view the work together and write Post-it comments using encouraging language. The comments must be specific, descriptive or supportive.

• Giants, Wizards, Elves

The group agrees on a pose for a Giant, a Wizard, and an Elf. Two teams are formed. Each team huddles and decides which creature it will be in the first round. Teams meet across the centerline, count to three, and make the chosen pose. Wizards fool Giants, Giants beat Elves, and Elves trick Wizards (functions like rock, paper, scissors). Members of the losing team must beat it back to their safety zone (about 20 feet behind the centerline) before the other team tags them. Those caught switch teams. Model tagging before playing.

• Gone Missing

Two students are sent out of the room. A third student hides out of sight. When the two sent out return, they have three guesses to name the missing player. They may work together or compete against each other. At times, more than one person may go missing; when playing this way, pairs or groups may be selected according to something they have in common such as:

> Those not wearing jeans
>
> Those without braces
>
> Those who had Mr. Rose for advisory last year
>
> Those who are members of student council

• Green Door

Leader chooses a topic but only reveals an example of the topic by saying, *You can bring a* (topic example) *through the green door.* Students deduce the topic by guessing what other things—objects, numbers, or ideas—they can bring through the green door, saying, *Can I bring a _____ through the green door?* Leader replies *Yes* or *No.* Play ends when everybody has made a correct guess and a student names the topic.

Example with topic—adjectives, followed by the nouns they modify:
Leader: *I can bring a red brick through the green door.*
Student 1: *Can I bring a football through the green door?* (thinking the topic is nouns)
Leader: *No, you cannot.*
Student 2: *Can I bring a red car through the green door?*
Leader: *Yes.*
(and, after more guesses from students)
Leader: *What is my topic?*
Student 7: *Your topic is adjectives, followed by the nouns they modify.*

• Group Juggle

Materials: 3 to 6 balls or beanbags

Students form a circle and stand. A student is selected to begin and is given a ball or beanbag. She tosses it to someone, who throws it to another, and so on, until each player has received the ball once. The last student to receive the ball tosses it to the student who started. She may stop or keep the ball in play by tossing it to the same person she picked the first time. When the group has mastered using one ball, introduce more into the game, until the group masters juggling several balls in the air simultaneously. Groups can try to complete a round as fast as possible and keep track of their best time. Brainstorm ways to improve the time and continue trying. Model and practice throwing the ball underhand and gently.

• Guess the Number

Leader writes a number on a piece of paper. He hides the number and tells students a range of numbers to guess between. Students take turns around the circle asking yes-or-no questions to determine the number. Guesses are allowed at any time, but a student may not ask a question after guessing incorrectly: in this case, the next student continues the questioning. Leader encourages students to think of questions that will give them information about the number, rather than questions that just eliminate one number. Instead of asking if the number is the number after fourteen, for example, students might ask if it's a two-digit number, whether it's larger than ten, or if it has a five in it. The game is great for developing questioning and listening skills, since players learn from answers to questions.

• Hands Up

Leader chooses a category and selects a student to begin. Whole group chants and claps in unison according to the instructions below, naming the category in the first blank and the student who will begin in the second. Going around the circle, each player then names an item in the category, maintaining the rhythm. If a player misses by repeating or breaking the rhythm, the activity starts over again with the chant naming the player who is next in the circle. The object is to get all the way around the circle without a miss.

Hands up (clap, clap) *for 20___! * (clap, clap) *Gonna name* (clap, clap) *some* _____! (clap, clap) *One apiece,* (clap, clap) *no repeats,* (clap, clap) *no hesitation,* (clap, clap) *no duplication,* (clap, clap) *starting with* (clap, clap) _____ (clap, clap).

Chanting stops at this point but clapping continues in exactly the same manner throughout play. The person named calls out a word that fits the category in the rest between the claps. The student to his right does likewise after the group's next two claps, and so on until everyone has had a chance to add a word to the category.

Topic examples:

> Adjectives, verbs, or nouns
> Instruments of measure
> Presidents of the U.S.
> Cities or countries in the world
> States or bodies of water in the U.S.

Variation: Post a list from which students can get ideas when you want to stretch them with a less familiar topic. The words are all there, but students must listen carefully to avoid repeating.

• Heads or Tails

Materials: a coin

Students stand. Object of the game is to see how many times in a row students correctly guess the side on which a flipped coin lands. Students signal their predictions prior to each coin toss by holding their hand on their head ("heads") or hip ("tails"). A coin is flipped. Those who guessed wrong must sit down. The game continues until one player remains. Leader may wish to ask students to predict how many consecutive correct guesses each will make, and/or how many will be necessary to "win."

• Helium Hoop

Materials: a hula hoop for each group of five to eight players

Groups of five to eight students gather around a hula hoop (a lightweight stick can also be used). Each student places both index fingers under the hoop's edge held at waist level and parallel to the ground. They work together to lower the hoop to the floor while keeping all fingers on the hoop or stick. The results will be "uplifting!"

• Hmong Courtship Game ("Pov Pob")

Students form two equal groups. Each group forms a straight line, its members standing side-by-side, a few feet across from partners from the other line. A tennis ball, koosh ball, or equivalent is given to each member of one of the lines. With a partner, leader models proper toss-and-catch techniques. Leader then holds a quick brainstorm session of possible getting-to-know-you questions. To play, the student in possession of a ball asks a getting-to-know-you question of his partner and tosses the ball to her. Recipient catches the ball, answers the question, and then asks a new question or says, *And you?* before tossing the ball back. Play continues, back and forth, with questions coming from both sides, for two minutes. Afterwards, leader may choose to end the game or move a line one or two positions, creating new partners, and resume play. Note: Leader may choose to call the game "Pov Pob" and leave it at that.

• Honey, Do You Love me?

Two teams are formed. One player (the initiator) from one side walks to the other side and asks one of the players (the responder), *Honey, do you love me?* The response then is, *Honey, I love you, but I just can't smile.* If the responder smiles or laughs while saying this, then he is "recruited" and moves to the other side. If the responder does not laugh, then the initiator is recruited by that team. The game continues until all players are on one side (or until you decide to stop playing!).

• I Never

Materials: 10 coins or tokens for each player (optional)

Students sit in a circle. A student is selected to begin. She states something she has never done. Each player who *has* done the thing named acknowledges it by stepping briefly into the center of the circle or by giving a token to the player who spoke. The game goes around the circle until everybody has had a chance to name something he or she has never done.

• I Sit in the Grass

Students sit in a circle in which there is one empty chair. Key to success: after all required movements at each phase of the game have been completed, *the person to the right of the empty chair is always responsible to continue the forward momentum of the game.* To start, the *student to the right* of the empty chair says, *I sit*, and moves one place to the left, occupying the empty chair. The *student to the right* of the newly vacated chair says, *In the grass*, and also moves one place to the left, occupying the empty chair. The *student to the right* of that newly vacated chair also moves one place to the left and says: *With my friend _____*, naming someone across the circle. The student named rises and moves to the chair vacated by the student who named him. In doing so, of course, his former chair becomes empty, *and the student to the right* of it starts the process all over again, by occupying it and saying, *I sit.* This continues until all students have been called a friend or until they are out of game time. As students begin to master the game, they may be required to speed it up.

• In the Manner of the Adverb

A student is selected to exit the room. The group comes up with an adverb that has an –ly suffix. The student returns. She then goes about determining the adverb in question by requesting that individual students pantomime doing something "in the manner of the adverb." The student making the requests has three guesses to identify the adverb. If she can't, additional clues may be given or the adverb could be revealed.

Requests of student guesser examples:
Jose, please wash dishes in the manner of the adverb.
Neela, please eat breakfast in the manner of the adverb.

• Inside-Outside Circle

Students form a circle within a circle. Those along the inside circle pair with partners along the outside. Leader presents a topic or asks a question. Partners share ideas for a moment or two. Leader asks the inside circle to move clockwise a given number of spaces and find new partners across from them. Leader may have new partners discuss the same topic or question or he may put forth a new one. Before beginning, leader may ask students to review how to greet and thank partners as they move from one to another.

Question examples:
Problem-solving focus: *What do we need to do so we can include a greater variety of people in our groups?*
Content Focus: *Should we continue spending money on the U.S. space program and why?*
Content Focus: *In your opinion, what was the most troubling issue for the colonists? What would you have done to solve it?*

• Inuit High Kick

Materials: a ball or other soft, swinging target for kicking, attached firmly to a pole

The group sees how much it can help a few of its members elevate. Students form a circle large enough to accommodate running and kicking. A student is selected to hold the target. Another volunteers to kick first.

Kicker starts several steps away from the target. Target is held a reasonably reachable height from the floor (roughly at waist level). Audience watches quietly. Student approaches and kicks target. Target is raised approximately six inches before student approaches and kicks target again. This is repeated two or three times, until target reaches a height which the student fails to kick. At that point, student tries a final time, with target at the same height, but with audience giving robust vocal encouragement by chanting in unison, AAAAAYYYYYYYYYYYYYYYYY-YA! Audience does its best to time the –YA! part of the chant to coincide with the actual kicking of the target. Usually, the kicker succeeds with the support of the group. Discuss the effect of group support. Repeat with two or three other volunteers.

• Is This Seat Taken?

A student is selected to stand in the middle of the circle. His vacated chair is removed. He approaches another and asks, *Is this seat taken?* If the answer is *no*, the two exchange places, and the student who gave up her seat begins another round. If the answer is *yes*, he must ask another. As the student is asking the question, others are quietly trading seats across the circle behind his back. Make sure switching players make eye contact before exchanging seats; also make sure they understand that once they make eye contact and begin to move, they must follow through and exchange seats with the person with whom they made eye contact. If the student in the middle sees them switching, he tries to take one of the seats that is temporarily vacant during the switch. If he is successful, the student left standing starts the next round. Discuss with students when might be a good time to answer *no* to the question. Students also could create a few guidelines on how to keep this game moving and avoid excluding some.

• Key Punch

Materials: 20 objects

(A key punch is a machine actuated by a keyboard and used to cut holes in punch cards. They were used in early computers.)

Number the objects (paper plates work well) from 1-20 and scatter them inside a circle (use a piece of string or rope or chalk to designate a circle). These twenty objects become the keys on a key-punch device. The group starts 15 to 20 feet away from the keys and must run to the keys and punch the numbers in correct sequential order. Teams must create a plan to do this. When students on a team arrive at the key-punch circle they must take turns entering the circle and punching a number. There should be only one student in the circle at a time. After the group has punched all the numbers, it must run back to the starting line. This is a timed event.

• Knots

Students stand in a circle and link right hands with someone across from them. They repeat this process with left hands, selecting someone other than the student with whom they joined right hands: the "knot" is complete. Next, students must untangle the knot without letting go of hands. By grabbing short strips of cloth or rope (stretchy is fun) instead of hands, proximity and touching are diminished, making this a safer option early in the school year.

• Line Ups

Students arrange themselves as quickly as possible in an ordered line according to a prompt given by the leader. Students can line up by height, by birthdays, age, number of siblings, alphabetically, according to a number given them on a slip of paper (numbers can be large and don't have to be consecutive), last four digits of their telephone number, etc.

Variations: To increase the challenge, students line up while whispering, silently, while speaking a language besides English, on a bench or log, or within a narrow space.

• Macaroni and Cheese

Students form groups of three. Each group chooses a pair of things that go together: macaroni and cheese, salt and pepper, chips and salsa, fish and chips, dogs and bones, ducks and water, horse and buggy, shoes and socks, left and right, etc. Standing in a circle, groups share their pairs, to make sure there are no repeats. Each student in the group has a job. For example, if the group's pair is macaroni and cheese, one student is the Macaroni and another is the Cheese. The third guides them together. To play, one of the pair, Macaroni, closes her eyes. The other, Cheese, finds a new spot to stand in, away from the other two members of her group. The third group member will serve as a guide for the one whose eyes are closed. The guide stays alongside the teammate she's guiding. Once everyone is ready, Macaroni yells out, *Macaroni!* And Cheese responds, *Cheese!* The macaroni uses the sound of the cheese's voice (and the guide) to find her. Calls may be repeated as needed. Switch roles within groups when finished and play again.

• Magic Ball

An acting game. Ball is imaginary and morphs into a different object each time it's passed from student to student. Students form a circle and stand. A student is selected to begin. She mimes molding a ball of malleable clay into an object—a watermelon, coffee cup, book, anything—and pretends to carefully hand it to the student to her right. Her neighbor pretends to carefully take possession of it before transforming it into a new object. Imaginary patting and/or sculpting the object into its new shape is mandatory. Dramatic acting can add to the effect: a heavy object may cause a student to struggle to handle it; a smelly object may cause one's nose to wrinkle, etc.

This activity is done silently. Guesses as to what each student intended the object to represent wait until after the game.

• Me Too

A student begins by saying something that is true about himself, e.g., *I live to play basketball*, or *I have two brothers*. If others in the circle share the stated sentiment, they may snap their fingers or stand up and say, *Me too!* The game goes around the circle until everybody has had a chance.

• Media Mania

Leader offers an assignment to partners or small groups. Groups are to choose from the menu of choices below and respond to this prompt: You are an advertising agency, and your job is to convince people in a 30-second TV ad to buy a product that makes them attractive by:

> Making their eyebrows grow continually
>
> Painting their noses different colors
>
> Wearing their clothes backwards
>
> Wearing huge shoulder pads
>
> Wearing many layers of clothes
>
> Wearing a bustle (men and women)
>
> Tattooing their faces in black, red, and white

• Mix and Mingle

Students move around in the center of the circle. At the leader's signal they stop and make physical contact in a prescribed way (touch thumbs, shoulders, elbows, toes, hips, back to back, etc.); as contact is maintained, pairs exchange a prescribed piece of information (birthday, number of siblings, names of siblings, names of pets, job they have, favorite food, song, kind of music they enjoy, a book they read recently, sport to watch, sport to play). Then the mingling resumes until the leader signals another connection.

• Mrs. Mumble

Students are seated in a circle. They hide their teeth while speaking by curling their lips over their teeth. A student is selected to begin. He starts by addressing his neighbor and asking this question: _____, *have you seen Mrs. Mumble?* The neighbor responds by saying, *No,* _____, *I have not seen Mrs. Mumble! but I'll ask my neighbor.* She turns to the next person and asks: _____, *have you seen Mrs. Mumble?* The answer is always the same. Play continues around the circle. See Mrs. Mumble, a children's book, as a resource.

• Name Game: Name Us All

Students attempt to name everyone in the room without looking. When the namer has said every person's name he can think of, ask students whose names haven't been said yet to raise their hands. They can greet the namer, and he can try to identify them by their voices.

• Name Game: Name with Gesture

Follows Choice of Gesture Greeting where students state their names along with a gesture. Recalling as much as possible from the greeting, ask for volunteers to try to name everyone and repeat their identifying gestures.

• Name Game: Toss a Name Game

Students form a circle. Begin by having each student say his or her name. Next, the leader holds a ball and repeats his own name, *I am Steve*, then names a student and tosses the ball to her, *and this is Kris*. Kris catches the ball and says, *That is Steve, I am Kris, and this is Amanda*, and then tosses the ball to Amanda. After the first student, each will say two names besides her own. The game continues until all have been called. Model and practice safe, efficient ball-tossing before beginning.

Variations: Play the game again, trying to beat the previous time or with multiple balls at the same time or with a cumulative name recitation in which each successive person names all who have had the ball before her.

• No, No, No...

One student is chosen to start a story with a ridiculous remark such as, *On your way to school this morning, did you see that bus full of quacking giraffes?* The next player says, *No, no, no....* and changes part of the story in an equally ridiculous way. For example, the next player might say, *No, no, no...that wasn't a bus of full of quacking giraffes! It was actually a boat full of roaring hamburgers!* The story continues to change as it goes around the circle and ends when everybody has had a turn.

Model and practice with the group how to start a wacky story and how to change it. To make the activity more challenging, have each player add to the story rather than changing it. Using the example above, the second player could say, *No, no, no... it wasn't a bus full of quacking giraffes; it was a boat full of roaring hamburgers and they were passing by a picnic of quacking giraffes!* The next player would add a third part to the story after repeating what had come before.

• Non-Verbal Messages

Two groups have a list of words that show feelings or states of mind to pantomime. They take turns acting out without speaking, and the other group tries to guess what's going on. Possible feeling states to communicate non-verbally:

I'm glad to meet you.	I feel terrific today!
I'm tired.	I'm so angry with you for being late.
I'm so excited.	I'm impatient.
I'm bored.	I'm in love.
I'm worried.	I'm not interested.
I'm nervous.	I can't see well.
I'm proud of my work.	I need help.
I'd like to meet you.	I'm so confused and lost.
Ouch, that's hot!	I'm really interested.

• Observation Olympics

Ten to 15 objects are laid out for students to observe. Then the objects are temporarily hidden, one (or more) is removed, and the group tries to guess which object is missing. In each round, all are observed again before the removal and guessing are repeated.

• Obstacle Course

Find a large space for this activity (gymnasium, playground). May be played with individual classes or in large groups of 100+. Leader has scattered objects around the space. Students form pairs; one of each pair is then blindfolded. Those not blindfolded must go to a designated area and verbally lead their partners through the scattered objects. The blindfolded partner must reach his partner without touching any of the objects. Have the partners switch roles when finished. Students may time how long it takes for teammates to navigate the course.

• One Frog

A cumulative game of concentration. Players stand in a circle. Play moves sequentially around the circle, each player saying one thing about a frog (or frogs). The group begins by considering various aspects of a single frog: how many eyes and legs it has, an activity all frogs enjoy (jumping into a pond), and how many "kersplashes" it would make were it to jump in the pond (a single one—KERSPLASH!)

Example:
Player 1: *One frog*
Player 2: *with Two eyes*
Player 3: and *Four legs*
Player 4: *Jumped into the pond*
Player 5: *KERSPLASH!*

Notice two things: The student whose turn comes after the student who counts frog legs will always say the same thing: *Jumped into the pond*. No counting will ever be necessary for this student. Also, notice that the student responsible for the first KERSPLASH need not count KERSPLASHES; she simply makes the noise a single frog might cause when it jumps into water.

Player 6 will move the group to considering Two Frogs, and the students who follow will have to adjust:

Player 6: *Two frogs*
Player 7: with *Four eyes*
Player 8: and *Eight legs*
Player 9: *Jumped into the pond* (this line never varies)
Player 10: *KERSPLASH!*
Player 11: *KERSPLASH!* (a second KERSPLASH is needed because there are two frogs leaping—these are untrained, non-synchronized diving frogs!)
Player 12: *Three frogs*
Player 13: with *Six eyes*
Player 14: and *Twelve legs*

Player 15: *Jumped into the pond*
Player 16: *KERSPLASH!*
Player 17: *KERSPLASH!*
Player 18: *KERSPLASH!*

Play continues in this fashion, with group working to concentrate and avoid making counting or naming mistakes. When a mistake is made, leader may decide to have the next player start over, or play may continue.

• One-Minute Talk

Students sign up for or are assigned times during advisory to speak to the class for one minute. Topics for talking may be assigned, may be chosen ahead of time, or may be given on the spot, depending on level of student readiness. Audience listens respectfully. Time for questions afterwards is optional, but questions during the one-minute talk are not allowed. Students may not use visual aids.

Variation: Invite students to name good topics for sharer. The sharer may choose one, or share on a topic of her own.

• Paper Toss

Divide the room in half. Make balls of paper and strew them along the dividing line. Divide into two teams. The object is to get the paper balls on the other team's side. Create rules for fair play and decide on a method of moving balls (throwing, swatting, kicking, flicking, etc.) before beginning. Set a timer for two minutes. When the time is up, count the balls of paper on each side to determine the winner.

• Park Bench

Two chairs are set up to resemble a park bench. Two student actors are selected and given a card with the "what happened" part of a news story. They have one minute to prepare a scene in which they pretend they just met each other and have a conversation about the event (who, when, where) without ever actually saying what happened. The prep time is short to keep the drama improvisational and spontaneous. After watching the actors talk and dramatize on the park bench for a short while, the audience guesses what the news story was about. The actors continue in the scene until the class names the event.

Examples:

> What: Tornado caused great damage
>
> Where: Iowa
>
> When: yesterday
>
> Who: people who lived in mobile homes

• Passing Game

Materials: small stick or pebble

A sleight-of-hand guessing game. Students sit in a circle, hands up, palms up. Each student's right hand lies on top of his neighbor-to-the-right's left hand. A pattern with a regular, even tempo is established, and in the rhythm, everyone makes the motion of picking something out of his own left hand and placing it in his neighbor's left hand. Practice this pattern until all can do it together.

Next, add the following chant to the passing motion (or make up your own, or have students create one):

Pebble pebble treble bass
Well done medium or rare.
Is it true? Regard his face!
We've left poor _____ standing there!

A student is selected to move to the middle of the circle. She will be the guesser. A small stick or pebble is passed around the circle, as the chant is said; students keep the pebble hidden from the guesser's sight and everyone feigns passing the pebble. Guesser has three tries to guess where the pebble is. When the guesser is correct, the person who was caught with the pebble goes into the middle.

• Passing the Hoop

Materials: hula hoops

Students stand in a circle, holding hands. A hula hoop is placed between any two students, resting over their clasped hands. Students pass the hoop around the circle while keeping hands held. The goal is to pass the hoop around the group without hands letting go at any point.

Variations: Add as many hoops as you like, going both directions, increasing the challenge as students master earlier versions. Challenge students to set a speed record!

• Pico Firme Bago

Materials: scratch paper, chart or board for writing

A game of logical deduction. Leader secretly selects a three-digit number. She also creates three columns (for ones, tens, and hundreds) on the board or chart that will be used during play. As students make a guess, leader writes their guesses in the columns. She then gives the group clues as to the accuracy of the guess, using the words Pico, Firme, and Bago to do so.

Definitions:

> Pico: wrong place, wrong digit
>
> Firme: wrong place, correct digit
>
> Bago: correct place, correct digit

Example: Leader's secret number is 357. First student guesses 691. Leader writes the number on the chart and responds, *Pico, pico, pico*, indicating that the numbers are altogether wrong. Second student guesses 542. Leader responds, *Firme, pico pico*, indicating that the 5 is correct but in the wrong place, the others altogether wrong. Third student guesses 785. Leader responds, *Firme, pico, firme*, indicating that the seven and five are correct but in the wrong places, the eight altogether wrong. Fourth student guesses 375. Leader responds, *Bago, firme, firme*, indicating the three is altogether correct, the seven and five correct but in the wrong places. Fifth student guesses 357. Leader responds, *Bago! Bago! Bago!* The fifth student may then select another secret three-digit number or another volunteer may choose one.

• Pictionary

Materials: paper, drawing materials

A student is selected to go first. Leader gives that student a word. The student makes a quick representational drawing of the word while the group watches. The first student to correctly guess "draws" the next word. Decide on a method of guessing before you begin. Play in teams once the group has mastered playing individually.

• Popcorn Acknowledgments

Students form a circle, standing. At random, students acknowledge others for deeds done recently. After each acknowledgment, the group may honor the student being acknowledged with a simultaneous clap, bow, chant, etc. See Cheers on page XX.

• Quiz Show

Leader creates questions and answers to be used in a game-show format. The game may be modeled on a television version—Jeopardy, for example—or be a new invention. The game may be played individually or in teams. After initial success, students may create their own questions and answers, or create their own format(s). To ensure success, model and practice how to respond to questions properly. Bells, buzzers, raising hands, etc. may be employed, but make sure the rules and procedures for responding are clear.

Variation: Students can recall news stories read to them. Divide students into teams of 2 to 4 members. Each team has a bell or other noisemaker. One person on team A reads a news story to the other teams. Another member of team A then calls out the categories, one by one: Who, What, When, Where, Why, pausing after each one to see if anyone can answer. When a listening team has an answer, its members ring their bell. The objective is to see if the listening teams can fill in all the details of the story.

• Ra-di-o

Students sit in a circle, with plenty of room on the outside to be used later. Leader teaches students a hand gesture that will accompany each of the three syllables in the word RADIO:

> Ra = one hand atop head, pointing left or right
>
> di = one hand under chin, pointing left or right
>
> o = pointing at any other student in the circle

A student is selected to begin. She says *Ra* and points left or right, placing her index finger atop her head. The student she points at must quickly say *di* and point to his left or right by placing his index finger under his chin. That student points to someone else in the circle while saying, *o*. The student indicated by the student saying *o* starts a new round of play by saying *Ra* and pointing either left or right (she must have her index finger atop her head when she does this!). If a student points incorrectly or takes too much time, she becomes "radio static" in the outer circle. These students try to distract the group with conversation, weird noises, etc. As their numbers grow, their power should make it increasingly difficult for those remaining to concentrate. Establish what appropriate "static" looks like, sounds like, and feels like (Y-Chart) before beginning.

• Rap a Rhythm

This is a call and response activity. While seated in a circle, leader "calls" by patting his knees, clapping his hands and/or snapping his fingers in a basic rhythmic pattern. The student to his right "responds" by creating a different short rhythmic pattern of his own. Leader then repeats his initial rhythm. Then everyone simultaneously repeats the response of the student to the leader's right. Leader then calls again (he uses the same rhythm each time he calls) and the next student responds with her unique rhythm. Continue around the circle: each student listens to the leader's call and responds with his own rhythm; then, after the call is repeated by the leader, everyone simultaneously repeats the response in question.

• Rare Birds

Materials: notecards

Leader gives a notecard to each student. On the cards, students write their names and answers to 2 or 3 questions/prompts from the leader. Leader collects the cards and reads the answers aloud. Students have 3 guesses to identify the "rare bird" described in the card. Remind students to respect differences. Our purpose is to celebrate uniqueness.

Prompt examples:

> List three things you like to do after school.
>
> List three of your favorite songs, foods, etc.
>
> Who is your favorite book character?
>
> What's your favorite piece of technology?
>
> What is something most people may not know about you?

You can read several Rare Bird cards as an activity and save the others for future advisories.

• Sausages

One student is chosen to stand and move to the center of the circle. The rest of the group asks her questions, one student at a time. She must respond to all questions by saying, *Sausages!* and must remain serious. The goal of the game is to get the student in the middle to smile. Once she smiles, she sits down and a new student is selected to move to the middle. While planning, include a rule about asking appropriate questions. Also, the students who is "It" can stay in the circle rather than standing in the middle (less risky).

• Shape Up

Materials: about five pieces of flat elastic, nine feet each; blindfolds (optional)

Leader forms students into teams of four, five, or six. Teams work together to recreate with a piece of elastic as exactly as possible a geometric shape drawn on a piece of paper by the leader. Leader displays one figure at a time; the figures are progressively more challenging. All team members must have contact with the elastic at all times. As teams master the figures, the leader may ask them to make increasingly complex ones, or blindfold all but one member, who can give instructions to the others.

• Shrinking World

Materials: hula hoops (preferably of different sizes) or pieces of rope to create circles.

Leader places many rope circles or hula hoops within the set boundaries, then gives the command, *Float!* Students move among the circles, greeting each other. Upon the leader's signal to *Find a piece of the world*, all students must get both feet off the area outside the circles (no foot can be touching the "water" outside of a circle). Next, at the leader's signal, everyone must "float" again, and upon the call to find a piece of the world to stand in, find another circle. Between signals, as players are moving around, the leader removes a circle or two so the world keeps shrinking and the challenge to get everyone onto a safe piece of land is greater. The game is over when the leader decides that the group has consolidated itself as much as possible or is advisable.

Note: Students should problem-solve methods of finding their pieces of the world while following the rules. For example, they may stand with one foot in one circle and the other in another, or they may be held by others inside the circle. It's more fun to play without brainstorming these ideas first; allow them to emerge in the course of the game.

• Shuffle 'em Up

Students write their names on large notecards. Leader says, *Shuffle 'em up!* Students switch cards with one or more other players, then hold the new one in front of them like a nametag. A student is selected to stand in the middle of the circle. He reads all the names and rearranges the cards in players' hands as quickly as possible so that each player is once again holding his or her own name card. Once all notecards and students match, the leader may say again, *Shuffle 'em up.* As variations, choose more than one student to stand in the middle to sort names, or use nicknames or last names (Mr. Naim, Ms. Cruz). As the group gets to know each other better, you can try using students' personal information instead of their names: their interests, favorite TV shows, birthplaces, etc.

• Simultaneous Clap

Students stand in a circle. Leader starts by clapping both hands with the student to his right, just once, "pat-a-cake" style; that student quickly turns to her right and repeats this with her other neighbor, and so on. After the clap makes it all the way around the circle, the challenge is to clap individually but simultaneously with the person next to you, one pair at a time, around the circle. Go faster to create more fun. At the end, see if the whole group can clap their own hands at the same moment.

• Snake Toss

Students form a single-file line a few steps apart from each other. The student in the back is given an object. She tosses it to the person in front of her; that student tosses it to the next student in line, and so on, trying to get the object to the front of the line. Whoever tosses the object then races to the front of the line, trying to beat the object there. To match the degree of running/tossing difficulty, additional running distance or challenges may be necessary. The person now at the end of the line begins the process again.

• Something Bad about Something Good

A student names something good in school, at home, or in life in general. The next person in the circle says, *Yes but something bad about that is* _____, describing something bad about what the first person has stated. The next person says, *Yes, but something good about that is* _____, describing something good about what the second person stated. This continues around the circle as students alternately describe something bad about something good and something good about something bad. The "somethings" have to be real, not fantasy. The activity pushes students to think hard and imaginatively. The first person may begin either with something good or something bad.

Example:

I've got to go to my aunt's house on Saturday—what a bummer!

Yes, but something good about that is that cousins might be there and you can hang out together.

Yes, but something bad about that is that if your cousins are there you will be stuck with the adults.

• Something's Changed

A student is selected to stand in the middle of the circle and slowly turn around. The students in the circle observe her carefully, trying to memorize the details of how she looks: what she is wearing, her hairstyle, any accessories she may be wearing, etc. She then goes out of sight and quickly changes one, two, or three things about her appearance. Upon her return, she turns around slowly in the middle of the group, inviting students to try to ascertain what she has changed. Collectively, three guesses are given.

• Space Station

Materials: flashlight, blindfold

Students form a large circle, moving as far as possible from the middle of the room. They count off into groups of four; each group adopts a name and announces it. A student from one of the teams is blindfolded and handed a flashlight and led to the middle of the room. She calls one team, and the members of that team scatter around the room. She turns on the flashlight and begins moving the beam around the room, trying to shine the beam on each of the members of the group she has called. Team members try to make it to the middle of the room and tag the student holding the flashlight, avoiding the light. If they are hit by the beam, they freeze. If one team member is able to tag the flashlight holder, a new student is selected to be in the middle and a new round can begin. If all four members of the team are frozen, a new round begins.

• Table Top

After mingling politely among each other, students spontaneously arrange themselves into groups of two, three, four, or more at leader's prompt. For example, if leader calls *Table for four!*, students quickly form into groups of four and stand still. They may not choose to exclude anyone from their group or go out of their way to create a group consisting of best friends. Once groups are formed, leader announces a topic to be discussed and amount of time for the discussion. For example, *Table for five, two minutes on the value of caring for a pet.* Groups discuss; leader times conversations and gives signal for quiet after time expires. Play can continue for multiple rounds. Students mix and mingle between rounds to insure the formation of a variety of groups. Leader can help guide conversations by appointing a group facilitator for each Table Top discussion.

• Tag Games

Materials: large space marked with game boundaries

Review safe tagging (shoulders, back, arms) and the Tagger's Choice rule (if the tagger says she got you, she did). Model and practice running safely in a crowd, linking elbows, and staying within the set boundaries before starting.

Variations:

Elbow Tag: students form pairs. Pairs randomly scatter across the playing area and stand still, side-by-side, one hand on hip and elbows hooked together. Leader selects one pair to separate; she gives one of the separated students the role of chaser. The other separated student is to try to avoid being tagged. To avoid being tagged, students can run among the pairs or hook onto an outside elbow of any student. Upon hooking elbows, the player being chased is safe; she has created a group of three linked students. When this occurs, the student on the other end of the newly-formed group of three must unhook elbows, break free, and run to try to avoid getting tagged. Whenever a student is tagged, she immediately takes over the role of tagger

Freeze Tag: after a player is frozen by the tagger, two single players can unfreeze him by holding hands and encircling him. In the meantime, however, the tagger may tag the partners who are trying to unfreeze the frozen player.

Partner Tag: students hold hands and try to tag other pairs, who freeze when tagged. Pairs can be unfrozen by other partners who each tag each of them.

Toilet Tag: this is Freeze Tag with a twisted twist! Leader assigns two or more inept "plumbers" (taggers) depending on the size of the group. The rest of the group consists of free-flowing "toilets" (players who try to avoid getting tagged). When a student is tagged by a plumber, she gets "clogged" (freezes) and raises one arm in the air. That arm becomes her "flush handle." A frozen student is "un-clogged" when another student approaches and "flushes" her arm. The frozen player then says, *Whoosh*, and twirls around once before she may roam freely. Play continues for a preset amount of time, or until all students are frozen. Leader may need to adjust the number of inept plumbers to create the proper balance of plumbers and toilets.

• Talk Show

A student is selected to be interviewed as if she were appearing on a talk show. She leaves the room, but remains within earshot. The rest of the class is given a moment to think of a few interesting, open-ended questions to ask. When everyone's ready, the selected student is introduced to the group by another student or by the leader. She enters and sits, as the others applaud. Then, anyone can ask a question, starting with, *What is a hobby of yours?* Additional questions may follow the hobby question or student may choose others, like, *What is your biggest dream in life?* or *Tell us about a time when you really enjoyed yourself.* Students also can brainstorm topics for future talk shows.

• Team Red Light, Green Light

Materials: small ball or beanbag

Students form teams of four to eight. A leader is selected for each team. Teams begin side-by-side, along a starting line, with leader several steps away; her back is towards them. A small ball or equivalent is placed behind her, in plain view of the team. When the leader says, *Green light!*, the team moves toward the leader, and on the command, *Red light!*, the team must freeze. Leader turns to face them, and tries to catch one of the players moving; if she does, she tells the whole team to go back to the start. If she doesn't, she turns her back to them, calls, *Green light!*, and play continues. Team tries to advance to the leader, capture the small ball, and return with it to the place from which they started. Once they are in possession of the ball, the fun begins. Leader continues to call out *Red light!* and *Green light!* as before; but now, when she turns to face the team, her challenge is to try to determine which team member is in possession of the ball after they freeze. If she is correct, then the entire team must move back and start over. If not, on the *Green light!* command, the group continues to pass the ball and move backwards to get back to the starting line with the ball. Team tries to hide the ball from the leader, strategizing on the fly to successfully get the ball from one student to another as they move back to the starting line.

• Telephone

Students sit in a circle. Leader introduces a statement to the group by whispering it to one student, who whispers it to the next student, and so on. Students try their best not to alter the message in any way; if a student isn't clear about the message after hearing it once, she may say, "Operator," indicating she'd like to have it repeated. When the message makes its way all the way around the circle, the final person announces her version of it.

Variations: Send different messages in opposite directions at the same time. Set a time limit for messages completing the circuit.

• Touch Someone Who

Students sit in a circle and close their eyes. Leader chooses four volunteer "Tappers." Tappers stand; remaining students continue to keep their eyes closed. Leader chooses from categories listed below, or may invent her own. Categories are preceded by the phrase, *Touch someone who....* Tappers move quietly around the room gently tapping the shoulders of students they feel fit each category. Leader gives ample time for tapping before announcing a new category. Play may continue for several categories. Leader selects new tappers at intervals, so that everyone gets a chance to be a tapper.

Category examples: *Touch someone who...*

> Is a good listener
>
> Will find a cure for cancer
>
> Will be a millionaire
>
> Will invent something
>
> With whom you would like to be stranded on a desert island
>
> You think has helped us with our hopes and dreams
>
> Is as good as . . .(gold, a chocolate sundae, etc.)
>
> With whom you would share a secret
>
> Would look good in pink
>
> Is a good friend
>
> You don't often work with, but would like to get to know better
>
> Helped you today
>
> Would make a good . . .leader, accountant, computer repair specialist, dancer, comedian
>
> Sometimes makes you laugh
>
> With whom you'd like to have lunch
>
> With whom you would like to play at recess
>
> You admire
>
> You would take on an all-expenses-paid trip to Fargo, ND, New York City, Hawaii, etc.
>
> Has taught you something
>
> You have seen using the CARES skills—cooperation, assertion, responsibility, empathy, self-control
>
> You'd invite to join your rock 'n roll band—singers, roadies, guitar players, bus drivers, etc.

Processing questions:
How did it feel being tapped? Why?
How did it feel being the Tapper? Why?
Do you have other ideas for categories we can ask?
How does this activity help us to make a more caring classroom?
Do you have any ideas on how to make it more fun or meaningful?

• Tug of War

Materials: a strong rope with a marker at its center

Leader divides students into two equal teams based on weight and strength. A line is drawn, or a scarf or string is tied, on a strong rope to indicate its midpoint. Teams grab hold of the rope at its opposite ends and begin pulling when the leader signals. The object is to be the first team to pull the other team toward them until the marker at the rope's midpoint moves a predetermined distance. Leader may choose to stop the game at any point to allow teams to strategize. Teams may want to create a name, slogan, and/or chant to use as they pull.

• Twenty Questions

Materials: notecards

A student is chosen to stand in the middle of the circle. A notecard naming a hobby (or person place or thing) is affixed to his back. He then asks up to twenty yes-or-no questions to try to figure out what is written on the card. He may address his questions to individuals or to the whole group. Guesses are allowed at any time, with a maximum of three guesses. After ten questions, the player may ask for clues from the class. To increase the level of difficulty, the group may agree to ban certain categories of questions.

• What Are You Doing?

A student is selected to begin. She stands in the circle (or in the center) and mimes someone engaging in an activity, for example, playing the violin. The student to her left or right in the circle asks her, _____ (name), *what are you doing?* The first student replies by naming an activity other than the one she is miming: *I'm painting a picture.* The first student then returns to her seat, while the student who asked the question commences to mime the activity that was named. This continues around the circle until all have had a chance to mime and tell someone else to mime an activity. To increase the fun (and the risk), students can do their pantomime in the center of the circle.

• What Would You Do?

Leader describes a scenario, filling in details up to a critical point of decision-making. He then poses the question to the group: *What would you do?* A student is selected to respond first; then other student responses are added, Whip Share style, around the circle. Students may pass, but leaders are encouraged to invite passers to continue to think about possible answers and return to them after all others have had an opportunity to respond.

Variation: Use this activity with academic content by describing an event in history, current events, science, or literature, and asking, *What would you do in such a situation?*

• What's in a Name?

Materials: paper, pencil

Leader announces and posts a current topic of study. Students form groups of four; each group receives a blank piece of paper. Students write their first names at the top of their group's paper. Groups then brainstorm words that both fit the selected topic and begin with letters of their names. When finished, each group stands and names its best three to five words. Players can also be acknowledged for having:

> The most words
>
> The longest word
>
> The most words with more than three letters

Topic examples:

> List as many words as you can that are associated with weather. Results: Tom ("t"ornado); Jane ("e"lectrical storm); Deshon ("d"eep snow, "s"now, "h"urricane)
>
> List as many mammals as you can
>
> List nutritious food
>
> List any/all plant terms studied this year

• What's Your Job?

Students sit in a circle. A student is selected to leave the room; her chair is removed. She'll return in a moment and begin to ask each person in the circle, *What's your job?* While she's out of the room, one student is selected to respond, *I'm a student*—the truthful answer. Remaining students come up with a pretend career to claim for themselves. When the student returns and begins to ask others what their jobs are, each student responds with the "pretend" job, but when the selected student responds, *I'm a student*, everyone gets up and exchanges chairs with someone across the circle. In that moment, the student in the middle attempts to find a seat. The student left without a spot leaves the room, a new student is selected to be "a student" (provide the truthful answer), everyone else chooses a new pretend career, and the game continues. Model and practice how to safely exchange seats and move in traffic before beginning.

Variation: Can be played with different categories, for example, **Where are you from?** What school do you attend? The key is to have only one student respond with the correct answer, while everyone else makes up a pretend answer.

• When the Cold Wind Blows

Students sit in a circle. One student is selected to stand in the middle of the circle and say, *When the cold wind blows, it blows for anyone who*_____, filling in the blank with a category such as *has a dog*. Everyone who fits that category quickly finds a new place to sit. The one student who doesn't find a seat now stands in the center of the circle and continues the game by saying, *When the cold wind blows, it blows for anyone who* _____, naming a new category. The activity continues for several rounds. You can limit categories to ones that relate to interests, hobbies, and family, or to a curriculum topic, rather than allowing students to focus, say, on clothing or appearance. Model and practice safe movement across the circle and how to claim chairs by tagging them. Can initially be played with an equal number of chairs and students in order to teach safety or review the process of the game.

• YES!

Students stand or sit in a circle and look around at each other's eyes. When eye contact is made, both players say, *Yes!* They then switch seats, high-fiving as they walk across the circle.

Variation: Leader asks players to look down and choose somebody's shoes on which to focus. Leader then slowly calls, *Waist, shoulders, eyes.* On the word "eyes," players look up and see if someone is looking. If so, they say, *Yes!*, and switch seats. *Yes!* may be substituted by other positive forms of recognizing another person.

• Zoom

A player begins the activity by saying, *Zoom!* (fast car sound) and turns her head quickly to a neighbor on either the right or the left. The neighbor passes the zoom to the next player and so on around the circle. The idea is to go as fast as you can. Challenge the players to go faster and time how long it takes to zoom around the circle.

Variations: Add the right to reverse the direction of the speeding car with an accompanying sound (*Screech* or *Eek*), or turn the corner onto another street (call out the name of a person in the circle—*Natalie Street*) or feign a bad driving move (by saying *Cell phone!*) and the next person must continue with *Zoom* without faltering, or add in *Bump*, which signifies that you skip over the next person in the direction that the Zoom is already going. Any mistakes restart the game and the object is to see how long you can keep it going without a mishap (crash). The group might choose to eliminate players when they make mistakes later on in the year.

• Zumi Zumi

More rhythmic fun! Groups of 7 to 10 students sit in circles. A student in each circle is selected to begin in the role of Zumi Zumi. Zumi Zumi has the highest status during the game. The person to the left of Zumi Zumi has the next highest, and so on around the circle. The chant starts with everyone saying: *AAAAAAAAHHHHHHHHH* while spiraling their hands upwards. Then the patting/clapping rhythm begins: pat your lap twice; clap twice; pat your lap twice; clap twice. This sequence is maintained throughout play, including during speaking, while the play moves to different people around the circle when their names are called. You say your own name on the pats and the other person's name on the claps. Here's what happens:

1. Warm-up:

Pat pat/*Zumi Zumi*

Clap clap/silence

(repeat until the rhythm is established)

2. Go around the circle once. Zumi Zumi starts the action:

Zumi: Pat pat/*Zumi Zumi*

        Clap clap/*Jack Jack*

Jack: Pat pat/*Jack Jack*

        Clap clap/*Maria Maria*

Maria: Pat pat/*Maria Maria*

        Clap clap/*Sophie Sophie*

And so on around the circle.

3. After making it successfully around the circle with no rhythmic glitches, Zumi Zumi continues play, this time saying *Zumi Zumi* and calling the name of any person in the circle. The person called must respond in rhythm, by saying her name twice and any other person's name. When a person delays or makes a mistake, he moves into the chair just to the right of Zumi Zumi (the lowest-status chair). The object of the game is to have any person with a status higher than you or Zumi Zumi make a mistake, so he must move out of the status chair, the person to his left becomes the new Zumi Zumi, and you are ready for a new round.

Example:

Zumi: Pat pat/*Zumi Zumi*

        Clap clap/*Greta Greta* (Zumi Zumi call on someone out of sequence in the circle)

Greta: Pat pat/*Greta Greta*

        Clap clap/*Clara Clara* (Jake calls on someone out of sequence in the circle)

Clara: Pat pat/*Clara Clara*

        Clap clap/*Zumi Zumi* (Clara calls on someone out of sequence in the circle)

If Zumi Zumi misses the beat or makes any mistake, he gives up his chair to the person on his left, the new Zumi Zumi, everyone shift up one seat, and the deposed Zumi Zumi goes to the lowest status chair, the one to the right of the new Zumi Zumi.

Variation: To increase the challenge, use numbers instead of names. Everyone except Zumi Zumi counts off starting with the student to Zumi Zumi's right, who is number One, student to her right is Two, and so on. The larger the number, the higher the status, so in a group of eight, Seven is second only to Zumi Zumi. Players then say numbers instead of names, except for Zumi Zumi.

Example:

Zumi: Pat pat/ *Zumi Zumi*

        Clap clap/ *to the Three* (Zumi calls on the person three spaces to his right)

Student 3: Pat pat/ *to the Three*

        Clap clap/ *to the Ten* (Student 3 calls on the person seven spaces to her right)

Student 10: Pat pat/ *to the Ten*

        Clap clap/ *Zumi Zumi* (Student 1 calls on Zumi)

CHEERS

• The Alligator

Stretch both arms straight out as if to make an alligator's jaws; then at the signal do one big clap.

• The Beatnik

The Beatnik harkens back to the coffee houses of the '60's. Students cross arms in front of themselves and snap fingers in unison.

• The Clam

Interlock fingers; at the count, clap palms of hands together.

• High Five

Pass a high five around the circle, down the row to your partners, etc.

• Invent Your Own

The best cheers will be the ones the students create. Have them design cheers that relate to the purpose of the acknowledgment. For example, to acknowledge somebody for helping her on the phone with homework, the student could mime picking up a phone, dialing, and saying, *Thank you, homework help line!*

• The Noiseless Cheer

Hearing-impaired people use this to acknowledge others. Open hands, palms out, are raised to ear level and shaken.

• Round of Applause

Clap while moving your hands in a circle.

• Two Snaps Up

As a group, start with hands waist high. At the count, raise hands to shoulder height and snap once. Then lower hands back to waist level. Raise hands again to shoulder height and snap once.

Additional Advisory Resources

ASKING QUALITY QUESTIONS

Use these questions during sharing or whenever you want to elicit thoughtful conversation on any topic.

Knowledge Questions

Who...?
When ...?
Where...?
What more do you know about...?
What did you learn from that?

Comprehension Questions

What do you think this means?
What is your understanding of this argument?

Application Questions

How does this apply to...?
How would this be useful?
How can this information help us?

Analysis Questions

How does this work?
What are the causes of this?
How does this compare to...?
Why did that happen?
What does this tell us about...?
What are some ways we could solve this problem?
What if...?
How does this look from another point of view?

Synthesis Questions

How are these related?
How would you organize this information?

Evaluation Questions

What would you do differently next time?
What are the strengths and weaknesses of this?
What did you like/dislike about that?
Why is that important to you?

BASIC REFLECTION QUESTIONS

Social Reflection Questions

What did you do to live by the social contract?

What did your group do well?

Were you listened to? What is your evidence?

Were you an active listener? What is your evidence?

What did you do to stay on task?

How did you help others stay on task?

How did your group support one another?

Academic Reflection Questions

What is something you're not satisfied with and intend to change?

What is one thing you learned from doing this work?

What were the parts from which you learned the most?

What do you think is the best part of the work you did?

What needs more work?

What would you do differently next time?

Was there a place where you got stuck? What did you do?

What is a problem you solved as you worked?

How did you solve it?

What strategy was effective for you today?

What was easy and fun?

What was hard?

What is some work you did today that you enjoyed?

STUDENT-FRIENDLY SHARE TOPICS

Share about a time when you were brave.

What is the best gift you ever gave to someone? To whom did you give it?

Describe the qualities of a good friend.

Name something that stresses you in life and tell how you handle it.

Describe the kind of person you would like to be when you are an adult.

What is your favorite season, and why do you like it?

What do you do to stay healthy?

If you could eat only one food for the rest of your life, what would it be?

Share the last random act of kindness you did.

If you had $1,000,000 and had to give it all away in one day to someone you didn't know, how would you give it away?

Whom do you admire? Why?

Share a family ritual.

Describe the best day of your life.

Tell what you would do differently if you were a teacher.

Describe your most successful class.

If you could eliminate one emotion from your life, which would it be?

What was your favorite birthday? What made it special?

Explain what is stressful to you about school.

In your opinion, what rule in school is the most important?

What rule is most important in your home?

What occupation (job) do you most admire?

Describe a perfect day for you.

What is your favorite holiday? How do you celebrate it?

What is the best meal you ever had? Who made it?

What scares you?

Tell what you would do differently if you were a parent.

Do you have a pet peeve (annoyance)? If so, what is it?

How do you repair a relationship when you break it?

Have you ever had a serious injury or illness? What was it, how did it happen, and what was the cure?

PERSONALITY INVENTORY

Instructions: In each box, circle the words or phrases that describe a consistent character trait that you possess. Total the number circled, double your score, and tally the results. Note the animal type in which you scored the highest.

For discussion: What blend of animal-types represents your personality? In which animal type did you score the lowest? Meet with classmates that have the same animal as you and discuss your inventories.

Lion

Assertive

Quick to act

Decisive

Enjoys challenges

Good motivator of others

Confident and firm

Strong willed and persistent

Takes charge, controlling

Competitive

Problem-solver

Goal-oriented

Independent

Total x 2 = _____

Bear

Practical

Dependable

Thorough

Follows rules

Weighs all sides of an issue, balanced

Careful

Controlled

Reserved

Sensitive

Analytical

Precise

Persistent

Total x 2 = _____

Deer

Allows others to feel important

Team player

Noncompetitive

Adaptable

Warm and relational

Sympathetic

Loyal

Nurturing

Sensitive

Calm and patient

Good listener

Peacemaker

Total x 2 = _____

Eagle

Visionary who sees the big picture

Likes to experiment and explore

Likes to create

Takes risks

Motivator

Inspirational

Optimistic

Enthusiastic

Fun-loving

Energetic

Promoter

Friendly

Total x 2 = _____

STICKY SOCIAL SITUATIONS

I want some positive attention from the opposite sex

Someone has a crush on me, but I don't reciprocate

I would like to speak to a certain person but am afraid to

I revealed my feelings for another to someone else, and then regretted it

I was with a certain person and didn't know what to say

A certain person said something to me and I was embarrassed

I told someone something and now wish I hadn't

I was the only boy (girl) who signed up for an activity

I was embarrassed when I was with a boy (girl) I like at the mall and my parents came by and asked to be introduced

I want to date, but my parents won't let me

A time I acted tough to impress my boyfriend (girlfriend) and s/he thought I was weird

I felt all eyes were on me when I arrived at the party

I thought I looked nice, and someone told me I didn't

I really looked bad and saw a boy (girl) I liked

I didn't want my picture taken but people kept taking it anyway

I was very self-conscious about my appearance at a dance

I want to change the way I talk (or dance or walk) but can't

I'm uncomfortable around people with physical handicaps

STUDENT CPR PLAN SHEET

Group members _____ _____ _____ _____

Greeting:

Who will facilitate? _____

How long? _____

Describe the greeting:

Sharing:

Who will facilitate? _____

How long? _____

What do you need to consider when facilitating this?

Activity:

Who will facilitate? _____

How long?_____

Describe the game and its rules:

Daily News:

Who will facilitate? _____

Write the chart exactly as it will appear on the back of this sheet. Include something for each one of the five required parts:

1. Greeting and the date:

2. A comment about what happened yesterday:

3. A comment about what is happening today:

4. An interactive question students can respond to in writing or drawing:

5. A closing salutation and your signatures:

Date to run meeting _____

Teacher signature _____

STEPS OF A ROLE PLAY

Explore an Issue

Declare and explore the importance of the issue; keep it brief and refer to the Social Contract.

Why is it important to...?

What does our Social Contract tell us about this kind of situation?

Action!

Set up and play a short scene that incorporates the dilemma of choosing between what you want and what you know is right.

Let's say that...

In our scene, ...

As the role play starts, ...

Cut!

Stop the scene at the decision point to think about what's happening.

What's happening in this scene?

What are the people thinking and feeling?

Problem-Solving

Think together about possible choices within the limits of the Social Contract, and choose a responsible option that also meets students' needs for competence, autonomy, relationship, and fun.

What could _____ do that would feel OK and also be the right thing to do in this case?

What action would support our rules and feel good?

Replay

Run through the scene from the beginning, incorporating the option chosen, and discuss.

Let's go back to the beginning and, this time, include our solution.

STEPS OF A CONFLICT RESOLUTION

Have a Way to Calm Down

Establish the rules of the conversation.
Are you ready to solve this problem?

Explain the Problem

Tell your version of the situation as matter-of-factly as you can, and include how you felt.

Listen to the Other Person

Listen to him and concentrate on remembering what he is saying.

Paraphrase What the Other Person Has Said

Retell what she said as if you were simply a reporter.

State Your Needs

Say how you feel and what you need and want.

Own Your Responsibility for the Problem

Honestly admit your part in the problem.

Unveil A Win-Win Solution

Figure out a way you both can get at least some of what you want.

Thank the Person for Working with You to Resolve the Conflict

Acknowledge each other for working to solve this problem.

Set a time to check in!

STEPS OF A PLANNING MEETING

Launching

Circle up. Establish relationship with a greeting, acknowledgment, or short activity.
State the topic. Read the Guidelines
Thumbs up if you are willing to stick to the Guidelines.

Brainstorm Ideas

Recorder makes a list on board or chart paper
Who has an idea for...?
What's one thing we might do on...?

Deciding on the Plan

Establish a consensus on a final version of the plan
Let's first choose our two favorite ideas so we can see which the group wants most to do.
Okay, we've got the list trimmed down and organized. Show me thumbs up if you're satis-
fied with the plan. Up is "Yes." Down is "No." Middle is "Yes, but." Be ready to share your
concerns.

Assigning Tasks

Students sign up for a responsibility they are willing to assume to execute the plan
Think for a minute, and then put you name next to the task you have chosen to work on.

Evaluating Our Meeting

With thumbs decide how well this meeting has gone
It's now time for us to think about how we did in our Planning Meeting.

STEPS OF A PROBLEM-SOLVING MEETING

Launching

1. We are willing to solve the problem.
2. We avoid naming.
3. We avoid blaming.

Establish relationship with a greeting, acknowledgments, or short activity.

Post and read rules of the meeting.

Check for understanding of the rules and show thumbs to indicate willingness to abide by them.

Getting to the Root

Share around the circle (whip share) in which everyone gets to describe her/his experience with the problem

Briefly describe a time when....
What have you noticed about...?
What's getting in the way of...?
What rules are being broken, and why?
What are the causes? What are the effects?

Brainstorming Solutions (List ideas)

What would help us to be more _____?
What would help us solve the problem?
What would help us follow our agreements?
Give us an idea for improving this situation.

Deciding

Students provide reasons for which solution they think is best.
The class votes to get the choices down to the top one or two.
Students make a consensus decision on which solution to try.
Which solution will work for us?

Keeping Track of How We're Doing

Set up a way to keep track of changes.
How will we know if we are improving?
How will we measure our success?
When will we check in to decide if our solution is working?

Evaluating Our Meeing

How did our meeting go?
Students use thumbs to indicate.

BUILDING CONSENSUS

When a group is working to build community, all important decisions that affect the whole group should be made by consensus. Creating a Social Contract, deciding on a solution to a class issue, or making decisions about where to go for an end-of-year field-trip are examples of decisions that would be best made via consensus to ensure that all voices are heard and respected.

The Process

To make a decision using consensus:

1. Propose the question or issue clearly and check for understanding. All group members must be clear about what is being discussed, because after consensus they will all be bound by the decision about how to handle the issue.

2. Let everyone who wishes to speak to the question or issue and offer solutions do so. Some students may speak more than others because they know more about or have a greater interest in the topic, but they should not dominate or intimidate others.

3. When you get down to a few possible solutions, you may wish to take a straw (non-binding) vote to see which solutions are generally the most popular. Eventually you will narrow down to one solution that seems to satisfy most people.

4. State what seems to be the most preferred solution and ask students to show their level of acceptance. Three thumb positions work well for this:

- Thumb up means "I agree and fully support the decision."

- Thumb sideways means "I am not in total agreement, I but can live with the decision."

- Thumb down means "I do not agree and need to be heard."

- Consensus requires that all group members give either thumbs up or sideways. If even one person is thumb down, more discussion is necessary.

When the group is struggling to come to agreement

When individuals or groups are unwilling to consent to a proposal, students will likely suggest that the group votes instead of using consensus to decide. Remind them that communities are inclusive, and as a community you are unwilling to leave anybody behind.

Here are some suggestions when the group is stuck and not making progress:

- Ask: *What do we need to change or add to the proposed decisions so we can all live with the solution?*

- Stop the process and take a break. *We need to take a break and continue our discussion tomorrow.*

- Suggest that each person who does not like the solution speak with a person who supports it, so they can see each other's point of view.

- Look for new insight. *We need to study our decision more. This evening, think about or discuss with someone new solutions or changes could make so everybody can agree.*

BOOKS THAT INSPIRE GOAL-SETTING

Chicken Soup for the Teenage Soul, Jack Canfield, Mark Victor Hansen, Kimberly Kirberger

Feathers and Fools, Mem Fox

Fly Away Home, Eve Bunting

The Glorious Flight: Across the Channel with Louis Bleriot, Alice and Martin Provensen

Oh, the Places You'll Go! Dr. Seuss

Salt in His Shoes: Michael Jordan in Pursuit of a Dream, Deloris Jordan and Roslyn M. Jordan

Snowflake Bentley, Jacqueline Briggs Martin, Mary Azarian

The Three Questions: Based on a story by Leo Tolstoy, Jon Muth

Tree of Hope, Amy Littlesugar

Uncle Jed's Barber Shop, Margaree King Mitchell, James Ransome

The War, Anais Vaugelade

FILMS THAT INSPIRE GOAL-SETTING

PRIDE

Knights of the South Bronx

Mad Hot Ballroom

Stand and Deliver

Hoop Dreams

Whale Rider

Akeelah and the Bee

Smoke Signals

Hoosiers

"GIRAFFE" STORY BOOKS: ABOUT PEOPLE WHO TOOK A STAND

The Escape of Oney Judge: Martha Washington's Slave Finds Freedom, Emily Arnold McCully

Pink and Say, Patricia Polacco

Thank you Mr. Falker, Patricia Polacco

Mr. Washington's Way, Patricia Polacco

Elijah of Buxton, Christopher Paul Curtis

Henry s Freedom Box, Ellen Levine

The Invention of Hugo Cabret, Brian Selznick

Shindler's List, Thomas Keneally

Aani and the Tree Huggers, Jeannine Atkins

Dream Freedom, Sonia Levitin

Elizabeth Blackwell: First Woman Physician, Tristan Boyer Binns

The Boy Who Dared, Susan Campbell Bartoletti

Dear Miss Breed: True Stories of the Japanese American Incarceration During World War II and a Librarian Who Made a Difference, Joanne Oppenheim

The Freedom Writers Diary: How a Teacher and 150 Teens Used Writing to Change Themselves and the World around Them, Freedom Writers and Zlata Filipovic

Freedom Walkers: the Story of the Montgomery Bus Boycott, Russell Freedman

The Hiding Place, Corrie Ten Boom

Passage to Freedom: the Sugihara Story, Ken Mochizuki

Strong Right Arm: the Story of Mamie "Peanut" Johnson, Michelle Green

BOARD GAME TEMPLATE

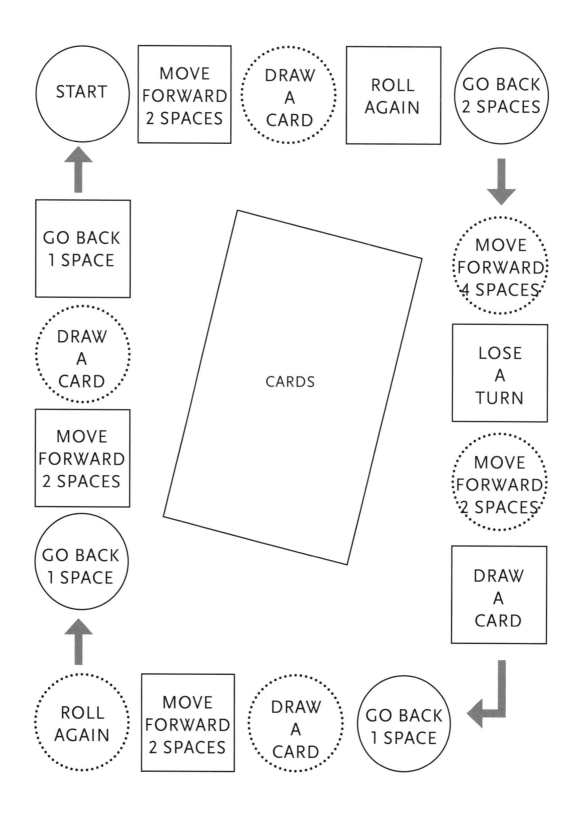

CARDS FOR BOARD GAME: "SAVE OR SPEND"

Write the following information on cards to create "save" or "spend" cards for the board game. The cards that players pick determine how much money each player has at the end. See page XX for a description of "Save or Spend."

Transportation	$45
Movies	$10
Presents	$150
Movie rentals	$10
Sports events	$30
Concert tickets	$30
Team gear	$200
Haircuts	$30
Make-up	$40
Video games	$250
Music	$25
Shoes	$95
Clothes and accessories	$300
Jewelry	$800
Sports equipment	$400
Food	$300
Electronic accessories	$300
Books and magazines	$75
Candy and pop	$10
Cell phones	$125

A FEW LESS-KNOWN CAREER POSSIBILITIES

Acupuncturist
Advertising executive
Agricultural/food scientist
Air traffic controller
Archeologist
Architect
Astronomer
Biochemist
Biophysicist
Biologist
Butcher
Carpenter
Cartographer
Cartoonist
Chemist
Choreographer
Civil engineer
Computer programmer
Computer systems analyst
Concierge
Coroner
Court reporter
Database administrator
Dental hygienist
Detective
Disc jockey
Economist
Editor
Electrician
Environmental scientist
Epidemiologist
Financial analyst
Fish & game warden
Geographer
Geologist
Graphic designer
Historian
Hypnotherapist
Immigration agent
Customs inspector

Psychologist
Interpreter/translator
Interior designer
Jeweler
Landscape architect
Legislator
Machinist
Management analyst
Marine engineer
Market research analyst
Mathematician
Microbiologist
Municipal clerk
Nuclear engineer
Greenhouse manager
Occupational therapist
Optician
Paralegal
Park naturalist
Pest control worker
Pharmacist
Pipefitter
Podiatrist
Potter
Professional photographer
Public relations manager
Radiologic technician
Railroad inspector
Real estate broker
Respiratory therapist
Sculptor
Set designer
Sheet metal worker
Silversmith
Sketch artist
Statistician
Surveyor
Systems analyst
Taxidermist
Technical writer

Tool & die maker
Tour guide
Upholsterer
Urban planner
Veterinarian
Webmaster
Welder
X-ray technician
Zookeeper
Zoologist

SCHOOL SERVICE JOBS

Post office: distribute weekly or daily mail from office to students and teachers

Environment: organize and collect recycling from around the school and bring to collection site

Birthday Committee: check school lists and provide a card, song, or public recognition for people's birthdays

School store: set up and operate a store for pencils, paper, notebooks, etc.

Communications: provide announcements over public address system or on a community message board

Buddies: partner with kindergarten or primary grade students

Product manufacture: make hacky sacks, cards, calendars, or other materials as needed for teachers

Get-well cards: make and send cards to ill students and teachers

Acknowledgments and appreciations: give oral or written acknowledgments to students who have contributed to others or accomplished something special

Staff support: assist in the office or with custodial tasks

All-school events: organize, prepare, and execute events

Student publications: collect stories, articles, poems, and photos for publication

Peer tutoring team (academic): help other students with academics

Peer coaching team (social): help new students adjust and loners make friends

Peer mediation team (conflict resolution): help students resolve conflicts peacefully

Displays: design, mount, and label public displays of student work

Joke book: Make a book of riddles and jokes to distribute to homerooms/advisories

Pet caregivers: feed and clean cages of classroom animals

Community connections: invite speakers, mentors, and tutors from the community to school events

Greeter: greet students, parents, and guests as they enter the school for an event

Lunch count: take the lunch count and turn into the office/lunchroom

Advisory representatives: for all-school planning, student council

POWER FOODS: FOODS WITH HIGHER NUTRITIONAL VALUE

Vegetables

broccoli, Brussels sprouts, cabbage, kale, collards, chard, spinach, onion, garlic, bell pepper, parsley, celery, mustard greens, arugula, yam, tomato, olive, cucumber, carrot

Fruits

blueberries, raspberries, strawberries, blackberries, mangos, avocados, limes, apples, pomegranates, grapes, oranges, bananas

Nuts and seeds

sunflower seeds, pumpkin seeds, sesame seeds, almonds, walnuts

Fish and seafood

Best: sardine, wild salmon, mackerel, tilapia (high in omega-3 fats, low in pollutants)
OK: limited amounts of Alaskan halibut, cod, sole, haddock, lobster, clams, mussels, oysters, shrimp

Meat

chicken, turkey; limited amounts of beef or pork

Legumes

lentils, split peas, adzuki beans, soy (tofu, miso); all other beans and peas are good sources, too

Whole grains

rice (especially brown), quinoa, barley, whole wheat

Milks

cow, soy, rice, almond

References

Anfara, Vincent A. 2006. Research summary: Advisory programs. *National Middle School Association*, July. http://www.nmsa.org/Research/ResearchSummaries/AdvisoryPrograms/tabid/812/Default.aspx (accessed May 24, 2010).

Bandura, Albert. 1994. Self-efficacy. In Vol. 4 of *Encyclopedia of human behavior*, ed. V. S. Ramachaudran, 71-81. New York: Academic Press.

Clark, S. and D. Clark. 1994. *Restructuring the middle level school: Implications for school leaders.* Albany: State University of New York Press.

Connors, N. 1991. Teacher advisory: The fourth r. *In Transforming middle level education: Perspectives and possibilities*, ed. J. L. Irvin, 162 -178. Needham Heights, MA: Allyn & Bacon.

Comer, James P. 2005. Child and adolescent development: The critical missing focus in school reform. *Phi Delta Kappan* (June): 757-763.

Dembo, M.H. and M. Eaton. 2000. Self-regulation of academic learning in middle-level schools. *Elementary School Journal* 100 (5): 473-490.

Dewey, John. 1938. *Experience and education.* London: Macmillan.

Durlak, Joseph and Roger Weisberg. 2007. A major meta-analysis of positive youth development programs. *CASEL Update. Collaborative for Academic, Social, and Emotional Learning* (December).

Fleming, Jane E., Thomas D. Coork, and Addison C. Stone. 2002. Interactive influence of perceived social contexts on the reading achievement of urban middle schoolers with learning disabilities. *Learning Disabilities Research and Practice* 17 (1): 47-64.

George, P. and L. Oldaker. 1985. *Evidence for the middle school.* Columbus, OH: National Middle School Association.

Glasser, William. 1998. *Choice theory: A new psychology of personal freedom.* New York: Harper Collins.

Goleman, Daniel. 2006. *Social intelligence: The revolutionary new science of human relationships.* New York: Random House.

Gresham, Frank and Stephen Elliott. 1990. *Social skills rating system manual.* Circle Pines, MN: American Guidance Service.

Fall, Kevin A., Andre Marquis, and Janice Miner Holden. 2004. *Theoretical models of counseling and psychotherapy.* New York: Brunner-Routledge.

Larson, Reed W. 2000. Toward a psychology of positive youth development. *American Psychologist* (January): 170-183.

Libbey, Heather P. 2004. Measuring student relationships to school: Attachment, bonding, connectedness, and engagement. *Journal of School Health* 74 (7): 274-283.

Mac Iver, D. 1990. Meeting the needs of young adolescents: Advisory groups, interdisciplinary teaching teams, and school transition programs. *Phi Delta Kappan* 71(6): 458-464.

Marantz Henig, Robin. 2008. Why we play. *New York Times*, February 17.

Payne, Diane and Terry Wolfson. 1989. *Turning points: Preparing American youth for the 21st century.* New York: Carnegie Council on Adolescent Development.

Rogoff, Barbara. 1990. *Apprenticeship in thinking: Cognitive development in a social context.* Oxford: Oxford University Press.

Ryan, Richard and Edward Deci. 2000. Self-determination theory and the facilitation of intrinsic motivation, social development, and well-being. *American Psychologist* 55 (January): 68-78.

Sousa, David. 2001. *How the brain learns.* Thousand Oaks, CA: Corwin Press.

Vaughan, Angela L. 2005. The self-paced student. *Educational Leadership* 62 (7): 69-73.

Wentzel, Kathryn R., Carolyn McNamara Barry, and Kathryn A. Caldwell. 2004. Friendships in middle school: Influences on motivation and school adjustment. *Journal of Educational Psychology* 96 (2): 195-203.

ABOUT THE AUTHOR

Linda Crawford is the executive director of Origins. She has taught at every grade level from kindergarten through graduate school. She was principal of an arts-integrated elementary school for five years, and has led professional-development seminars and workshops for educators for nearly thirty years. She is co-founder of the *Developmental Designs* approach to integrated social and academic learning for adolescents. She is the author of *Classroom Discipline: Guiding Adolescents to Responsible Independence*; *To Hold Us Together: Seven Conversations for Multicultural Understanding*; *Lively Learning: Using the Arts to Teach the K-8 Curriculum*; multicultural education through the arts books  and videos; and numerous articles on the integration of social and academic learning. She has a BS in English-Education from the University of Wisconsin and an MA in English Literature from the University of Minnesota.

Index

╲╷╭╱
ORIGINS
⁄⁀╲DEVELOPMENTAL DESIGNS®
An integrated approach to social and academic learning

This book was developed through the work of Origins, a nonprofit educational organization, and its research-grounded approach to teaching known as *Developmental Designs*. The *Developmental Designs* approach offers practical structures designed to keep young people safe, connected, responsible, and engaged in learning. Because many adolescents struggle to focus on work or to manage assignments or to generally exercise the self-control needed to learn, they are not likely to succeed in school unless someone consciously teaches them social and emotional skills. Teachers use *Developmental Designs* structures to help young people learn how to learn.

DEVELOPMENTAL DESIGNS TEACHING PRACTICES

Community-building Advisory—The Circle of Power and Respect (CPR) and Activity Plus (A+) are meeting structures for building community, social skills, and readiness for learning.

Goals and Declarations—Students declare a personal stake in school to anchor their learning in a meaningful commitment to growth.

Social Contract—Based on their personal goals, students design and sign an agreement that binds the community to common rules. Its principles are modeled and practiced every day.

Modeling and Practicing—Social competencies are learned by seeing and doing. Nothing is assumed; all routines are practiced.

Reflective Loop—Ongoing, varied reflective planning and assessments ensure continuous, conscious growth.

Empowering Teacher Language—Gesture, voice, and words combine to create a rigorous, respectful climate for building responsible independence.

Pathways to Self-control—When the Social Contract is broken, teachers have an array of strategies, such as redirections, fix-its, loss of privilege, and Take a Break. Social skills grow without loss of dignity.

Collaborative Problem-solving—Students and teachers use social conferencing, problem-solving meetings, conflict resolution, and other problem-solving structures to find positive solutions to chronic problems.

Engaged Learning Strategies (including Power Learning)—Social interaction, experiential learning, choice, exhibition, reflection, and other practices help connect young adolescent needs and the school curriculum, so students are deeply engaged in learning.

Power of Play—Play is designed to build community, enliven students, and restore their focus, ensuring more time on task.

LEARN MORE ABOUT
THE DEVELOPMENTAL DESIGNS APPROACH

Professional Development Opportunities

- One-day, half-day, and 90-minute overviews
- One-day follow up workshop
- Week-long workshops: *Developmental Designs* 1, 2, 3, and Building Academic Communities Through the Arts
- Classroom and school-wide consultation providing on-site training, implementation coaching, and support for school-wide sustainability

Publications and Resources for Middle Level Educators

- Books supporting building community, establishing order, and engaging learners
- Free newsletter with articles by classroom teachers and *Developmental Designs* consultants
- Free, informative e-notices supporting *Developmental Designs* implementation
- Website with articles, teaching ideas, and other information: www.OriginsOnline.org

For details, contact:

⅏ORIGINS

3805 Grand Avenue South
Minneapolis, Minnesota 55409

612-822-3422 / 800-543-8715
Fax: 612-822-3585
www.OriginsOnline.org
Origins@OriginsOnline.org